Sloganization in Language Education Discourse

Full details of all our publications can be found on http://www.multilingual-matters.com, or by writing to Multilingual Matters, St Nicholas House, 31–34 High Street, Bristol BS1 2AW, UK.

Sloganization in Language Education Discourse

Conceptual Thinking in the Age of Academic Marketization

Edited by
Barbara Schmenk, Stephan Breidbach and Lutz Küster

MULTILINGUAL MATTERS
Bristol • Blue Ridge Summit

DOI https://doi.org/10.21832/SCHMEN1862
Library of Congress Cataloging in Publication Data

Library of Congress Cataloging in Publication Control Number: 2018026959

A catalog record for this book is available from the Library of Congress.

British Library Cataloguing in Publication Data
A catalogue entry for this book is available from the British Library.

ISBN-13: 978-1-78892-186-2 (hbk)
ISBN-13: 978-1-78892-185-5 (pbk)

Multilingual Matters
UK: St Nicholas House, 31–34 High Street, Bristol BS1 2AW, UK.
USA: NBN, Blue Ridge Summit, PA, USA.

Website: www.multilingual-matters.com
Twitter: Multi_Ling_Mat
Facebook: https://www.facebook.com/multilingualmatters
Blog: www.channelviewpublications.wordpress.com

Copyright © 2019 Barbara Schmenk, Stephan Breidbach, Lutz Küster and the authors of individual chapters.

All rights reserved. No part of this work may be reproduced in any form or by any means without permission in writing from the publisher.

The policy of Multilingual Matters/Channel View Publications is to use papers that are natural, renewable and recyclable products, made from wood grown in sustainable forests. In the manufacturing process of our books, and to further support our policy, preference is given to printers that have FSC and PEFC Chain of Custody certification. The FSC and/or PEFC logos will appear on those books where full certification has been granted to the printer concerned.

Typeset by Nova Techset Private Limited, Bengaluru and Chennai, India.
Printed and bound in the UK by Short Run Press Ltd.
Printed and bound in the US by Thomson-Shore, Inc.

Contents

Contributors		vii
1	Sloganization in Language Education Discourse: Introduction *Barbara Schmenk, Stephan Breidbach and Lutz Küster*	1
2	We Innovators *David Gramling*	19
3	The Only Turn Worth Watching in the 20th Century is Tina Turner's: How the Sloganization of Foreign Language Research Can Impede the Furthering of Knowledge and Make Life Difficult for Practitioners *Dietmar Rösler*	42
4	Slo(w)ganization. Against the Constant Need for Re-inventing the Discourse on Language Education: The Case of 'Multiple Intelligences' *Gerhard Bach*	57
5	Just Another Prefix? From Inter- to Transcultural Foreign Language Learning and Beyond *Britta Viebrock*	72
6	On Common 'Exposure' and Expert 'Input' in Second Language Education and Study Abroad *John L. Plews*	94
7	What on Earth is 'Language Commodification'? *David Block*	121
8	Superdiversity and Why It Isn't: Reflections on Terminological Innovation and Academic Branding *Aneta Pavlenko*	142
9	Sloganization: Yet Another Slogan? *Barbara Schmenk, Stephan Breidbach and Lutz Küster*	169
Index		176

Contributors

Gerhard Bach is Professor Emeritus of TESOL methodology at the University of Bremen, Germany. There he directed the Institute for Foreign Language Learning and Multilingualism (INFORM) and its international research branch and doctoral program (LANGSCAPE) until 2009. He now works as an independent research consultant, focusing on career planning, academic publishing and referrals. Gerhard has given keynote presentations at international conferences in Canada, England, France, Hong Kong, Ireland, Israel, Japan, Scotland and Spain. His numerous books and articles in scientific journals relate to research interests in the culture curriculum, CLIL methodology, theories of task-based learning, student-centered classroom approaches, the pedagogy of multiliteracies and empirical research methodologies.

David Block is ICREA Research Professor in Sociolinguistics at the Universitat de Lleida (Spain). He has published on a variety of language-related topics, which he examines drawing on scholarship in political economy, sociology, anthropology, geography and education. He is author of *Second Language Identities* (Continuum/Bloomsbury, 2007/2014), *Social Class in Applied Linguistics* (Routledge, 2014) and *Political Economy and Sociolinguistics: Political Economy, Neoliberalism and Social Class* (Bloomsbury, 2018). At present David is writing *Post-Truth, Ignorance and Corrupt Discourses* for Palgrave Macmillan. He is a member of the Academy of the Social Sciences (UK) and editor of the Routledge book series *Language, Society and Political Economy*.

Stephan Breidbach worked as a secondary school teacher of English as a foreign language for several years. He received his PhD from the University of Bremen before joining the Humboldt-Universität zu Berlin, where he has worked as Professor of English Language Education and Pedagogy since 2009. Stephan's research interests include conceptualizations of language education, content-and-language-integrated learning (CLIL), language teacher identity and professional development. He also takes a special interest in language education policies in transforming societies. He is co-coordinator of LANGSCAPE together with Lutz Küster.

David Gramling researches primarily in applied linguistics, translation studies and literary studies. With Chantelle Warner, he has edited the interdisciplinary journal *Critical Multilingualism Studies* (cms.arizona.edu) since 2012. He is the editor of the Translations section of *Transgender Studies Quarterly* and writes regularly on queer approaches to translation and multilingualism. With Aron Aji, he translates the work of the Turkish-Kurdish poet Marathon Mungan. David's monograph *The Invention of Monolingualism* (Bloomsbury, 2016) won the Book Award of the American Association for Applied Linguistics in 2018. He currently serves as Director of Graduate Studies in the Department of German Studies at the University of Arizona, where he is an Associate Professor.

Lutz Küster is Professor of Teaching Romance Languages and Literatures at Humboldt-University of Berlin, Germany. He is co-coordinator of LANGSCAPE, an international research network for the study of multilingualism and language teaching methodology, co-editor of *Fremdsprachen Lehren und Lernen*, a journal on topics in foreign language education, and director of Klett Akademie für Fremdsprachendidaktik – Französisch. Lutz's main research areas are multiliteracies and education, intercultural learning, identity and motivational aspects of foreign language learning, and literary studies.

Aneta Pavlenko is Research Professor of Applied Linguistics at the University of Oslo. Her research examines the relationship between multilingualism, cognition and emotions. She has testified in court as an expert in forensic linguistics, lectured widely in North America, Europe and Asia, and authored more than a hundred articles and 10 books, the most recent of which is *The Bilingual Mind: And What it Tells us about Language and Thought* (Cambridge University Press, 2014). Aneta is former President of the American Association for Applied Linguistics and winner of the 2006 BAAL Book of the Year Award and the 2009 TESOL Award for Distinguished Research.

John L. Plews is Professor of German at Saint Mary's University, Halifax, Canada, and Director of the Canadian Summer School in Germany. He earned a PhD in German literatures, languages and linguistics and a PhD in secondary education, both from the University of Alberta. His recent co-edited books include *Second Language Study Abroad Programming, Pedagogy, and Participant Engagement* (with K. Misfeldt, Palgrave Macmillan, 2018), *Translation and Translating in German Studies* (with D. Spokiene, WLU Press, 2016) and *Traditions and Transitions: Curricula for German Studies* (with B. Schmenk, WLU Press, 2013). John researches second language curriculum and teaching, learner identities and study abroad.

Dietmar Rösler studied at the FU Berlin (German and media studies), where he was later awarded a PhD. He worked as a junior member of staff in the German departments of University College Dublin and the Freie Universität Berlin and as Reader in the German department of King's College, University of London. In 1996, he was appointed Professor at Giessen University, where he was responsible for two postgraduate degree courses on German as a foreign language and on foreign language learning and language technology. In 2017, Dietmar was awarded the Otto-Behaghel Senior Professorship by Gießen University. His main research areas are intercultural learning, learning material design and the role of new media in foreign language learning.

Barbara Schmenk is Professor of German/Applied Linguistics at the University of Waterloo, Canada. She taught at high schools in Germany and at Clemson University, Trinity College Dublin and Ruhr-Universität Bochum. Barbara's research publications include books and articles on gender and language, learner autonomy, governmentality and language education, conceptions of cultural learning, drama in education and teacher cognition.

Britta Viebrock is Professor of TEFL Theory and Methodology and Dean of the Faculty of Modern Languages at the University of Frankfurt/Main, Germany. Her research interests include content and language integrated learning (CLIL), inter- and transcultural learning, digital und multimodal literacies, film in English language teaching, teacher professionalism and qualitative research methodology as well as research ethics. Britta has published several books and numerous articles in these areas.

1 Sloganization in Language Education Discourse: Introduction

Barbara Schmenk, Stephan Breidbach and Lutz Küster

Think different. Just do it. Because you're worth it. A diamond is forever. Vorsprung durch Technik. Par amour du gout. La meta está en ti. Chi mi ama mi segue. I'm lovin' it. We are surrounded by slogans. They grab our attention, they are memorable and they sell. Any successful marketing strategy involves the development of a slogan, a tagline that captures the attention of potential consumers. Slogans, according to the *Entrepreneur Small Business Encyclopedia*, are 'catch phrase(s) or small group(s) of words that are combined in a special way to identify a product or company' (Entrepreneur Media, 2017). As a linguistic packaging strategy, creating an appealing and effective slogan is an essential part of product branding.

The emergence of slogans is by no means new. As Urdang and Robbins (1984), in their collection of more than 6000 slogans, explain:

> [t]hroughout history, as long as language has been employed in any form, slogans have been formulated and promulgated. As a means of focusing attention and exhorting to action they long have been and still remain most effective; as an aspect of language they are illustrative of the intimate relationship of thought, word, and deed. Although the word *slogan* itself takes its origin from the Gaelic sluagh-ghairm 'host-cry,' a battle cry of the Scottish clans, its meaning has broadened to include the catchwords and phrases used by religious, political, and other groups. Recently, we have witnessed a huge proliferation of slogans with commercial purpose, saturating print and electronic media. (Urdang & Robbins, 1984: 17, emphasis in original)

More than 30 years after the publication of Urdang and Robbins' collection of slogans, we are witnessing an ever-increasing need to marketize almost every aspect of life, at an ever-increasing pace. The need to create new slogans has become imperative in almost all sectors of society and institutions, a development that seems inevitable in a world that is predominantly constructed in current neoliberal discourses as a marketplace

(Crouch, 2011, 2013; Fairclough, 1993; Holborow, 2015; Urciuoli, 2010). Education is but one example. Driven by what Martha Nussbaum (2010) refers to as the 'profit motive', educational landscapes, including the world of academia, have been subject to transformations geared chiefly towards marketability and profitability. Branding has become an integral part of their endeavors to thrive, or merely to survive.

This trend has made its way into academic work as well. Possible motives driving this development are many and diverse, and may include, for example: the need to apply for research funding; the obligation to keep the production of research output at a competitive level ('publish or perish'); preparing mission statements and mottos for educational institutions; promoting educational programs in an age of national and international rankings; developing new (*innovative*) approaches and solutions to meet today's challenges; spelling out what a program, a conference or a research project will contribute to institutional or societal goals in the age of accountability; and rallying teachers behind an approach that will presumably facilitate, modernize, humanize or otherwise legitimize their classroom practices or professionalize their occupation. All this effort requires what was considered unacademic until a few decades ago: selling, advertising and branding, alongside the conventional work involved in the development of, for example, research projects, programs, conferences, courses, and the general academic activities of thinking, reading, writing, rethinking, rereading and rewriting. The creation and use of slogans seems inevitable in this context, if not necessary. In order to convince others (administrators, funding sources, etc.) of the usefulness of particular projects, changes or new proposals, one often has to employ effective sales strategies, which frequently involve the use of slogans.

Yet, as Billig (2013: 5) points out, the practice of self-branding has become commonplace because the 'culture of competition and self-promotion is seeping into the content of our academic writing. This is a culture in which success and boasting seem to go hand in hand.' This volume takes this concern as its starting point. The field of language education, with its predominant focus on the future and the perceived need to develop more and better – *innovative* – educational programs, practical applications, useful approaches and timely answers to political challenges, is profoundly susceptible to competitive branding and the creation of slogans.

Slogans and Language Education Discourse

The development of language education discourse over the past few decades has been characterized by a significant rise in the number of publications and a concomitant thematic diversification and general broadening of the field (e.g. de Bot, 2015; Jakisch *et al.*, 2013). In the course of its development, language education discourse has seen the emergence of several trends or fashions. Over the course of the past few decades, we have observed the rise of a series of fashionable, high-frequency terms in language education discourse that have made their way into school and university curricula, policy papers and other educational domains.

Similar to the world of fashion, new trends (often referred to as 'turns') have emerged in academic discourse over the past 50 years. Since the rise of the *linguistic turn* in the 1970s, a growing number of *turns* have entered scholarly discourses in the humanities and cultural studies. In quick succession, scholars declared a series of turns: the *interpretive turn*, the *performative turn*, the *reflexive turn*, the *postcolonial turn*, the *spatial turn*, the *pictorial* or *iconic turn* and the *translational turn* (Bachmann-Medick, 2014, 2016), to name but a few. Each of these turns generated a plethora of publications and scholarly debates, and each promised to bring about innovative theoretical models and analyses, all considered to be necessary in order to capture the challenges and complexities identified by the respective 'turn makers' and 'turn takers', as fundamentals that had not been adequately addressed in previous (i.e. 'pre-turn') theories, frameworks or approaches.

Similar developments can be observed in language education discourse. At a macro-level, different teaching paradigms have emerged and, in some cases, disappeared: audiolingualism, communicative language teaching, task-based language teaching or intercultural language teaching, each referring to or triggered by developments in psychology, cognitive theory or linguistics (e.g. behaviorism, pragmatics, sociocultural theory). At the micro-level, a number of leitmotifs, concepts and principles have entered educational discourses: authenticity, language awareness, learner autonomy, the intercultural speaker, learner centeredness or lifelong learning, which also made their way into language curricula and policy papers in many regions of the world. Situated at the intersection of linguistics, social sciences, education and cultural studies, the field of language education is inherently interdisciplinary, and so it comes as no surprise that language education discourses draw heavily on theoretical models and concepts developed in disciplines such as general education, cognitive psychology or the social sciences, leading to an ever-increasing number of innovative teaching methods or new turns and paradigms in the wider field of applied linguistics.

What is remarkable about these developments is that they can be observed across cultural and linguistic boundaries. Communicative language teaching (CLT), for instance, has had a profound effect on language education worldwide (e.g. Richards, 2006; Savignon, 2013), as have intercultural learning (e.g. Byram, 1997, 2008) and learner autonomy (e.g. Benson, 2001, 2013), although their definitions and practical applications vary considerably across different curricula and policy papers and in scholarly work. With regard to CLT, for instance, Richards (2006: 2) asserts that its popularity among language educators worldwide stands in stark contrast to the lack of globally accepted or shared definitions of the concept. 'Perhaps the majority of language teachers today, when asked to identify the methodology they employ in their classrooms, mention "communicative" as the methodology of choice. However, when pressed to give a detailed account of what they mean by "communicative," explanations vary widely' (see also Schmenk, 2017). This variation leads to the problem at the core of this volume.

The volume is concerned with a development called the *sloganization* of key terms in language education discourse. Sloganization is meant to denote a tendency to use a range of popular terms in scholarship, policy papers, practical applications and curriculum development *as if* their meaning were obvious and shared across the globe. Assuming that the meaning of a popular term is obvious and globally shared leads to foregoing precise definitions, ignoring the whereabouts of concepts, overlooking the variety and inconsistencies of different meanings attached to them, and perpetuating seemingly straightforward and unproblematic terms that would sometimes more appropriately be considered *slogans*. As participants in the scholarly discourse of language education and applied linguistics, the editors of this volume felt increasingly uneasy about a noticeable tendency towards slogan dropping in publications, at conferences or in policy papers on language education.

In order to illustrate what we mean by the process of sloganization, we will discuss one example in more detail: the sloganization of 'learner autonomy'.

An Example of Sloganization: Learner Autonomy

Already in 1994, David Little noted in a critical appraisal of research into learner autonomy in second/foreign language education that the term was in danger of becoming a new buzzword in applied linguistics, and he explicitly warned that 'any technical term that gains currency as a buzzword is in danger of losing its original, perhaps rather precisely grounded, meaning and *becoming an empty slogan*' (Little, 1994: 430f., emphasis added). Little illustrates his point with reference to two words that had in his view become buzzwords in many contexts of language education: 'communicative' and 'authentic', and he concludes: 'There are some signs that "learner autonomy" is on the way to achieving the same status in the 1990s as "communicative" and "authentic" achieved in the 1980s' (Little, 1994: 431).

Little's premonitions turned out to be true. Learner autonomy has indeed become one of the most widely – and globally – used buzzwords in language education discourse, and it has become a slogan in many contexts (Schmenk, 2008), in language education and beyond. The notion of autonomy is often encountered in relation to self-access learning, individualization, lifelong learning, language learning strategy use and computer-assisted learning – all of which usually hail autonomous language learning as a particularly timely, effective, efficient and desirable kind of learning. Yet a closer look at the notion of learner autonomy and its worldwide career as a buzzword reveals that, more often than not, autonomy is not clearly defined and theorized, nor is it adequately contextualized. The growing popularity of the phrase played a major part in its sloganization, as did the fact that its definition was not as precise as Little's quote suggests. This can be shown when we trace back the 'career' of learner autonomy in language education discourse.

Henri Holec coined the term 'learner autonomy' in a seminal publication for the Council of Europe (Holec, 1980 [1979]). At the time, Holec was the Director of the Nancy language center (Centre de Recherches et d'Applications Pédagogiques en Langues, CRAPEL); his aim was to spell out the prerequisites for successful self-directed learning. In this context, he listed a set of capacities characterizing what he called an 'autonomous learner':

> To say of a learner that he [sic] is autonomous is (...) to say that he is capable of taking charge of his own learning (...). To take charge of one's own learning is to have, and to hold, the responsibility for all the decisions concerning all aspects of this learning, i.e.:
>
> - determining the objectives;
> - defining the contents and progressions;
> - selecting methods and techniques to be used;
> - monitoring the procedure of acquisition properly speaking (rhythm, time, place, etc.);
> - evaluating what has been acquired.
>
> The autonomous learner is himself capable of making all these decisions concerning the learning with which he is or wishes to be involved. (Holec, 1980: 4)

This definition is precise to the extent that it details five areas of learner responsibility. If a learner is capable of taking responsibility for these five areas of decision making, s/he can be considered autonomous. In retrospect, Holec's definition appears quite unrealistic given the broad range of competencies and knowledge required for a learner to make decisions regarding learning goals, contents and progressions, monitoring and assessment or techniques and methods. Decision making in these areas requires knowledge of curriculum development, assessment, second language acquisition, cognitive psychology and more, all of which are rarely found among learners of languages. The demanding prerequisites may have contributed to the fact that Holec's definition, although referenced in virtually every publication on learner autonomy, was soon reduced to its first sentence, which provided merely a general (and superficial) description of learner autonomy as denoting 'taking charge of one's own learning'. Judging from the sheer number of publications on learner autonomy to date, the shortened version of the definition set up the notion of learner autonomy for global success and paved the way for its sloganization.

'Taking charge', after all, remains a vague though catchy phrase which can be employed in many contexts of language learning and language use. Holec himself did not consider the fact that when he coined the phrase 'learner autonomy', he entered a philosophical and educational discourse that was worthy of further reflection, nor did he take into account the rich cultural history of 'autonomy', and so it can be argued that 'learner autonomy' was based on a simplified notion from the start. We shall return to this point further below.

The simplification of autonomy, also referred to as its 'mainstreaming' (Pennycook, 1997: 40) in language education discourse resulted in a popular description of learner autonomy as chiefly a matter of strategical choice and studying on one's own, i.e. 'as an act of learning a language outside the framework of an educational institution and without the intervention of a teacher' (Benson, 1997: 19). An example of this can be found in the *Common European Framework of Reference for Languages* (CEFR; Council of Europe, 2001):

> [O]nce teaching stops, further learning *has* to be autonomous. Autonomous learning can be promoted if 'learning to learn' is regarded as an integral part of language learning, so that learners become increasingly aware of the way they learn, the options open to them and the options that best suit them. (Council of Europe, 2001: 141, emphasis in original)

The CEFR promotes what Pennycook referred to as the 'mainstreamed' notion of autonomy. Given the enormous impact of the CEFR worldwide, it has likely contributed significantly to the global circulation of this notion, and will continue to do so.

One of the effects of the vagueness of the popular understanding of autonomy as 'taking charge' is that it was soon taken to denote all kinds of learning that learners engage in *on their own*, regardless of what exactly they are doing or learning on these occasions (Benson, 2001). The advance of the personal computer and of computer-assisted language learning programs further fueled the promotion of vague notions of autonomy. It was tempting to attach the fashionable label 'autonomous' to any kind of learning that enabled people to study on their own, such as using digital media, which infamously led many administrators to reduce the number of teaching staff, as the notion of autonomous, computer-assisted learning allowed them to align the rhetoric of innovation with budget cuts. In retrospect, it seems evident that the rise of digital media helped learner autonomy become a buzzword in language education.

The simplification of learner autonomy has often been critiqued and contested, and several scholars have developed alternative models, concepts and approaches to the study of autonomy in language education (e.g. Barfield & Brown, 2007; Benson, 2011, 2013; Murray, 2014, to name but a few). These efforts to theorize autonomy in more depth, however, could not put a halt to the global spread of popular simplified notions of it. The sloganization of autonomy can thus be regarded as a counterforce that undermines the work of many colleagues concerned with fostering autonomy in language education and seeking to develop more elaborate models and theories.

To be sure, we do not intend to say that work on learner autonomy is generally flawed due to a lack of adequate theorizing, or generally based on simplified notions of autonomy. Neither do we believe that many of the ideas about, approaches to and studies of autonomy in language education are solely based on a slogan. On the contrary, we argue that in order to do justice to autonomy as an educational concept that can reasonably be pursued, theorized and studied in language education, it is necessary to acknowledge the fact *that* the term is widely used as a slogan. For this reason, it is important to look at the sloganization of autonomy more closely.

In what follows, we identify several points that have contributed to the sloganization of the term: its idealization; its frequency of use; its common-sense appeal; its popularity in other educational, scholarly and political discourses as well as across disciplinary boundaries; and its decontextualization.

Idealization and common-sense appeal

The immediate appeal of the notion of autonomy lies in the fact that it is widely considered an ideal. As Pennycook (1997: 39) argued, it is 'not an easy task to write critically about learner autonomy in language learning, principally because autonomy seems such *an unquestionably desirable goal*' (emphasis added). The idealization of autonomy is reinforced due to its common-sense appeal, which renders it a prime candidate for sloganization. Autonomy dovetails well with grand Western narratives of freedom and independence, making it singularly attractive and turning it into an 'ideological placebo' (Fineman, 2004: 6). From the point of view of sloganization, it can be argued that autonomy is prone to become a slogan precisely because it is widely considered 'unquestionable and desirable'. Not only does it seem dubious – if not impossible – to be against autonomy; the idealization of the term has also led to its sacrosanct status as unquestionably positive. In scholarly discourse, ignoring, and so implicitly or explicitly subscribing to, the unquestionably positive associations of autonomy and its emotional appeal inevitably contributes to its sloganization. Simply affirming that learner autonomy is a good thing and a desirable goal in language education may seem obvious or even natural to many, yet if the notion itself ceases to be subject to questioning, critical discussion and scrutiny, the term turns into a slogan: catchy, appealing, memorable, marketable and profitable. Little's early warning that autonomy may turn into a buzzword and thus be 'in danger of (...) becoming an empty slogan' (Little, 1994: 430f.) referred to this development, and in retrospect we can identify additional points that have contributed to the sloganization of autonomy in language education discourse and beyond.

Popularity in other discourses

An additional factor that has contributed to the sloganization of autonomy is its use in a variety of other discourses, some of which overlap or are compatible with language education discourse. Such overlaps can be found, for example, in many current narratives on the global, digital age, which is widely touted as a new era of the 'knowledge economy' (e.g. Powell & Snellman, 2004; OECD, 1996; Williams, 2010). As Benson (2001: 19) observed, '[s]ocio-economic and ideological changes are rapidly bringing the notion of the autonomous learner into harmony with dominant ideologies of what it means to be a fully functioning member of a modern society'. This supposedly harmonious merger is most obvious in discourses of the knowledge economy and in the role of the individual who is to take responsibility for their own (lifelong) learning, as promoted in publications by, for example, the Commission of the European Communities (EC) and the Organisation of Economic Co-Operation and Development (OECD). What is envisaged here is a development towards a learning society whose members strive to increase human capital and to take responsibility for their learning. Autonomy becomes a cornerstone of this imagined 'high-technology knowledge society' which demands that 'learners must become proactive and more autonomous, prepared to renew their knowledge continuously and to respond constructively to changing constellations of problems and contexts' (EC, 1998: 15).

> In the knowledge economy, memorization of facts and procedures is not enough for success. Educated workers need a conceptual understanding of complex concepts, and the ability to work with them creatively to generate new ideas, new theories, new products, and new knowledge (...). *They need to be able to take responsibility for their own continuing, life-long learning.* (OECD, 2008: 1, emphasis added)

This programmatic call for fostering autonomy goes hand in hand with a demand for increasing individual responsibility and lifelong learning. Surely no-one would object to individual responsibility or to the idea that people learn throughout their lives. The point of the chapters in this volume, however, is that such bland, vacuous statements propagate individual responsibility, lifelong learning and autonomy as slogans, while aligning them with economic meanings that sell the political vision of the knowledge economy and the need for each member of society to contribute 'proactively' to the production of goods and services – and leave unsaid on whose behalf and for whose profit. Recommending autonomy sounds significantly more appealing than asking people to obey the rules of the knowledge economy.

This sheds light on some of the implications of the sloganization of autonomy when it is understood to refer to a set of behaviors and activities whose common denominator is doing something on one's own, regardless of what exactly this 'doing' entails and whose interests it serves. Ignoring such problems results in a shallow notion of autonomy which turns a blind eye to the power structures, tensions and desires involved in seemingly autonomous actions and behaviors, glossing over the fact that, more often than not, what we do on our own may not be self-determined. Our individual actions and behaviors may be more or less independent and self-determined, or they may be instances of compliance and obedience – as is the case in many learning environments. If 'doing them on our own' is considered a sufficient condition for autonomy, then virtually any behavior or activity can count as autonomous. Sloganized versions of autonomy demonstrate a lack of conceptual clarity which is first and foremost related to the theoretical decontextualization of the term.

Decontextualization

The decontextualization of autonomy can be observed historically, culturally and theoretically-conceptually. Autonomy is historically decontextualized when its origins and its histories are overlooked, it is culturally decontextualized when its meanings in different times and cultural environments are ignored, and it is theoretically-conceptually decontextualized when theories of autonomy and their respective conceptions of the term (all of which are themselves historically and culturally contingent) are not taken into account.

As mentioned above, when Holec coined the phrase *learner autonomy*, he did not reflect on autonomy as a term that had a rich cultural history in education and Western thinking. Perhaps it was due to this omission that the phrase quickly became popular, because it was easily adaptable to other discourses of the sovereign, free, self-determined Western subject. Especially in educational philosophy, autonomy had been an important notion since Immanuel Kant (1998 [1785]) first applied the term to the individual in moral philosophy. Formerly, it had had a collective meaning. For example, in Ancient Greek, autonomy was used to refer to political groups that had the right to govern themselves, a familiar meaning even today when we talk about the quest for Palestinian or Quebecois autonomy, for instance. Not until the Enlightenment did the notion of personal autonomy become the hallmark of the sovereign subject in Western educational thinking, celebrated by many and more recently critiqued widely. Ignoring the many histories of autonomy in education, as well as its celebration and critiques, inadvertently leads to promoting a notion of autonomy that remains historically and culturally blind (Schmenk, 2005).

In postwar Western Germany, the notion of autonomy became particularly influential when Theodor W. Adorno (2005 [1971]) declared it the single most important educational goal that might enable people to resist totalitarianism. Autonomy was invested with political meanings and used synonymously with emancipation and maturity (Meyer-Drawe, 1990; Rieger-Ladich, 2002). In his reflection on 'Education after Auschwitz', Adorno spelled out his educational agenda in the opening sentence: 'The premier demand upon all education is that Auschwitz not happen again' (Adorno, 2005: 191). He then declared that education must be geared towards fostering autonomy: 'The single genuine power standing against the principle of Auschwitz is autonomy, if I might use the Kantian expression: the power of reflection, of self-determination, of not cooperating' (Adorno, 2005: 196).

According to this definition, autonomy entails the ability to resist and say no, to think independently and critically, to not obey or comply. This kind of autonomy can be read as a call for disobedience that seeks to overcome what has widely been termed *Untertanenmentalität* (submissive mentality), which is characterized by subordination, the willingness to obey, silence in the face of authority – which many blame for the rise and survival of Germany's Nazi government. The political significance of Adorno's words in the postwar German-speaking world cannot be underestimated. In Germany, the worldwide uproar and political protests of the 1960s took on a specifically German focus geared chiefly towards learning from history and coming to terms with the recent past (*Vergangenheitsbewältigung*). The significance of Adorno's educational credo is that it called for educating the next generation in ways that prevented them from repeating the mistakes and atrocities committed, tolerated or passively witnessed by many of their parents and grandparents.

With this charged historical and cultural background it is all the more astounding that the discourse of learner autonomy in language learning – including German-speaking debates – rarely acknowledges this or other cultural histories of the term (see also Benson, 2007). Instead, an ahistorical understanding of autonomy prevails and ‚as noted above, much of what is promoted as autonomous learning remains confined to a kind of learning that resembles independence and critical thinking only on the surface. Even when learners complete tasks and other learning activities on their own, they may well be doing what they are supposed to do and what is expected of them (by teachers, parents, peers, potential employers, etc.). In other words, they may indeed be saying yes, rather than saying no, to any number of things that are simply not for them to decide. By labeling such learning on one's own as autonomy, examining the thorny question of how much – and what kind of – autonomy is really involved in actual practice is pushed aside.

In order to address these thorny questions, it is also important to take into consideration the *limitations* of personal autonomy, a topic long discussed in educational philosophy. In philosophical thinking, pure autonomy is not considered a realistic or existing state of persons. Rather, autonomy is always complemented by its opposite, heteronomy (Meyer-Drawe, 1990). Overlooking the heteronomous, other-determined conditions under which subjects act and live leads to a unidirectional view of the sovereign subject which ignores the network of power relations within which subjectivity is shaped and shapes itself. In other words, the belief that autonomy is possible – in life or in educational contexts – is itself problematic and leads to unrealistic assumptions about people and possibilities. Educational philosopher Meyer-Drawe (1990, 1998) observes in her publications on the history of autonomy as an educational ideal, that it has become increasingly difficult to distinguish between heteronomy and autonomy because much of what people do seems to originate from their own desires and wishes, yet often these have been fabricated elsewhere and successfully internalized by the subject. She terms this phenomenon 'illusions of autonomy' and argues in favor of an educational agenda that no longer ignores these illusions but rather aims to foster people's ability to see – and to question, if necessary – the heteronomous conditions and networks within which they are situated. Only if people have learned to inquire about and attempt to see heteronomy, Meyer-Drawe concludes, can they begin to assess the scope of their agency and their potential for autonomous thought and action.

To come back to the world of language education and learner autonomy, at the theoretical-conceptual level, the focus on the self-determined individual learner completely blocks out the many heteronomous dimensions of learning. Ignoring the dialectics of autonomy and heteronomy inadvertently results in theoretical-conceptual decontextualization. Heteronomy, or other-determination, is rarely considered in descriptions of learner autonomy or similar discourses hailing the autonomous subject that 'takes charge'. Yet heteronomy is arguably present, and often prevails, in learning arrangements that involve people completing tasks or communicating with each other, either face to face or via digital media. As a result of ignoring the heteronomous conditions under which learning takes place (for example, self-study, classroom learning, online communication or the use of digital media in general), many descriptions of learner autonomy in language education discourse would more appropriately be considered depictions of *illusions of autonomy*. This implies what Simons and Masschelein (2008: 51) and Peters (2001: 67) have called 'responsibilization', i.e. the tendency to enforce or impose responsibility on the individual, which turns on its head much of what educational philosophers have associated with autonomy.

The notion of learner autonomy as 'taking charge' bears only scant traces of Adorno's critical educational ideas. It also ignores the original Kantian theory of personal and moral autonomy, which entails the need to respect the autonomy of others. As long as the buzz about learner autonomy hinges on the use of an idealized and unquestioned slogan, questions about theoretical-conceptual precision or cultural and historical contingency cannot arise.

About this volume

The editors' uneasiness with the sloganization of terms such as autonomy or CLT was the starting point of our *sloganization* project. In May 2014 we organized a conference on the topic at the Humboldt-Universität zu Berlin, Germany. Many international scholars attended and shared their views of sloganization in language education discourse, encouraging the plan to produce an edited volume on the topic. The chapters in this volume include some of the topics presented at the Berlin conference, as well as additional contributions.

In Chapter 2, David Gramling investigates *innovation*, one of the most popular slogans in current educational rhetoric. Starting from current usages of innovation in language education and management, Gramling sets out to scrutinize innovation as a presentist, 'affirmative, depoliticized and essentialist' (Gramling, this volume: 26) notion and to reconstruct some of its histories. Turning towards examples of purported innovation in early, mid- and late 20th century language education discourse and beyond, Gramling illustrates several instances of the sloganization of the term *innovation*, alongside its increasing popularity in discourses of education and research marketing. His chapter reveals that the current, inherently positive and progressivist understanding of *innovation* makes it one of the most popular descriptors of what is considered (and/or promoted) as new, forward-looking and promising, and of what is geared towards a market that requires constant reinvention and novelty. These connotations differ markedly from earlier usages of the term, for example in Ancient Greece, where it denoted a sacrifice or 'fresh cut into a living being' (this volume: 37), meanings that 'belie the contemporary aura of beneficence' surrounding *innovation* today.

In Chapter 3, Dietmar Rösler focuses on notions that are often used alongside the epithets of innovation, namely, *paradigm shifts* and *turns* in language education discourse. He casts a critical eye over the trend to announce new turns and paradigm shifts, arguing that Kuhn's (1962) original conceptualization of *paradigm shifts* is largely ignored in attempts to brand new ('innovative') ideas for language education theory and practice. Taking the *communicative turn* and the German-speaking debate on *constructivism as a new paradigm* in language education as examples, Rösler demonstrates the inflated use of *turns* and *paradigm shifts* in the characterization of methods or theories that more appropriately should be regarded as extensions or further elaborations of existing frameworks and approaches. Declaring seemingly new (and often one's own) suggestions and ideas *paradigm shifts*, Rösler concludes, denigrates Kuhn's theory of scientific revolutions and what he referred to as paradigms and shifts, and prevents scholars from reflecting on the continuity, and thus the history, of issues and challenges in language education. As a result, the sloganization of *paradigm shifts* also contributes to the ahistoricity of language education discourse.

Gerhard Bach (Chapter 4) relates the sloganization of terms to the rapid pace at which scholars produce new ideas. Taking as his starting points Nadolny's (1987) novel on John Franklin's slowness, which contributed to his discovery of the Northwest Passage, and Kahnemann's (2011) thoughts on fast and slow thinking, Bach showcases how sloganization can result from the need to produce new ideas and theories quickly. He investigates Gardner's (1993) notion of 'multiple intelligences' (MI) and its application in language education discourse. This application, Bach argues, is problematic for a variety of reasons. It merely attaches new labels onto what was formerly known as language learning strategies or styles and does not add to our understanding of language learning; it ignores the complexity of language learning and teaching; and it universalizes learning and teaching to such an extent that it completely ignores their social and cultural embeddedness. He concludes that MI models for teaching serve 'the current dynamic for the marketization of ideas (even those that are not new), a process bearing the label of "sloganization"' (this volume: 69).

In Chapter 5, Britta Viebrock looks at the notions of *intercultural and transcultural learning* and discusses the use of these terms and their reception in German-speaking discourses of language education. She traces the sloganization of these terms in scholarly discourse, arguing that the lack of conceptual clarity of the term *culture* leads to simplistic and reductionist notions of inter- and transcultural learning. Viebrock expands her critical analysis to include educational policy papers and their (sloganized) use of intercultural and transcultural learning, and she reports on a study she conducted with language teachers demonstrating the impact of sloganization on practitioners' views and concepts. Inter- and transcultural learning, she concludes, is often sloganized in scholarly discourse and this tendency is reinforced on their uptake in educational policy papers, which usually operate with general and undifferentiated terms. Practitioners, on the other hand, tend to define the two notions in idiosyncratic ways that are informed neither by scholarly writings nor by educational policy papers. Sloganization of inter- and transculturality occurs in all three instances, but it takes on different forms due to the different stakeholders' interests and goals.

In Chapter 6, John Plews traces the notion of exposure in scholarly works on second language acquisition (SLA), language education and study abroad research. He scrutinizes the use of the term exposure and its different meanings in scholarly contributions and popular discourse, following Williams' (1985) work on cultural keywords. Similar to Williams, Plews sets out to explore 'the available and developing meanings of known words (...) and the explicit but as often implicit connections which people were making, in what seemed (...) particular formations of meaning' (Williams, 1985: 15). In order to investigate the semantics of *exposure*, Plews takes as a starting point the discrepancy between the frequent use of the term by students, parents or in the popular media, where it represents the widely held belief that the best way to learn a language is through exposure, that is to say, going to a country where the language is spoken, and a markedly decreasing use of the term in scholarly discourse. In his close readings of scholarly publications mentioning exposure, he identifies a range of meanings attached to the term, and traces the advent of a new slogan, 'input', which has largely replaced exposure. Popularized by Krashen's (1985) 'input hypothesis', what had previously been termed 'exposure' fell out of favor in academic circles. Plews concludes that the rise of the seemingly more scientific term 'input' demonstrates that 'common "exposure" is too indecent for the field of second language education. It cannot be observed easily as a controlled classroom environment' (Plews, this volume: 107).

Chapters 7 and 8 look at terms that have only recently entered debates in applied linguistics and language education. David Block investigates *language commodification*, a term that Monica Heller (2002, 2003) originally introduced and that has since gained considerable currency in critical works on language in the age of neoliberalism. Going back to Marx's thoughts and his concepts of materiality and labor, Block contextualizes 'commodity' and 'commodification' in theories of political economy and argues that the recent sociolinguistic discourse on the 'commodification of language' seems to be based on vague notions of both commodity and language. Given the marketization of language that is implicit in phrases such as employers' demands for applicants who possess excellent 'communication skills' or 'English', language itself becomes a (sellable) entity that needs to be broken down into manageable pieces (skill sets), which can then be demanded or sold. Critiques of linguistic marketization of this and similar kinds, Block argues, remain problematic as long as they focus on language commodification because 'any work that extends the semantic space of commodification as a construct is, in effect, based on acceptance of the market metaphor for all' (Block, this volume: 130). Commodification, he concludes, needs to be theorized more rigorously, because otherwise its 'seductive appeal' (this volume: 138) may render it a prime candidate for sloganization.

Aneta Pavlenko (Chapter 8) scrutinizes *superdiversity*. She argues that this notion has never been theorized appropriately in the first place, and so it cannot even be said to have undergone a process of sloganization. Rather, *superdiversity* has been marketed as a slogan from the outset. She undertakes a rigorous investigation of the term, demonstrating that *superdiversity*, due to its simplicity, memorability and emotional appeal, can be viewed as a successful slogan in sociolinguistics. Pavlenko traces the considerable success story of the term since its first coinage by Vertovec (2007) and identifies several branding strategies scholars have employed to appropriate and circulate the new term widely in a very short period of time. Turning to the question of what the term actually means and how it has been defined in scholarly discourse, Pavlenko examines many definitions and explanations in publications on superdiversity and observes a marked gap between the popularity of the term on one hand, and its conceptual clarity and precision on the other. Having branded *superdiversity* as 'the "it" word in the field' (Pavlenko, this volume: 144), Pavlenko argues that proponents of *superdiversity* operate with definitions of the term that seem to 'free us from the need to define categories' and instead declare the term simply a 'feature of our age' (this volume: 154), a 'sociocultural fact' that does not warrant further elaboration or questioning.

In the concluding chapter of the volume, the editors outline the pertinent questions and problems about sloganization in language education discourse arising from the individual chapters in this book. Because this volume introduces a new term (sloganization) to current discourses of language education, the conclusion takes stock and discusses the potential contribution of the study of sloganizations in the field of language education.

Finally, a word about the title of this volume: readers from or familiar with the English-speaking world may wonder why it is not entitled 'Sloganization in applied linguistics discourse'. One of the ongoing challenges of the project has been the fact that the field of scholarly inquiry that is the focus of this volume, *language education*, is not a discipline in its own right in many regions of the world, but rather is labeled and categorized differently in different cultural and institutional contexts. In English-speaking contexts, for instance, the volume's focus would fall into the wider domain of applied linguistics, but in the German-speaking world it would be classified as *Fremdsprachenforschung* (second/foreign language research and education). The German term *Angewandte Linguistik* (the direct translation of the English term) and the English *applied linguistics* are, linguistically and culturally speaking, false friends. *Angewandte Linguistik* is used for language research that is not predominantly concerned with multilingualism and foreign/second languages. Because the editors of this volume all have ties to the German-speaking world, we chose as an umbrella term in the title of this volume the term 'language education', because it overlaps with the English 'applied linguistics' but is not as broad in thematic range. Language education includes the domains of language use, discourse analysis and multilingualism, as well as foreign and second language learning and teaching.

Besides the contributors to our conference and the authors of the chapters in this volume, the editors extend their sincere gratitude to Aneta Pavlenko for her encouragement, support and initiating contact with Multilingual Matters, to the Humboldt-Universität zu Berlin for hosting the conference and to Anna Roderick from Multilingual Matters for her patience and support of this project. Heartfelt thanks also go to Andrea Speltz, Ann Marie Rasmussen, Paul Malone, John Plews and Alexander Sullivan for their help with the manuscript and their invaluable comments and suggestions for parts of the volume.

References

Adorno, T.W. (2005) Education after Auschwitz. In T.W. Adorno (ed.) *Critical Models: Interventions and Catchwords* (trans. H.W. Pickford) (pp. 191–204). New York: Columbia University Press. Originally published (1971) as *Erziehung zur Mündigkeit*. Frankfurt am Main: Surkamp.

Bachmann-Medick, D. (ed.) (2014) *The Trans/National Study of Culture. A Translational Perspective*. Bonn and Boston, MA: De Gruyter.

Bachmann-Medick, D. (2016) *Cultural Turns: New Orientations in the Study of Cultures*. Bonn and Boston, MA: De Gruyter.

Barfield, A. and Brown, S.H. (eds) (2007) *Re-interpreting Autonomy in Language Education*. London: Palgrave Macmillan.

Benson, P. (1997) The philosophy and politics of learner autonomy. In P. Benson and P. Voller (eds) *Autonomy and Independence in Language Learning* (pp. 1–12). London and New York: Routledge.

Benson, P. (2001) *Teaching and Researching Learner Autonomy in Language Learning*. London and New York: Routledge.

Benson, P. (2007) Autonomy in language teaching and learning. *Language Teaching* 40, 21–40.

Benson, P. (2011) What's new in autonomy? *The Language Teacher* 35 (4), 15–18.

Benson, P. (2013) Drifting in and out of view: Autonomy and the social individual. In P. Benson and L. Cooker (eds) *The Applied Linguistic Individual. Sociocultural Approaches to Identity, Agency and Autonomy* (pp. 75–89). Sheffield: Equinox.

Benson, P. and Voller, P. (1997) Introduction: Autonomy and Independence in Language Learning. In P. Benson and P. Voller (eds) *Autonomy and Independence in Language Learning* (pp. 18–34). London and New York: Routledge.

Billig, M. (2013) *Learn to Write Badly: How to Succeed in the Social Sciences*. Cambridge: Cambridge University Press.

Byram, M. (1997) *Teaching and Assessing Intercultural Communicative Competence*. Clevedon: Multilingual Matters.

Byram, M. (2008) *From Foreign Language Education to Education for Intercultural Citizenship: Essays and Reflections*. Clevedon: Multilingual Matters.

Council of Europe (2001) *The Common European Framework of Reference for Languages. Learning, Teaching, Assessment*. Strasbourg: Council of Europe. See https://rm.coe.int/1680459f97 (accessed 1 July 2017).

Crouch, C. (2011) *The Strange Non-Death of Neoliberalism*. Cambridge and Malden, MA: Polity.

Crouch, C. (2013) *Making Capitalism Fit for Society*. Cambridge and Malden, MA: Polity.

de Bot, K. (ed.) (2015) *A History of Applied Linguistics. From 1980 to the Present*. London and New York: Routledge.

EC (1998) *Education and Active Citizenship in the European Union*. Luxembourg: Office for Official Publications of the European Communities.
Entrepreneur Media (2017) Slogan. *Small Business Encyclopedia*. See https://www.entrepreneur.com/encyclopedia/slogan (accessed 23 November 2017).
Fairclough, N. (1993) Critical discourse analysis and the marketization of public discourse: The universities. *Discourse & Society* 4 (2), 133–168.
Fineman, M.A. (2004) *The Autonomy Myth. A Theory of Dependency*. New York: New Press.
Gardner, H. (1993) *Multiple Intelligences: The Theory of Practice*. New York: Basic Books.
Heller, M. (2002) Globalization and the commodification of bilingualism in Canada. In D. Block and D. Cameron (eds) *Globalization and Language Teaching* (pp. 47–63). London: Routledge.
Heller, M. (2003) Globalization, the new economy and the commodification of language. *Journal of Sociolinguistics* 7 (4), 473–492.
Holborow, M. (2015) *Language and Neoliberalism*. London and New York: Routledge.
Holec, H. (1980) *Learner Autonomy*. Strasbourg: Council for Cultural Co-operation of the Council of Europe. Originally published (1979) as *Autonomie et l'apprentissage des languages étrangeres*. Strasbourg: Conseil de l'Europe.
Jakisch, J., Königs, F.G. and Küster, L. (eds) (2013) Standpunkte der Fremdsprachenforschung. *Fremdsprachen lehren und lernen* 42 (1) (Special Topic Issue).
Kahnemann, D. (2011) *Thinking, Fast and Slow*. New York: Farrar, Straus & Giroux.
Kant, I. (1998 [1785]) *Groundwork of the Metaphysics of Morals* (trans. M. Gregor and J. Timmermann). Cambridge: Cambridge University Press.
Krashen, S. (1985) *The Input Hypothesis*. London: Longman.
Kuhn, T.S. (1962) *The Structure of Scientific Revolutions*. Chicago, IL: University of Chicago Press.
Little, D. (1994) Learner autonomy. A theoretical construct and its practical application. *Die Neueren Sprachen* 93, 430–442.
Meyer-Drawe, K. (1990) *Illusionen von Autonomie. Diesseits von Ohnmacht und Allmacht des Ich*. Munich: Kirchheim.
Meyer-Drawe, K. (1998) Streitfall 'Autonomie'. Aktualität, Geschichte und Systematik einer modernen Selbstbeschreibung von Menschen. In W. Bauer, W. Lippitz, W. Marotzki, J. Ruhloff, A. Schäfer and C. Wulf (eds) *Fragen nach dem Menschen in der umstrittenen Moderne* (pp. 31–49). Baltmannsweiler: Schneider Verlag Hohengehren.
Murray, G. (ed.) (2014) *Social Dimensions in Autonomy in Language Learning*. Basingstoke: Palgrave Macmillan.
Nadolny, S. (1987) *The Discovery of Slowness* (trans. R. Freedman). New York: Viking.
Nussbaum, M. (2010) *Not for Profit. Why Democracy Needs the Humanities*. Princeton, NJ: Princeton University Press.
OECD (1996) *The Knowledge-based Economy*. Paris: Organisation for Economic Co-operation and Development. See https://www.oecd.org/sti/sci-tech/1913021.pdf (accessed 25 March 2017).
OECD (2008) *Teaching, Learning and Assessment for Adults: Improving Foundation Skills*. Executive summary. Paris: Organisation for Economic Co-operation and Development. See https://www.oecd.org/edu/ceri/40026459.pdf (accessed 21 March 2017).
Pennycook, A. (1997) Cultural alternatives and autonomy. In P. Benson and P. Voller (eds) *Autonomy and Independence in Language Learning* (pp. 35–53). London and New York: Routledge.
Peters, M. (2001) Education, enterprise culture and the entrepreneurial self: A foucauldian perspective. *Journal of Educational Enquiry* 2/2, 58–71.
Powell, W.W. and Snellman, K. (2004) The knowledge economy. *Annual Review of Sociology* 30, 199–220.

Richards, J.C. (2006) *Communicative Language Teaching Today*. Cambridge: Cambridge University Press.
Rieger-Ladich, M. (2002) *Mündigkeit als Pathosformel. Beobachtungen zur pädagogischen Semantik*. Konstanz: Universitätsverlag.
Savignon, S.J. (2013) Communicative language teaching. In M. Byram and A. Hu (eds) *Routledge Encyclopedia of Language Teaching and Learning* (pp. 134–140). London and New York: Routledge.
Schmenk, B. (2005) Globalizing autonomy? *TESOL Quarterly* 39 (1), 107–118.
Schmenk, B. (2008) *Lernerautonomie. Kariere und Sloganisierung des Autonomiebegriffs*. Tübingen: Narr.
Schmenk, B. (2017) Myths of origin and the communicative turn. *Critical Multilingualism Studies* 5 (1), 7–36.
Simons, M. and Masschelin, J. (2008) Our 'will to learn' and the assemblage of a learning apparatus. In A. Fejes and K. Nicoll (eds) *Foucault and Lifelong Learning. Governing the Subject* (pp. 48–60). New York: Routledge.
Urciuoli, B. (2010) Neoliberal education. Preparing the student for the new workplace. In C. Greenhouse (ed.) *Ethnographies of Neoliberalism* (pp. 162–176). Philadelphia, PA: University of Pennsylvania Press.
Urdang, L. and Robbins, C.D. (eds) (1984) *Slogans*. Detroit: Gale Research.
Vertovec, S. (2007) Super-diversity and its implications. *Ethnic and Racial Studies* 30 (6), 1024–1054.
Williams, G. (2010) *The Knowledge Economy, Language and Culture*. Bristol: Multilingual Matters.
Williams, R. (1985) *Keywords: A Vocabulary of Culture and Society* (revised edn). New York: Oxford University Press.

2 We Innovators

David Gramling

The slogan innovation *seems a harmless enough word, although the emergence of coded descriptors like* innovation-friendly *or governmental initiatives like the EU's 'innovation union' (EC, 2015) hint that the term is undergoing a period of aggressive repurposing and social dissemination. This essay surveys the term 'innovation' between 1930 and 2015 as a particularly flexible cipher in the 'regime of anticipation' (Mackenzie, 2013) of US higher education language studies and foreign language instructional research. Using data from curricular program materials, mission statements, historical debates and commercial sector handbooks, I document the evolving and ever-newly coded functions, metonymies and connotations that 'innovative research and teaching' in this arena have accrued, particularly in the context of the US financial crisis of 2008 and the 'War on Terror'.*

In *applied linguistics and language studies contexts, methodological 'innovation' tends to play a more prominent role in research rhetoric than, say, in literary and cultural studies, where an ethos of historical extensivity most often still structures prevailing notions of good scholarly practice. This chapter will make several observations about how language studies research has come to trade on the dynamics and conceits of innovation, leading it to a presentist bias that generates disattention to historical continuities, underrepresents practices perceived as not contemporarily relevant, and consents to a progressive historical logic of knowledge supersession that automatically elevates certain traditions of language learning over others. In the spirit of Hannah Arendt's 1943 essay 'We refugees' and Lauren Berlant's monograph on* Cruel Optimism *(2011), the essay explores how the positive affect around innovation clouds enduring aspects of multilingual subjectivity in the context of economic globalization.*

> Oh! Powerful god, Apollo Aguieus, who watchest at the door of my entrance hall, accept this innovation; I offer it that you may deign to soften my father's excessive severity; he is as hard as iron, his heart is like sour wine; do thou pour into it a little honey.
> Aristophanes, *Wasps*, 422 BCE (Aristophanes, 1938)

> For centuries language learning has not been the place of innovation.
> Diane Larsen Freeman (Argondizzo, 2013: 12)

This chapter seeks a critical understanding of the role, usage and history of the word *innovation* in recent, and less recent, language education discourse. By proceeding backwards chronologically – from its most contemporary instances in scholarship to the term's counterintuitive Hellenic origins, I claim that applied linguists and second language studies researchers today have good reason to be cautious about the term *innovation*, which is far from a neutral, transposable catalyst for insight and action. I will further claim that the blithe or opportunistic use of the word – as in book or journal titles on the model of *Innovations in X* – participate (often unwittingly) in a supply-side logic about how, and upon whose temporal scale, foreign language teaching is thought to acquire and retain relevance. Because of its discursive collusion with the ethos of free-market *creative destruction*, sometimes known as (Joseph) 'Schumpeter's gale' (Schumpeter, 1942), *innovation*-based conceits about language education can profoundly undermine recent findings about subjectivity in language, whether those emerging from ecological (Steffensen, 2015), dynamic (Jessner, 2003), complexity-based (Larsen-Freeman, 1997), affective (Vinall, 2012; Pavlenko, 2006) or symbolic lines of thought (Kramsch & Whiteside, 2008).

The primary questions I will pursue are as follows. What discourses are language educators and researchers implicitly underwriting when we frame our work – seriously or casually – through *innovation*? Secondly, how have previous generations of modern language researchers and applied linguists approached, confronted, embraced or theorized *innovation* in their specific institutional and historical contexts? Lastly, what features of language learning and teaching are quietly but consequentially obscured, when they are pursued under the heading of *innovation*? What the current volume calls 'sloganization' is, I will claim, a process designed and then honed to suppress inconvenient counterevidence and counterdiscourses, precisely in such practically volatile and ideologically diverse global arenas as instructed language learning. It is therefore one of the tasks of this chapter to highlight instances where, even in 'innovation'-affirmative presentations of language education research findings, counterdiscourses are nonetheless in ample evidence – either in the words of study participants themselves or in the rhetorical and methodological tensions at large in the research presentation.

Contemporary Usages 1: The Aegis of Innovation

For most foreign language teachers over the course of a work week, the word *innovation* presents as a mild anodyne, unworthy of worry or reflection. Merely one more Latinate fixture amid the complex shibboleths of grant application or program review language, *innovation* is often uttered alongside *impactfulness* and other morphologically infelicitous neologisms – an uncherished pragmatic means towards a cherished vocational end. Already disposed to see it as our *professional* responsibility to translate our daily work into the lexicon of an audit culture that we struggle to decode, intuit or admire, some of us say *innovation* in meetings or write it in our institutional prose, whether or not we 'get it', and move on. This volume offers an opportunity to pause upon this word, and to review a number of historical instances in which innovation has come into meaningfulness (or meaningful meaninglessness) in diverse and contradictory ways for language education discourse.

As an opening touchstone from recent years, I should like to take to hand a fine collection of essays edited by Carmen Argondizzo, Italian linguist and President of the Italian Association of University Language Centers (*Associazione Italiana dei Centri Linguistici Universitari*). Entitled *Creativity and Innovation in Language Education*, this 2013 volume comprises three prefaces, one editor's introduction and 19 chapters covering everything from neuroscience education in multilingual settings to corpus linguistics approaches to fairy tales. Impeccable on their own methodological terms, these 19 essays collectively betray, however, a rather arms-length relationship to *creativity* and *innovation*, the titular aegises under which they are collected. Excluding running headers and verbatim invocations of the book's title, there occur (over the 372 pages of research findings) only 25 unique mentions of *innovation/innovative*, in their various nominal and adjectival forms. Of the 19 essays, only two deal in a sustained and substantive way with the concept of innovation; eight essays mention it only in their introductory paragraphs, in a gracious effort to tie into the collection's theme; seven essays do not speak of innovation at all. Of the 25 uniquely collocated mentions of innovation throughout the volume, the majority arise in the midst of a list of terms where innovation appears either undefined or otherwise spirited into a catalog, for instance: 'creativity and innovation' (Myers, 2013: 45), 'innovation, community, and feelings' (Myers, 2013: 51) or 'administration, law, marketing, patents, innovation' (Argondizzo, 2013: 181).

Innovation contra magic

Among the two essays in the collection that do discuss, theorize and explore innovation as such, before investigating language education phenomena under its celebratory auspices, one is Marie Myers' study of peer communication in a French as a second language teacher preparation course in Canada (Myers, 2013: 45). Apparently taking a cue from the volume's speculative theme, Myers includes 'innovation' among the three primary qualitative categories ('innovation, community, and feelings') through which she aims to understand the self-reported experiences of Canadian French teachers-in-training and their relationships to their peers. Interestingly, however, Myers finds that 'innovation', in the end, has played a decidedly unimportant role in her subjects' self-conceptions during training, relative to the other two categories of experience, 'community' and 'feelings'. The two instances where participants have volunteered personal experiences that Myers understands as reflecting 'innovation' in their work as teachers are as follows:

(1) Honnêtement jusqu'à date on n'a pas suivi les directives du Ministère, on fait les choses un peu différemment. [Honestly, to date we haven't followed Ministry directives, we do things a little differently.]
(2) Je veux être professeur à Hogwarts (l'école de Harry Potter). C'est plus simple de contrôler les élèves avec la magie. [I want to be a teacher at Hogwarts (Harry Potter's school). It is easier to control pupils with magic.] (Myers, 2013: 58)

While 'innovation' is the term of art Myers calls upon to analytically house these two statements, these teachers appear actually to be foregrounding practices inimical to 'innovation' in its commonest sense. The teacher-in-training speaks in the first case of bucking the dictates of the Ministry of Education and doing as one pleases, and in the second case, of wizardry, magic, mind control and Quidditch. Thus it appears that while Myers is prompting her informants with the token 'innovation', they are ill-disposed to take it up – politely offering up their own conceptual counter-bids. It would certainly be possible in such a light for a researcher who is bullish about innovation to claim that what these teachers are doing is *translating* innovation into their own experiences, thereby propagating a further, *innovative* form for the innovation discourse itself. Such is indeed one of the key characteristics of a winsome slogan: in addition to its wiles at suppressing counterevidence, a sturdy slogan is equally eager to *appropriate* counterevidence, spontaneously and as needed.

What else is at work in this multiply disengaged 'engagement' with innovation, as instantiated by the discursive occasion of this collection of essays? I wish to reiterate that, despite the curious way 'innovation' is handled in the volume, the research within it makes a wide-ranging and important contribution to language education discourse generally. The articles themselves suffer no glaring methodological drawbacks, and are not overly compromised by the volume's collective nod to the slogan *innovation*. Indeed, good research is taking place here under its graces. But, in a collection dedicated to innovation, even the essay that takes this category most seriously finds that its research subjects have little interest in the concept or phenomenon itself.

Key, perhaps, to understanding this puzzle is that the gathering that gave rise to the volume – clearly a very productive meeting indeed – was titled '1st Conference on Creativity and Innovation in Language Studies', so as to correspond with the 2009 European Year of Creativity and Innovation, whence the funding for the gathering issued. There has not been a second CILS conference since this 'first' event in 2009. A certain tableau slowly emerges here that, in its socio-epistemological aspects, seems to indicate the scene this volume calls 'sloganization': eager and dedicated researchers gathering to dialogue about their current work, under cover of a slogan that neither they nor their research subjects express much interest in theorizing or embodying. (I should mention that the slogan 'creativity' endures an equally disinterested treatment throughout the collection, although it is retained in the four overarching section titles throughout the book, while 'innovation' is dropped from these altogether.)

This initial case study provides us with two characteristics with which we might work towards an understanding of sloganization processes within language education discourse. First, slogans benefit from an extraordinary capaciousness when it comes to suppressing and subsuming counterevidence in a given discursive scene. Secondly, practitioners often gather under the aegis of a slogan – traveling often thousands of miles to present their research in its name – without themselves displaying any particular affection or commitment to the conceptual specificity of the slogan. In this sense, slogans operate almost like a centripetal mating call, drawing even the most noncommittal interlocutors into their orbit for enough time to establish in-group/out-group conceits.

Contemporary Usages 2: The Imperative of Innovation

An apparent counter-example to the tableau of the sloganization process above is John Trent's (2014) Hong Kong-based study of 'Innovation as identity construction in language teaching and learning', which leads off with an engaged and explicit investment in innovation as a logistical, methodological and institutional value.[1] Drawing on Everett Rogers' (1962) germinal book, *Diffusion of Innovations*, now in its fifth printing (2003), Trent is keen to understand the 'divorce of innovation from successful implementation or diffusion' and the 'bleak picture of the adoption of educational innovation within the classroom' (Trent, 2014: 56). Surveying other researchers' findings on this question, Trent notes that the problem of non-innovation appears to stem either from teachers' 'overt resistance' to innovation or from 'token adoption, whereby teachers claim to have changed their classroom beliefs and practice yet leave their actual day-to-day engagement in teaching unaltered' (Trent, 2014: 56–57). Accordingly, Trent seconds Numa Markee (2001) in suggesting that these misfires of practice arise from 'neglect of the implementation process' (Trent, 2014: 57), a gap which Trent hopes to bridge by pursuing 'an integrated framework for understanding teacher identity' (Trent, 2014: 58). The remainder of Trent's multiple case study follows three full-time, early-career English language teachers in Hong King, anonymized in the article with the outwardly Anglophone names of Daniel, Claire and Andrew, along with three department heads, Tim, Pauline and Ronald. During Trent's brief presentation of these research subjects, the topic of their own ethnic, linguistic and institutional positionalities is elided completely. Nonetheless, 'teacher identity' is proposed as the overarching category through which to investigate frictions in implementing educational innovation.

This is, of course, an interesting axiomatic assumption. While we do learn *en passant* about Hong Kong's five-band assessment system of primary school meritocracy (Cheng, 2009), itself a legacy of British colonial rule, any further attention to the structural, material and economic details of these teachers' positions recedes, in Trent's analysis, behind the selectively problematized aperture of 'teacher identity' and a generally psychologizing approach to teacher 'pessimism' (Trent, 2014: 58). The resulting, and ostensibly vexing, friction between innovation and implementation, which Trent hypothesizes as lying in the intransigencies of teacher identity, offers itself up without ado to the 'managing innovation' models of other researchers such as Alan Waters (2009, 2014). Concerned with similar human x-factors to those of Trent, Waters regrets that, although English 'has become a major "growth area" in recent years', the implementation of innovation 'has often been less successful than intended' (Waters, 2009: 421). Here, at last, the underlying idiom of commercial saturation and cognitive capitalism – of 'major growth areas' and unoptimized consumer adoption habits – is in plain sight.

For their part, Trent's early-career teacher informants on this topic of innovation appear to have been approximately as interested in the phenomenon as had been Marie Myers' French teachers-in-training – who were, we will remember, inclined to champion the role of magic and resistance in their work, but not innovation. In the course of data collection, Trent asked his six participants to 'discuss their beliefs about language teaching and learning, their understandings of innovation in language teaching and learning, and how they planned to introduce innovative teaching and learning activities within their schools' (Trent, 2014: 64). This data collection design means that, from the outset, participants were given the discursive token 'innovation' affirmatively, and their responses thus tended to orient themselves – in accordance with the pragmatics of politeness – around reciprocating or accommodating that particular token 'innovation' in various ways. Moreover, the research questions presuppose *that* the teachers 'plan (…) to introduce innovative (…) activities' and, accordingly, skip directly to the *how*. This is a salient methodological detail when one considers that said teachers may not have planned to do anything of the sort, or that they might have generally preferred (prior to the interview) to introduce into their classrooms, for instance, 'good' activities or 'proven', 'time-honored' or 'sound' activities instead of 'innovative' ones. For applied linguists, of course, such terminological divergences at this minute scale are not mere accidents of spontaneous formulation or vernacular interpretation. The choice of 'good' over 'innovative', for instance, may index entire categories of experience – even entire cosmologies, ethical frames and axiologies of being.

When prompted in this way in the interview context, Daniel, Claire and Andrew do indeed labor to identify themselves and their teaching practices along a spectrum between innovative and 'boring' (Trent, 2014: 66), and they tend accordingly to counter-distinguish their own outlook and efforts from those of 'lots of traditional Hong Kong teachers', as Daniel puts it (Trent, 2014: 66). Here we see a third feature of sloganization at work: the establishment of in-group versus out-group membership – of those who 'get it' versus those who 'don't (yet) get it' – often accomplished implicitly on ethnic, gendered, generational and classed axes. While Daniel cites his drama-based methods in a bid to style himself 'innovative', in reciprocation of the research questions posed to him, Claire likewise does so by referencing her commitments to communicative language teaching (CLT; Trent, 2014: 68).

Although drama pedagogy and CLT are on their own merits widely recognized and time-honored classroom methodologies, here they spontaneously acquire the status of innovation *only* in negative relation to what traditional Hong Kong teachers are alleged to have been doing meanwhile – a set of practices that remains unspecified throughout the article, as none of those negatively characterized teachers was asked about their experiences. It becomes gradually clear in the data analysis that 'innovation' is implicitly ethnicized and discursively coded, as that which teachers who were trained in (or symbolically affiliated with) Anglophone programs abroad – like for instance the 2009 European Year of Creativity and Innovation discussed above – are poised to deliver, while 'traditional Hong Kong' practitioners reportedly continue to put up barriers to implementation. Particularly given the appeal here to the broad category of 'teacher identity', the sloganization process around innovation thus begins to show itself to be ethnicized and racialized in complex ways. A similar neocolonial, neo-Orientalist dynamic can be traced in other 'innovation'-affirmative research arenas in Asian English learning settings, for instance in Pickering and Gunashekar's (2014) collection, *Innovation in English Language Teacher Education*.

At the close of his study, Trent reiterates that 'The objective of this critical reflection then is not to replace any particular discourse of language teaching and learning with another but to allow all teachers to not only see how they are constituted by discourse but also to explore the possibility of moving beyond constructed binary categories such as "innovative" and "traditional" teacher' (Trent, 2014: 75). This is a helpful discourse-critical caveat, but it cannot undo the underlying features of the incitement to discourse about innovation that the study performs. First, the focus on 'teacher identity' and self-perception tends to obscure the material and structural means by which supply-side forces make it nearly impossible for early-career practitioners to forego rhetorical paradigms like 'innovation'. Secondly, the post- and neocolonial dynamics of market saturation of English as a 'major growth area' (Waters, 2009) are underspecified and undertheorized in the argument, while the ethnic and linguistic positionalities of the teaching subjects are selectively effaced. Thirdly, as in Argondizzo's and Myers's research contexts discussed previously, the word 'innovation' takes on the incantatory function of a shibboleth, in compliance with which respondents perform their in-group or out-group relation vis-à-vis an innovation paradigm that is presupposed to be beneficial, benign, progressive and characteristic of professional behavior as such.

Without the presumption that *innovative* by definition means *benefit*, these studies would necessarily look quite different. It is, however, this presumption that drives such humane, engaged and otherwise thoughtful research as Trent's and Myers' studies, a presumption that rests upon a necessarily unspecified understanding of innovation as such. Trent (via Waters, 2009), for instance, relies on West and Farr's equally non-specific characterization of innovation as the 'attempt to bring about beneficial change' (West & Farr, 1990: 9). Such a shorthand definition of innovation is itself sloganistic, in that it appears poised above all else to recruit users to the very signifier it sets out to define. This curiosity makes sense, once viewed in light of the fact that Michael H. West is a management professor who, according to his faculty website at Lancaster University, specializes in 'the links between enlightened people management and performance'.[2] His sloganizing definition for innovation no less than 'performs' a social link between the word innovation itself and an in-group of enlightened, managed people.

Working with such an affirmative, depoliticized and essentialist definition as West and Farr's – cleansed of the dynamics of power, coloniality, relations of production, cognitive capitalism and globalized market saturation – Trent, Waters and Myers unintentionally allow the concept of 'innovation' to hitchhike (by way of their studies) from management school to language classrooms for free, without accounting for the profound acts of conceptual translation and effacement that this transposition has necessarily required. These studies thus sloganize *innovation* to the extent that they underspecify, conflate or suppress certain aspects of the supply-side economic history of innovation discourse, thus turning the term into what Bonnie Urciuoli (2000: n. p.) calls a 'strategically deployable shifter'. The laundered result is a slogan to which hardly anyone can articulate a reasonable impromptu objection, without coming across as what Adelheid Hu, writing from the European language proficiency assessment context, characterizes as 'a denier, a refuser, a troublemaker, an antediluvian, or a ditherer' (Hu, 2012: 72).

In addition to the characteristics of sloganizations we noted in the first section of this chapter, 'Contemporary Usages 1: The Aegis of Innovation', namely their substantively suppressive and socially centripetal force, the case just discussed adds three further features: (1) slogans are often ethnicized, classed, gendered and racialized in ways that ensure interactional hegemony for in-group users; (2) slogans are most effective when they are underspecified and underdefined, because they then benefit from the presumption of benevolence and progress; (3) slogans are a certain kind of sign. They are not indices, symbols or icons, but they possess a deictic quality: recruitment tools to a 'here and now' of utterance, interested in multiplying their own enunciation in the mouths and writings of others.

Historical Usages

The early War on Terror era

Each of the primary studies discussed above emerged from post-2010 research contexts, in European and Asian educational settings. We now turn to historical usages of the word 'innovation' in language education discourse in the US context. Richard Kiely's 2006 essay on 'Evaluation, innovation, and ownership in language programs' is exemplary for its (more upbeat than urgent) recourse to innovation, over other alternative values or slogans, in moments of institutional crisis, such as during the early US-led War on Terror (2001–2006) and its national, securitarian reinvestment in critical languages:

> Through the development and evaluation of innovations we can generate critical engagement with the FL curriculum, invest time in clarifying constructs of teaching and learning, establish an internal driver of program development to counter any dominance from external mandates, and facilitate opportunities for teachers' own professional and academic development. (Kiely, 2006: 597)

Noteworthy here is that it is difficult to find any plausible counterargument to Kiely's suggestions. Critical engagement with the FL curriculum is an objective that no-one can oppose. Innovation for Kiely is, however, less an action or a measure than a kind of conversation starter, a prompt, a disposition of social readiness that augurs a 'total mobilization' of personnel and resources that otherwise, one assumes, would remain mired in doubt, contradiction and disorderliness. The incitement to innovation, in turn, offers an opportunity to perceive and define oneself clearly, because this is what students, stakeholders and markets require:

> Their value is not so much in their success as in their inception and implementation. They illustrate teams of teachers developing their programs from the inside, in response to changing market situations. The position taken in this department was to evaluate and innovate in a cycle of engagement with different stakeholder perspectives and present the detail of this approach to external inspectors and monitors. The innovation reflex engendered a capacity to cope with changes in recruitment patterns, student profiles and needs, as well as emerging technologies. (Kiely, 2006: 601)

Again, the spirit of an 'innovation reflex' as outlined here is obviously admirable, and one hopes that the department in question did indeed experience success as a consequence of it. The logic of 'ownership', however – i.e. the charismatic diorama of 'teams of teachers developing their programs from the inside' – makes two presumptions: (1) that teamwork and internally generated change had been demonstrably absent prior to the advent of an innovation reflex; and (2) that participating in this cycle affirmatively was the 'smart' way to retain autonomy in a changing landscape.

Although Kiely's early War on Terror call for readiness for institutional change is unimpeachable, he shared the flexible discursive space of 'innovation' of the 2000s with colleagues who felt relatively unabashed in invoking innovation purely as a pragmatic discourse marker or opportunistic self-stylization, rather than as an ethical value of some kind. In his 2005 ethnographic essay 'Power, politics, and the pecking order: Technological innovation as a site of collaboration, resistance, and accommodation', the French language scholar James Davis relates a scene shared by one of his informants which dramatizes the range of magical effects the word innovation can have in an academic social setting. One of Davis' subjects in the study recalls an academic social interaction among a pre-tenure faculty member, a department chair, dean and a provost, all of whom are assembled to 'tour' a new language teaching technology, which the pre-tenure faculty member had helped to pioneer. The faculty member informant recalls as follows:

> So the provost (...) he's a lawyer, gets right down to it, he was clicking along, I was showing him the thing, kind of talking about it and explaining things to him (...). He finally pushed himself away and said, ([the informant] changed his tone of voice and accent) 'This is great! This is great! This is just what we need to be doing! This is innovation, blah, blah blah.' (...) And he said, 'I just got one last question for you.' I said, 'Well, OK. What is it?' And he said (...) 'I wanna know if this stuff will help you *git* tenure'. (Davis, 2005: 171, emphasis in original)

Having confidently categorized the work that the faculty member had presented to him as 'innovation', rather than something else – perhaps 'research', 'service', 'community outreach' or 'creative output' – the provost shifts the frame of the conversation from the 'friendly tour' genre to the 'promotion strategy meeting' genre. Utterly convinced of the current exchange value of the language learning technology (as innovation) in a certain market register, the provost is, however, himself not quite sure how to convert it into the older currency of tenurability, where a more conservative sense of scholarly output (articles and monographs) still held sway at his own institution. Understanding the implicature in the air, the faculty member had the presence of mind to realize this wasn't a question he personally could answer, and passed it over to his chair and dean. The dramatized account continues:

> There was like this pregnant pause, and it was great, and I was sitting in the middle of it. And, so, finally, the dean said (in a halting voice), 'Well, of course, what we're interested in is innovation and', you know (laughter), and the provost said (again, [the informant] changed his voice and banged on his desk in imitation of the provost), 'Well, I'm glad to see that because I think this is important, and for us to promote this kind of technological change, it's gonna have to count for tenure. Lemme tell you. This has been interesting. Gotta go.' And, then he left. (Laughter). (Davis, 2005: 171)

After sharing these data, Davis does not go into particular detail in his analysis of this exchange, allowing it to speak for itself. But the potency of the token 'innovation' in the exchange deserves some prolonged attention, as it demonstrates some particularly sloganistic qualities. The provost has ventriloquated the word from someone else's discourse, establishing ironic and cynical distance from the truth claim that 'this is what we need to be doing'. If English had a subjunctive mood, the indirect-speech nature of the provost's response would be even clearer. Yet even this formulation is fascinating, as it implicitly projects the 'doing' into an unrealized, aspirational future, rather than recognizing the present work that the faculty member seated before him has already done. Innovation is thus that which is deferred into the imminent future as the next necessary step, rather than the step already taken. It is what Adrian Mackenzie calls a 'regime of anticipation' (Mackenzie, 2013).

Having appropriated the category 'innovation' from an unascribed source of general contemporary knowledge, and having used 'blah blah blah' to establish an in-group presumption that his subordinates share his perspective, the provost has nonetheless paid little sustained attention to the substance of the contribution presented. Having then counterposed the newfangled value of 'innovation' with the old-school ritual of 'git[tin'] tenure', the provost nonetheless succeeds in getting the dean to repeat the token 'innovation', thereby committing his college to new tenure guidelines in which innovation becomes a specified and quantifiable category of output. The sudden and binding nature of this performative transformation *in situ* among four colleagues positioned vertically on an institutional hierarchy shows how 'innovation' has acquired a flexibly performative stature in various institutional settings – and that, despite the on-record cynicism and dismissiveness the provost shows towards the concept and substance behind the word itself. I have gone, somewhat pedantically, through the steps of an interaction like this so as to propose that innovation bears a particular kind of contemporaneity that prohibits many practitioners from either critiquing it or subscribing to it in any substantive way. It is a word that forces speakers into a pose of cynicism that they would rather be spared; perhaps this is why the provost was so eager to beg off to his next meeting?

Mid-century usages: How the rise of innovation co-occurred with the method wars

One might be tempted to imagine the idea of 'innovation' to be a rather recent implantation into the world of language teaching discourse, emerging in confluence and consonance with 'new work order' (Gee *et al.*, 1996) bursts in privatization, responsibilization and flexibilization narratives. But the conjuncture of innovation over invention (and other alternatives) occurred around WWI Austria, thanks to one particular strain of industrial and commercial thinking. Generally regarded as the father of innovation studies, the Austrian Joseph Schumpeter, however, did not make use of the concept itself in his earlier work in German, for instance in his 1911 *Theorie der wirtschaftlichen Entwicklung*, in which he generally refers to 'combination' as the major driving force in economic development. In a second 1926 printing, the English translation *Theory of Economic Development*, however, does speak of innovation, in terms of 'newness' (Schumpeter, 1934). By the end of the Great Depression decade of the 1930s, Schumpeter (1939: 84) was willing to consider as innovation as 'any doing things differently', although this principle held no promise of beneficence, as for instance West and Farr's latter-day sense would. This 'any doing things differently', for Schumpeter, broke down into five categories: commodities, methods, forms of organization, sources of supply, new markets. The focus for Schumpeter, however, as Godin notes, was still on combination and not technological advancement or commercialization. Meanwhile, anthropologists such as H.G. Barnett (in his 1953 book, *Innovation: The Basis of Cultural Change*) adapted the Depression-era, war-era and postwar-era axiom of innovation-as-'any doing things differently' as a theoretical constant for culture at large, rather than merely for commerce. The ensuing decades saw the further diffusing of the innovation impulse from economics into commerce and into cultural analysis at large. Being new and being different had become not only a market desideratum, but a historical inevitability.

Bringing the concept back to its founding discipline, Chris Freeman's (1974) *The Economics of Industrial Innovation* proposed that only a 'professionalized industrial R&D [Research and Development] system' (Freeman, 1974: 25) would be able to ensure the 'introduction and spread of new and improved products and processes in the economy' (Freeman, 1974: 18). In the same spirit as Kiely writes above of the 'innovation impulse' and the 'cycle of engagement' in his foreign language department, Freeman developed Schumpeter's early sense for combination into a sustainably commercializable cycle, which required constant followers and adopters. Innovation was no longer the *production* of the new technology, advancement or difference, but the *adoption* of it among end-users. From Schumpeter to Freeman, then, the moment of innovation shifts from the locutionary end of the performative axis to the perlocutionary. In Freeman's distinction, 'An invention is an idea, a sketch or a model for a new or improved device, product, process or system. (…) An innovation in the economic sense is accomplished only with the first commercial transaction' (Freeman, 1974: 22). According to this reorientation, a research-intensive sector is designed, beginning in the mid-1970s, so as to stimulate a 'higher rate of technical change' (Freeman, 1974: 277).

The provost in Davis' (2005) study is a fine exemplar of the ultimate success of this stimulatory imperative, as he was primed to change a time-honored institutional constant (tenure) to accommodate something he had spontaneously identified as an innovation. In this sense, the potency of the rate of change is the essence of innovation, rather than the nature of that change. Chris Freeman is, however, aware that the successful uptake among end-users 'depends upon understanding, and an important part of this understanding relates to economic aspects of the process, such as costs, return on investment, market structure, rate of growth and distribution of possible benefits' (Freeman, 1974: 32).

As noted thus far, the slogan *innovation* seems a harmless enough word on spec, but the term is undergoing a period of aggressive repurposing in globalized cognitive capitalism and the monetized mobilization of intellectual property across traditional market frontiers. In applied linguistics and second language studies, scholars are relatively familiar with the perennial rituals and rhythms of novelty. In these disciplines, methodological 'innovation' has played a more prominent role over the last half century in research rhetoric than, say, in literary and cultural studies, where an ethos of historical circumspection and extensivity most often still structures prevailing notions of scholarly practice. Yet scholars in second language acquisition have grown somewhat weary of the cycle of innovation and its promises, leading some to embrace a 'post-methods' stance. Kumaravadivelu writes, 'Since the audiolingualism of the 1940s, TESOL has seen one method after another roll out of Western universities and through Western publishing houses to spread out all over the world. On each occasion, teachers in other countries and other cultures have been assured that this one is the correct one, and that their role is to adapt it to their learners, or their learners to it' (Kumaravadivelu, 2003: 20).

Innovation is a difficult word to track and then mark in the social sciences and humanities, primarily because it often acts as a 'strategically deployable shifter' (Urciuoli, 2000: n. p.). Reflecting on such lexemes as *critical thinking*, *communication*, *skills*, *citizenship*, etc., in the 'recruitment register' of collegiate marketing programs, Urciuoli asserts that:

> Contemporary U.S. social life is full of speech situations in which what appear to be 'the same' lexemes are distributed across a range of discursive fields and are, so to speak, naturalized (over the course of pragmatic sedimentation) into those fields in ways that make their meaning appear quite transparent among its users. In this way, 'the same' lexemes can come to mean quite different things in different fields. But since social actors, especially in the U.S., are notoriously resistant to the idea that context shapes (or indeed, has any right to shape) the 'real' meanings of words, actors operate as if meanings are constant across contexts. (Urciuoli, 2000: n. p.)

In his study, *Beyond Methods*, Kumaravadivelu cites Mackey's jeremiad on another such word, *method*, which means simultaneously 'so little and so much' to teachers, administrators, learners, funders and program coordinators alike (Kumaravadivelu, 2003: 23). Talk of 'method', according to Mackey, betrays a 'willful ignorance of what has been done and said and thought in the past'. The reason for this 'lies in the state and organization of our knowledge of language and language learning [, and] in the vested interests, which methods become' (Mackey, 1965: 139). Innovation is most certainly also such a pragmatically sedimented lexeme, which traffics on the presumption that 'we all know what it means'. But particularly for a relatively specialized arena of thought like language education, there is good reason to look briefly beyond its disciplinary usage and into the lengthy past of the concept of innovation itself.

Early 20th century usages: Innovation in modern languages discourse

A glance at the first 50 years of *The Modern Language Journal* from 1916 onwards belies any presentist assumption that innovation is a newcomer on the scene of language education discourse. 'Innovation' was an ambivalent and ambiguous chess piece in language teaching research throughout the 1920s and 1930s, particularly in its tense relation to the effects of the Great Depression and the 1929 'Coleman Report', officially 'The Teaching of Modern Foreign Languages in the United States, chaired by Algernon Coleman'. This report, which cast doubt on the practicality and practicability of conversational language instruction (as opposed to reading-based methods) incited blustery debates between Colley Sparkman and Elton Hawking in 1932 about whether the Coleman findings offered any 'innovation' whatsoever. Meanwhile, other US and Canadian foreign language teachers (Bockstahler, 1932; Gullette, 1934: 384; Vail, 1933) were focused on presenting ad hoc 'innovations' of classroom method that would not burden students' already strapped

Depression-era pocketbooks. Innovation in this sense was – similarly to Kiely's context – about doing more with less, a leaner-and-meaner, optimistic, bootstrapping logic that deliberately flew in the face of pre-Depression institutional orthodoxies about method and professionalism in foreign language teaching. Promoting his cost-free innovations at Queens University, Bockstahler, for instance, wrote: 'One of the reasons why students of languages do not progress faster is lack of interest in the work caused by dry as dust methods of teaching and the use of poorly selected material' (Bockstahler, 1932: 16).

Prior to the Great Depression, 'innovation' in language education discourse had tended to refer to broader, more expensive infrastructural developments, such as the introduction of the Junior High School system (Stroebe, 1920: 42) or Columbia University's decision to move language classes out of the traditional core curriculum and into the extension services (Zeydel, 1924: 493). By 1941, scholars and teachers had witnessed a full gamut of sensibilities around 'innovation' in North American language education discourse – from the tactical-survivalist to the strategic-expansionist. Contemporary retrospectives on the mutable career of 'innovation' took various forms, but one in particular deserves in historical hindsight the kind of admiration that it most certainly did not receive at the time of publication, namely John Scott Irwin's 'idle idyll' from 1941, published in *The Modern Language Journal*, entitled 'Little Read Writing-Hood and Gramma Translation'.

Resisting innovation in Great Depression-era modern languages

A fairytale à clef, which must have appeared to Irwin's contemporaries as something of an uncharitable bromide, John Scott Irwin's send-up of 1930s language education debates makes for a fascinating ethnographic artifact 75 years hence, animating as it does (in fairytale form) most of the noble elements available on the disciplinary field – including form, empty formality, content, method, social sciences, aspiration, knowledge and indeed 'innovation'. Noteworthy from the start of his tale is that Irwin foregoes any mention of specific foreign languages, national antagonisms or fields of political allegiance. The story is told rather around the *loci amoeni* of Happy Valley (presumably the community of monolingual learners) and Knowledge Mountain (the goal of liberal discovery through multilingual investigation). Gramma Translation, we are told:

> was a kind but old-fashioned and rather gruff old lady who lived on a hill outside the village, and kept flowers, goats, bees and canaries, and loved to entertain children. They would flock to her on baking days, and, once the younger members had overcome their fear of her goat, Form, she would reward them with great slices of warm bread, fresh from the oven, and dripping with butter and honey. (…) She was an extrovert. She lived life steadily and she lived it whole, and she expected the children to do the

> same. (...) To the poor in spirit, Gramma would often remark, quite casually, that not since the middle ages (or was it the seventeenth century?) had it been customary to regard mountain travel merely as a necessary evil, and that the men of the Renaissance really enjoyed it. (Irwin, 1941: 375–376)

The tale, thus far, seems to hinge on no particular sociopolitical or commercial context other than perhaps modernity writ large. It was penned, however, after a decade of crushing fiscal and material privation in North America, during which the Works Progress Administration and Progressive politics more broadly sought to offer new, revenue-generating solutions for flailing public and semi-public institutions, like high schools and universities. Happy Valley, Gramma Translation and Knowledge Mountain – in this context – track very closely to the daily needs and struggles of those institutions.

> Once, indeed, an offensively well-dressed young man with slick, perfumed hair and a flattering smile, had entered [Gramma's] front gate, and, striding boldly, hat in hand, up the path past the beds of blue bells and foxglove to where she sat knitting on her porch, had tried to sell her, on the installment plan, a book prepared by educational experts and containing such phrases as 'multiple approach,' 'multi-sensory perception,' 'higher frequency brackets,' and the like. Gramma Translation didn't let him get very far before she seized a broom and drove the invader for that considerable speed, in a manner worthy of Aunt Betsy Trotwood. 'Such gibberish,' she exclaimed, with a flash of fire in her eye. (Irwin, 1941: 376)

Gramma Translation's contemptuous and violent resistance to the advantages of slick young methodologists is not in itself particularly revealing, and while the man with the perfumed hair is certainly a salesman and a knowledge merchant, 'innovation' itself cannot immediately be said to be at hand here. Gramma Translation continues teaching her learners, without the help of any commercial wares, how to avoid getting stung by the bees, and 'as the children grew in size and ability, she led them on expeditions of increasing length over the hills back of her house, and even into the mountains themselves. These expeditions became known as "Gramma Translation Exercises"' (Irwin, 1941: 376). Growing tired over the years, she does, however, later succumb to a suggestion from a Doctor of the Social Sciences that she accompany him on a 'cultural excursion to the top of Knowledge Mountain on new Neo-Progressive Funicular Railway' (Irwin, 1941: 379). At the summit,

> Gramma noticed with dismay that none of the young people ever seemed to look out of the window at the scenery. They spent their time eating and drinking, playing cards or looking at movie magazines. An innovation of which the railway company was very proud was the Half-Way House, with its game room, where passengers who so elected could stop off,

omitting the remainder of the trip, and play ping-pong in competition for silver loving cups. When Gramma ventured to suggest that these activities might just as well be carried on at home, the Doctor answered, 'Yes that is true. But if we limited these personally conducted tours to specialists like yourself, how many people would receive the cultural benefit of our democratic institutions? And how could we pay dividends to our stockholders?' (Irwin, 1941: 380)

Again, the fact that Gramma Translation objects to the 'fun' innovations of the Progressivist era of language learning methodology is less relevant to the current study than is the response to her objection from the Doctor of the Social Sciences. Expressly denoted as 'innovations', the domesticated simulations of multilingual exploration that replace the precarious mountain climbing activities are justified not on the basis of their merits of logic, but on the basis of enrollments and dividends. It is worth pausing to imagine, for instance, how the 1941 formulation 'how many people would receive the cultural benefit of our democratic institutions?' translates into the funding parlance of 2017. Meanwhile, all of the technological attempts to provide a faster, straighter line to knowledge are justified on the basis of that securitarian notion that the Wolf of Empty Formality will devour the child adventurers, and that it's safer for them to stay inside and look at 'a detailed list, classified, and with brief, explanatory comments, of all the birds, flowers, trees, waterfalls and other wonders that the mountain contained' (Irwin, 1941: 380).

In the end, the Wolf of Empty Formality eats Gramma Translation and her goat Form, and when Little Read-Writing Hood visits the bedridden figure she thinks is Gramma to read her some Virgil, a well-known exchange ensues, but in a new rendition that raises the girl's affective filter:

> 'What big eyes you have, Gramma.'
> 'The better to scare you out of your wits with', said Empty Formality, 'Boo!'
> 'What great ears you have, Gramma.'
> 'The better to hear your mistakes with, my child. Can you recite the rule for the agreement of particles backwards ten times in six seconds without making a mistake? Grrrrrr!' (Irwin, 1941: 383)

Through Irwin's pre-WWII droll we can trace the intense and acerbic relation between language program development and market-driven innovation in a period of intense socio-economic precarity in the United States, as well as political uncertainty about the incipient rise of fascism in Europe. Readers of *The Modern Language Journal* were expected to understand intuitively, and be intuitively skeptical of, both the affirmative, intercultural rationales of innovators as well as their tendencies towards securitarian scaremongering. Fun and innovation, as delivered by expert discourses, were understood as the answer to doubt and uncertainty on the part of foreign language learners, and if these expert discourses channeled funds towards stockholders, all the better. Meanwhile, the ecology of multilingual culture and knowledge about and around which such innovations were monetized is put increasingly at bay, or converted into extractable form. That these were such explicit concerns in the 1930s language education sphere helps remind us not only of the history of innovation in this context, but – for the broader purposes of this volume – about the long history of aggressive and opportunistic sloganization that indeed long precedes the current era.

Around the time of the composition of Irwin's wistful and sardonic send-up of innovation in 1941, the field that would eventually become 'innovation studies' started producing its own first popular monographs, as technological innovation as a discourse emerged out of mainstream quantitative neoclassical economics in the 1930s (Godin, 2015: 261–262).

Hellenic and Roman Usages: New Cuts in the Silver Mines

Amid all this mythic contemporaneity around innovation, it is unlikely that contemporary researchers would have any reason to remember that the past 2500 years since Aristophanes have not been particularly friendly to the idea. On this point, Benoît Godin (2015) wishes to set the record straight:

> For most of history, innovation has nothing to do with economics (technology) or with creativity. Innovation is a political concept, first of all in the sense that it is regulated by Kings, forbidden by law and punished – although Kings constantly innovate. Advice books and treatises for princes and courtiers support this understanding and include instructions not to innovate. Books of manners and sermons urge people not to meddle with innovation. From the Renaissance onward, innovation was also a linguistic weapon used by political writers and pamphleteers against their enemies. Today, innovation has a definite relation to politics too, as an instrument of industrial policy. (Godin, 2015: 5)

This caveat is helpful, because it cautions us not to mistake innovation for invention, advancement or progress. Since Xenophon's silver mine example, innovation has been a deeply political domain – gradualist, literal and strategic. Aristotle thought innovation as such to be too risky, and advised against its tendency to promote 'constitutional upheavals' (*Politics* II: viii, 1268b). Plato held equally unfavorable opinions towards innovation, on the basis that innovations make it difficult for children to learn acknowledged standards (*Laws* VII). The intervening two millennia have indeed accordingly seen overwhelming resistance to the idea of innovation – except in some radical religious texts (Godin, 2015: 42–43). It wasn't until the late 19th century that innovation and scientific advancements were understood as belonging to the same register of discourse.

I opened this essay with an epigraph from Xenophon, a tiger's leap into the ancient history of what is now known as 'innovation studies' (Godin, 2015). In doing so, I hoped to evoke the range of contradictory and deeply felt things that 'innovation' has meant for thinkers, teachers and policy makers from Aristophanes to Joseph Schumpeter. Cited in the epigraph is a distress call, uttered by the protagonist of Aristophanes' *Wasps*. Young Anticleon so wished to heal his father's ailments – addiction, insomnia, obsession with the law courts – that he presented to the God of truth and prophecy an 'innovation', a *kainotomia*, which in this rare case of Hellenic writing is invoked metaphorically. Innovation here means 'fresh sacrifice', a fresh 'cut' into a living being. With this first documented debut of the concept in the Western literary tradition, innovation is identified with the infliction of pain, the experience of uncertainty and the plaintive reliance on external power. Innovation is an act of audacious desperation for Anticleon, after all other attempts of persuasion, logic and pressure have failed to heal his father's pathologies.

Around 75 years later, Xenophon – still more or less a contemporary of Aristophanes – becomes the first known writer to use 'innovation' in an expository way, doing so in his short treatise on Athenian economics, *Ways and Means* (354 BCE, see Godin, 2015: 19–25 for a summary discussion). This first known expository usage of 'innovation' is set in the silver mines outside of Athens, which – for lack of labor power – had long been underutilized, despite the Athenians' unabating thirst for wrought silver jewelry and weapons. 'Why, it may be asked, are fewer new cuttings [kainotomia, "innovations"] made nowadays than formerly?', writes Xenophon, ready to answer his own question. 'Simply because those interested in the mines are poorer. (…) A man who makes a new cutting incurs a serious risk [(…) and] people nowadays are very chary of taking such a risk' (cited in Godin, 2015: 21). Xenophon's solution to this supply-side problem was for the State to acquire and sponsor public-use slaves, who will make these risky, difficult, life-threatening innovations, or 'new cuts', in the silver mines, for the benefit of Athens' citizenry. In Xenophon's political/market-oriented usage, innovation is thus also associated with danger, potential damage, fear and uncertainty, as it had been with Aristophanes' metaphorical usage. Here, however, those who will necessarily face the downsides of innovation are not the sacrificial animal in *The Wasps*, but the actual workers in the mines – who will strike into the rock, hoping to find silver to sell in urban Athens, and hoping not to see the rock ledges above them start to buckle and fall towards them, thanks to their 'innovation'. These Hellenic senses of innovation belie the contemporary aura of benign beneficence and ease-of-use that characterizes innovation, reminding us that innovation in pre-modern usage was by definition threatening, violent and expropriative.

Conclusions and Implications: A Scholarship of Maintenance?

Beyond language education discourse, other research fields and commercial studies are likewise beginning to tire of the frontal mandate to innovate. Under the title *The Maintainers: How a Group of Bureaucrats, Standards Engineers, and Introverts Made Technologies that Kind of Work Most of the Time*, scholars gathered at the Stevens Institute of Technology in 2016 for a conference that sought not only to critique the aura of unassailable beneficence, forward thinking and progressive values that has accrued to *innovation* across the disciplines.[3] The conference title was itself a send-up of Walter Isaacson's (2014) book, *The Innovators: How a Group of Hackers, Geniuses, and Geeks Created the Digital Revolution*. One of the presenters at The Maintainers conference, the scholar of technology in American cultural history Matt Thomas, asked that his colleagues consider taking up a 'scholarship not just *on* maintenance but *of* maintenance' (Thomas, 2016), in the spirit of the mid-century Americanist Gene Wise, who proposed a 'dense-facts' mode of scholarly maintenance work:

> [T]hat a work of scholarship makes a 'contribution' to knowledge is less important than that it reveals in information meanings that had not been seen before. The dense-facts model is committed less to the 'production' of new information and more to effective 'consumption' – that is, to the fuller intellectual digestion of whatever information is at hand. Facts of course are seldom 'lean'. (Wise, 1979: 529)

Such a dense-facts model for understanding the experiences and realities of students, languages and institutions may help relativize the imperative to advocate for ever more creative destruction through an accelerated implementation of new models. As Kumaravadivelu suggests about a 'beyond methods' approach to macro-strategies in language learning, it may be time for language education discourse and applied linguistics to go 'beyond innovation' – or to forgo it, as Gramma Translation tried to do in Irwin's 1941 'idle idyll' for modern language education discourse. In order to do this we may draw on alternate historical sensibilities around newness, novelty and invention that forego the impulse to 'stimulate the rate of change', producing ever better and more promising models of linguistic competence. Whereas innovation strives to make adoption and implementation easy and more manageable, part of our pedagogy, programming and curricular development may need to be dedicated towards honoring linguistic barriers to such adoption and adaption. Taking a cue from the ancients, we might find it germane to focus on finding ways to allow the patent newness and uncanniness of foreign languages to remain sublime, experiential, textured and often difficult for our students, such that, as Lucretius writes in *De Rerum Natura*, what we find worth studying and learning might remain 'incredible at first sight' and 'audacious to conceive for the imagination (...) the first time' (*Rerum Natura* 2:

1020–1040, cited in Godin, 2015: 38). Were (foreign) languages designed to be adopted and adapted according to an innovation-based economy, they would not be foreign for long.

Notes

(1) For similarly engaged pieces see, for instance, Edge & Mann (2013, 2015), Henrichsen (1989), Nicholls (1983), Waters (2009, 2014).
(2) See http://www.lancaster.ac.uk/lums/people/michael-west#activities.
(3) Unlike the 2009 '1st Conference on Creativity and Innovation in Language Studies' discussed in the first section of this chapter, this conference convened a second time in April 2017. See http://themaintainers.org/maintainers-ii-program/ (accessed 16 April 2017).

References

Arendt, H. (1996 [1943]) We refugees. In M. Robinson (ed.) *Altogether Elsewhere: Writers on Exile* (pp. 110–119). New York: Harvest Books.
Argondizzo, C. (ed.) (2013) *Creativity and Innovation in Language Education*. Bern: Lang.
Aristophanes (1938) *The Complete Greek Drama, Vol. 2* (trans. E. O'Neill, Jr.). New York: Random House.
Barnett, H.G. (1953) *Innovation: The Basis of Cultural Change*. New York: McGraw-Hill.
Berlant, L. (2011) *Cruel Optimism*. Durham, NC: Duke University Press.
Bockstahler, O.L. (1932) Editorial. *The Modern Language Journal* 16 (8), 681–684.
Cheng, Y.C. (2009) Hong Kong educational reforms in the last decade. Reform syndrome and new developments. *International Journal of Educational Management* 23, 65–86.
Coleman, A. (2012) *The Teaching of Modern Foreign Languages in the United States: A Report Prepared for the Modern Foreign Language Study*. Literary Licensing, LLC.
Davis, J.N. (2005) Power, politics, and pecking order: Technological innovation as a site of collaboration, resistance, and accommodation. *The Modern Language Journal* 89 (2), 161–176.
EC (2015) *Innovation Union: A Europe 2020 Initiative*. Brussels: European Commission. See http://ec.europa.eu/research/innovation-union/index_en.cfm (accessed 30 October 2017).
Edge, J. and Mann, S. (eds) (2013) *Innovations in Pre-Service Education and Training for English Language Teachers*. London: British Council.
Edge, J. and Mann, S. (2015) Innovation in the provision of pre-service education and training for English language teachers: Issues and concerns. In G. Pickering and P. Gunashekar (eds) *Innovation in English Language Teacher Education* (pp. 38–49). New Delhi: British Council.
Freeman, C. (1974) *The Economics of Industrial Innovation*. Harmondsworth: Penguin.
Gee, J.P., Hull, L. and Lankshear, C. (eds) (1996) *The New Work Order*. Boulder, CO: Westview Press.
Godin, B. (2015) *Innovation Contested: The Idea of Innovation Over the Centuries*. New York: Routledge.
Gullette, C. (1934) The awkward age in high school language study. *The Modern Language Journal* 18 (6), 361–365.
Henrichsen, L.E. (1989) *Diffusion of Innovations in English Language Teaching: The ELEC Effort in Japan, 1956–1968*. New York: Greenwood Press.

Hu, A. (2012) Academic perspectives from Germany. In M. Byram and L. Parmenter (eds) *The Common European Framework of Reference: The Globalization of Language Education Policy* (pp. 66–75). Bristol: Multilingual Matters.

Irwin, J.S. (1941) Little Read Writing-Hood and Gramma Translation: An idle idyll. *The Modern Language Journal* 25 (5), 375–384.

Isaacson, W. (2014) *The Innovators: How a Group of Hackers, Geniuses, and Geeks Created the Digital Revolution*. New York: Simon & Schuster.

Jessner, U. (2003) The nature of cross-linguistic interaction in the multilingual system. In J. Cenoz, B. Hufeisen and U. Jessner (eds) *The Multilingual Lexicon* (pp. 45–56). New York: Kluwer.

Kiely, R. (2006) Evaluation, innovation, and ownership in language programs. *The Modern Language Journal* 90 (4), 597–601.

Kramsch, C. and Whiteside, A. (2008) Language ecology in multilingual settings: Towards a theory of symbolic competence. *Applied Linguistics* 29, 645–671.

Kumaravadivelu, B. (2003) *Beyond Methods: Macrostrategies for Language Teaching*. New Haven, CT: Yale University Press.

Larsen-Freeman, D. (1997) Chaos/complexity science and second language acquisition. *Applied* Linguistics 18 (2), 141–165.

Mackenzie, A. (2013) Programming subjects in the regime of anticipation: Software studies and subjectivity. *Subjectivity* 6, 391–405.

Mackey, W. (1965) *Language Teaching Analysis*. London: Longman.

Markee, N. (2001) The diffusion of innovation in language teaching. In D. Hall and A. Hewings (eds) *Innovation in English Language Teaching. A Reader* (pp. 118–126). London: Routledge.

Myers, M. (2013) Evaluating creativity and innovation in second language teachers' discourse. In C. Argondizzo (ed.) *Creativity and Innovation in Language Education* (pp. 45–62). Bern: Lang.

Nicholls, A. (1983) *Managing Educational Innovations*. London: Allen & Unwin.

Pavlenko, A. (2006) *Emotions and Multilingualism*. Cambridge: Cambridge University Press.

Pickering, G. and Gunashekar, P. (eds) (2015) *Innovation in English Language Teacher Education*. New Delhi: British Council.

Rogers, E.M. (2003 [1962]) *Diffusions of Innovations* (5th edn). New York: Free Press.

Schumpeter, J. (1934) *The Theory of Economic Development: An Inquiry into Profits, Capital, Credit, Interest, and the Business Cycle*. Cambridge, MA: Harvard University Press.

Schumpeter, J. (1939) *Business Cycles: A Theoretical, Historical, and Statistical Analysis of the Capitalist Process, Vol. 1*. New York: McGraw-Hill.

Schumpeter, J. (1942) *Capitalism, Socialism, and Democracy*. New York: Harper & Brothers.

Steffensen, S.V. (2015) Distributed language and dialogism: Notes on non-locality, sense-making and interactivity. *Language Sciences* 50, 105–119.

Stroebe, L. (1920) The real knowledge of a foreign country. *The Modern Language Journal* 5 (4), 38–44.

Thomas, M. (2016) *Against Innovative Scholarship: The Monastic, Benedict, and Wiseian Options*. Conference presentation: The Maintainers. Stevens Institute of Technology, Hoboken, NJ, 2 April.

Trent, J. (2014) Innovation as identity construction in language teaching and learning: Case studies from Hong Kong. *Innovation in Language Learning and Teaching* 8 (1), 56–78.

Urciuoli, B. (2000) Strategically deployable shifters in college marketing, or just what do they mean by 'skills' and 'leadership' and 'multiculturalism'? *Language & Culture* 6. See http://language-culture.binghamton.edu /symposia/6/ (accessed 30 October 2017).

Vail, C.C.D. (1933) Modern language objectives. *The Modern Language Journal* 17 (4), 249–259.
Vinall, K. (2012) ¿Un legado histórico?: Symbolic competence and the construction of multiple histories. *L2 Journal* 4 (1), 102–123.
Waters, A. (2009) Managing innovation in English language education. *Language Teaching* 42 (4), 421–458.
Waters, A. (2014) Managing innovation in English language education: A research agenda. *Language Teaching* 47 (1), 92–110.
West, M.A. and Farr, J.L. (1990) *Innovation and Creativity at Work: Psychological and Organizational Strategies*. New York: Wiley.
Wise, G. (1979) Some elementary axioms for an American culture studies. *Prospects* 4, 517–547.
Zeydel, E.H. (1924) Elementary modern language instruction in American colleges. *The Modern Language Journal* 8 (8), 491–495.

3 The Only Turn Worth Watching in the 20th Century is Tina Turner's: How the Sloganization of Foreign Language Research Can Impede the Furthering of Knowledge and Make Life Difficult for Practitioners

Dietmar Rösler

Mainly focusing on the rise, establishment and ensuing sloganization of the communicative approach, this chapter discusses the concepts and mechanisms that lead to the rise of self-proclaimed new paradigms and the negative side-effects that accompany the displacement of previously available knowledge. Five possible ways to avoid or at least to reduce these losses of complexity are discussed: de-trivialization of the meaning of the term 'paradigm' and returning to how it was used by epistemologists like Kuhn through the academic community rejecting the inflationary use of it and the term 'turn' in academic self-advertising; acknowledging and appreciating the contributions to foreign language learning by the self-styled new paradigms as augmentation of existing knowledge rather than as a revolution; a vibrant meta-discussion about the points at which new ideas degenerate into slogans; accepting research which looks into the side-effects of self-proclaimed paradigm shifts as serious and relevant; and accepting the insight that there is rarely one single solution to any given challenge.

Spatial, iconic, translational, performative ... 20th century cultural studies like turns. Suppressing mischievous thoughts that people who have nothing left to talk about have to talk about how they talk and interpreting this in a benevolent manner, one could argue that this inflation of turns reflects the fact that cultural studies looks more and more at the different facets of the world and employs 'turn' terminology to denote changes in perspective which lead to an increase in knowledge on particular subjects. This view is possibly a bit too positive,[1] as initiating, defining and defending a particular turn and gate-keeping its 'correct' execution is linked to high academic status and a high impact factor, which could lead to a higher ranking for the institution that purchased the turn maker in order to feature prominently in the next research assessment.[2]

Compared to areas like cultural studies, language education research might seem to be less prone to succumbing to such developments, as it lacks the high status of cultural studies in academia and appears grounded in a practical area in a way that should prevent dizziness due to spinning. Language education researchers are often involved in teacher training, so noticing the complexity of learning and teaching languages in educational institutions could, theoretically, serve as an antidote to proclaiming new general approaches, paradigms and turns. This, however, is not the case.

Paradigm Shifts and their Sloganization in Language Education Research

Three examples,[3] taken mainly from the German debate on foreign/second language education, will illustrate ways in which sloganization operates:

(a) Marketing a new idea as a new paradigm. This can begin alongside the earliest debates on a subject, as was the case with the German *Interkulturelle Germanistik* (intercultural German studies)

When German as a foreign language (GFL) constituted itself as an academic subject at the end of the 1970s in Germany,[4] Alois Wierlacher (1980), one of the first chairs in this field, published an article entitled 'Deutsch als Fremdsprache. Zum Paradigmawechsel internationaler Germanistik' (German as a foreign language. On the paradigm shift in international German studies). In the history of science, paradigm shifts as discussed by authors like Kuhn (1970) or Feyerabend (1975) referred to academic developments which had happened in the past. Looking back across centuries gives the viewer a chance to classify research activities in relation to their reception and assess whether their contribution to the development of knowledge could be described as paradigmatic. To attribute the term 'paradigm' to the appearance of a fledgling academic subdiscipline (and especially to one's own

contribution to it) is, to say the least, a serious devaluation of the concept of paradigm as used in the debate about the history of science.
(b) Caricaturing an established approach as inferior by ignoring its diversity and branding it with a pejorative name, as happened in the rise of constructivism which insisted that the then dominant paradigm, the so-called instructional approach, was purely teacher-centered.

When the German-speaking community of foreign/second language education researchers discovered the notion of 'constructivism', it was hailed as a new paradigm, as suggested by titles like 'Der Konstruktivismus: Ein neues Paradigma in der Fremdsprachendidaktik?' (Constructivism: A new paradigm in foreign language pedagogy?) (Wolff, 1994).[5] As this debate coincided with the emergence of digital media in language learning – at that time usually called 'new media' and discussed widely – the two debates soon merged.[6] This sometimes led to rather superficial claims for the advent of learner autonomy, which focused more on the learners' newly found freedom to choose the time and place of their learning activities than on the learning process itself, on the contents of learning or on the educational dimension of autonomy (cf. the critical reconstruction in Schmenk, 2008).
(c) Rejecting and denouncing preceding approaches and practices in order to frame new approaches as radically different.

The history of foreign language teaching methods can sometimes be told like a Punch and Judy show. There is the 'evil' grammar translation method whose wrongdoings had to be rectified in the 20th century. The so-called direct method reacted to overemphasizing the learners' mother tongue by propagating a strict adherence to monolingual, target language teaching. How successful this dogma became is reflected in the observation by Butzkamm and Caldwell (2009)[7] on how deeply rooted the focus on monolingual teaching had become in the teaching community. Referring to the professional stakeholders – 'teacher educators, inspectors, applied linguists, members and chairs of examination boards and curriculum and syllables committees, leaders of language teachers' professional organizations, leaders of workshops, speakers at conferences, writers of journal articles and authors' (Butzkamm & Caldwell, 2009: 24) – they describe the state of the art of monolingual classroom discourse as follows:

> The monolingual approach has become a matter of faith with them, deep faith. It is little wonder that for a long time the main voices heard and heeded have been those that advocate monolingual teaching – with or without the usual concessions. Whenever the MT [mother tongue] is mentioned there is a neurotic fear that incompetent teachers, so embarrassing to the profession, are involved, that the dams will break and the MT will pour into the FL [foreign language] classrooms. Since a profession needs to see itself as well trained and competent, we believe that the profession

has fallen victim to a huge historical neurosis. Why else should a self-crippling mistake have held sway for such a long time? What teachers need is near-native proficiency in the FL, but definitely not a mother tongue phobia. It bears repeating: The baby has been thrown out with the bathwater. (Butzkamm & Caldwell, 2009: 24)

This critique, one should add, was not intended to promote a return to grammar translation methods, but it was to illustrate the momentum the direct method and its mantra of monolingual classroom discourse had gained.

Another 'paradigm shift' in language education discourse in the 20th century, namely communicative language teaching (CLT), also used the grammar translation method as the foil against which it could show its innovative potential, although its focus was less on the use of the first language (L1) than on a turn towards communication and authenticity in language teaching. This approach took off in the 1970s in West Germany, heavily influenced by Piepho's (1974) book entitled *Kommunikative Kompetenz als übergeordnetes Lernziel im Englischunterricht* (Communicative Competence as an Overarching Learning Goal in EFL Teaching). Using 'communicative competence' as a key concept, Piepho linked contemporary West German debates in politics and the social sciences (cf. Habermas, 1971) about necessary changes in German society to the world of language education. He thus connected the somewhat pedestrian debate on how best to learn and teach languages with a rather more 'exciting' post-1968 political and educational mainstream discussion on how egalitarian discourse could bring about social change and, in doing so, ensured that this approach to foreign language teaching and learning would be seen as a most timely new paradigm in West German language education.

It is also worth looking at the time of publication. This establishment of a new paradigm and its ensuing sloganization took place when empirical research carried out by Smith (1970) and van Elek and Oskarsson (1975) had just shown that there could be no such thing as a single best new method or approach. And the debate among West German researchers on foreign language learning focused on the individual learner, on the differences between learners and on learning styles.[8] Looking back, it is astounding how the communicative approach managed to live with the paradox that it was at the same time based on a set of beliefs which guided researchers and teachers towards a particular way of thinking about learning and teaching, and an educational ideology which proclaimed openness and self-determination. It is also astounding to see how little of the original concept of the communicative approach is sometimes left in, for example, textbooks that claim to adhere to CLT: often, a few signature practices such as role-play or games seem to be sufficient indicators for learning materials and teaching practices to qualify as CLT. Clearly, the notion of CLT has undergone a process of sloganization, as will be illustrated further in the following section.

The Communicative Approach as a Leading Paradigm and its Collateral Damage

The development of the communicative approach is well documented[9] and does not need to be rehearsed again here. In contrast to many of the prevailing teaching practices at that time, it was like a breath of fresh air which introduced or at least increased the status of many of the concepts that have by now become part of the everyday routine in many language classrooms: negotiation of meaning, relevance of the curriculum for everyday lives, role play, games and simulations, authenticity, transcending the classroom, task-based learning, cooperative learning, integrated grammar teaching, etc. The side-effects of the grammar-translation method, such as the downplaying of contents and an overemphasis on correctness, were to be countered by active learners interacting not only with each other but also with the real world, making use in a meaningful way of whatever bits of target language they had learnt at any given time and thereby increasing their command of the language. Project-oriented work like Legutke's (2006) widely known airport project[10] exemplified how a communicative approach could change the educational landscape.

Soon it became clear that a divide was opening up between the claim that foreign language teaching could and should contribute to the emancipation of society, and the everyday practice of the communicative approach that favored activities such as role play and dialogues. Looking back in 2005, Schmenk concluded, for instance, that Piepho's assumption that role plays in EFL classrooms are a means to practice democracy was rather naïve, and that the connection between Habermas' utopian concepts and foreign language learning produced a foreign language learning Arcadia:

> Piephos Vorstellung, dass ideale Sprechsituationen im Englischunterricht qua Rollenspiele realisierbar wären, wirkt allerdings – und das zumal aus heutiger Sicht – allzu blauäugig. Der Glaube daran, dass herrschaftsfreie Diskurse im Fremdsprachenunterricht simuliert werden könnten, (…) ist dabei nur zu deutlich als Ausdruck der Tatsache erkennbar, dass das Lernziel kommunikative Kompetenz utopische Qualitäten angenommen hatte. Der Übertrag von Habermas' gesellschaftspolitischer Utopie auf den schulischen Fremdsprachenunterricht stellt insofern eher die Schaffung eines fremdsprachendidaktischen Arkadien dar. So verführerisch diese Vorstellungen auch gewesen sein mögen – sie muten heute doch als von der Realität des Fremdsprachenunterrichts allzu weit entfernt, als mythisch-verklärt an. (Schmenk, 2005: 71–72)[11]

Furthermore, the intellectual stimulus that the communicative approach had received from its respective sources – i.e. Jürgen Habermas mainly in the German debate and Dell Hymes in the English-speaking world – faded away and so gave way to rather utilitarian approaches which replaced political and educational dimensions of communicative competence by a compilation of notions and functions to be used in textbooks and implemented step by step in the classroom:

> Somit fand eine eher utilitaristische Auffassung von kommunikativer Kompetenz Verbreitung, die man weder aus dem sozialphilosophischen Konzept Habermas' noch aus dem ethnographisch-soziolinguistischen Begriff Hymes' herleiten kann: Man beschränkte sich zunehmend darauf, kommunikative Akte so zu beschreiben, dass sie in überschaubaren Listen von Notionen und Funktionen portioniert und entsprechend in Curricula zusammengestellt und 'abgearbeitet' werden könnten. (Schmenk, 2005: 73)[12]

In addition to this, the scope of certain concepts became problematic. Relevance to everyday life, for instance, was taken to mean relevant to everyday life in the area in which the new language was spoken. This was an appropriate interpretation of the concept for a large number of language learners who would likely travel to places where the target language was a viable option. However, as in the case of GFL which is usually learnt far away from German-speaking regions, it is questionable whether this was really an appropriate interpretation of 'relevance to everyday life'. Similarly, many textbooks introduce words referring to parts of the body in the context of 'going to the doctor'. While this may make sense for learners who are or will be staying in the area where the new language is spoken, it is less obvious why a medical examination or a visit to a doctor may be of any relevance to those learners whose medical needs will in all likelihood be attended to by local doctors only. Thus, learning how to say that one has a headache or a sprained ankle may not necessarily be of primary concern to learners whose everyday life contact with the German language happens to be confined to conversing with visitors to their own country, to whom they might want to explain the peculiarities of their own everyday life or tell them about the cultural artifacts of the local environment. A role play at the doctor's is not a meaningful preparation for either of these two situations.[13]

As far as teaching grammar was concerned, the long-overdue reassessment of dealing with grammar not as an end in itself but as a necessary means of support for learners in order for them to be able to perform specific communicative acts – in German referred to with the widely used phrase of the *dienende Funktion der Grammatik* (the serving function of grammar) – was accompanied by a tacit devaluation of dealing with grammar in general, both in the classroom and in academic discourse. Königs considers the co-occurrence of the new focus on communication and the neglect of focusing on form as a side-effect of thinking in paradigms and the inherent tendency to extreme pendulum swings:

> Die Verlagerung des unterrichtlichen Schwerpunkts weg von der Formbetrachtung und hin zur funktional angemessenen Verwendung der Fremdsprache lässt bei vielen Betrachtern die Vermutung aufkommen, dass 'Kommunikation' und 'mündliche Ausdrucksfähigkeit' gleichbedeutend mit der Negierung der formalen Sprachbetrachtung seien – dies war weder intendiert noch sinnvoll, gehört aber offenbar zu den sich typischerweise einstellenden Erscheinungen, wenn Paradigmenwechsel anstehen und damit zu Extremen neigende Pendelbewegungen in der Forschung auslösen. (Königs, 2011: 77)[14]

The 'utilitarian' focus of some varieties of the communicative approach on role play or lists of lexical material with the intention to provide the means for students to express specific (presumed) intentions often resulted in the production of banal dialogues that can be considered a by-product of the focus on everyday life, especially for older learners of a second or third foreign language. This problem was addressed by proponents of the communicative approach, who argued that task-based language learning (TBLL) would help prevent communicative banalities. According to the strong version of TBLL, tasks have to be sufficiently complex so as to prevent the communication they trigger from turning shallow. According to Müller-Hartmann and Schocker-von Ditfurth, tasks

> motivate learners to get involved (1), they are complex (2), they support the learning process by an integrated focus on form (3), they provide individual and co-operative problem-solving in interactive scenarios (4), and they sequence the task process and balance task demand and task support (5). (Müller-Hartmann & Schocker-von Ditfurth, 2013: 688)

This strong[15] claim disregards traditional, more isolated exercises, thereby continuing the narrative of the communicative approach as something distinctly different from and superior to previous approaches:

> Die so genannte kommunikative Wende führte in den 70er Jahren zu einer Abkehr von mechanistischen und nach dem behavioristischen Denkmodell konzipierten Übungsformen hin zu Aufgaben, die das Bedeutungspotenzial von Sprache und damit einen Sprachgebrauch fokussierten, der die verschiedenen Fertigkeiten integrativ verband. (Müller-Hartmann & Schocker-von Ditfurth, 2005: 4)[16]

Just like the mother tongue became banned in the dogmatic monolingual approach described above, the focus on something new and exciting – in this case complex tasks – leads to the devaluation of a traditional tool. This can be seen as yet another case of throwing out the baby with the bathwater, as Hans Barkowski (2004) wrote at about the same time, when he stated that not only was practicing neglected within the communicative approach, but this neglect actually prevented the envisaged objective from being reached. He argued that the communicative approach:

> hat, aus meiner Sicht und in Auswertung vieler Hospitationserfahrungen, die Kommunikative Wende mit ihrer allzu radikalen Abkehr von Lerntechniken wie z. B. dem imitativen Einüben sprachlicher Bausteine und Wendungen oder auch der pattern practice diese als 'Kinder' behavioristischer Lernauffassungen quasi 'mit dem Bade' ausgeschüttet: im Interesse an lebhafter, thematisch interessanter Unterrichtskommunikation (...) wird das Üben vernachlässigt – was übrigens im Endeffekt wiederum verhindert, dass kommunikative Kompetenz wirklich erreicht wird. (Barkowski, 2004: 83–84)[17]

The devaluation and thus omission of 'practicing' in the design of learning arrangements was accompanied by a lack of research into the nitty-gritty of dealing with grammatical aspects in CLT. Not only did materials developers move any focus on form to the end of the task cycle[18] (instead of integrating it so students have the chance to shift their focus towards formal aspects of language whenever they deem it functionally appropriate in a given task cycle),[19] but a focus on form was also pushed to the end of the queue by TBLL theorists and researchers. Looking back at this development, Schmelter points out:

> Antworten auf die Frage, welche Formen der Präsentation, der Kognitivierung, des Bewusstmachens, des Einübens und so weiter beim Aufbau der funktional-kommunikativen und sprachstrukturellen Kompetenzen (besonders) wirksam sind, finden die Lehrenden selbst in aktuellen Publikationen zum Thema nur selten. (Schmelter, 2013: 75)[20]

The focus of research shifted instead towards interactional aspects – interaction between learners, interaction between learners and teachers – and the competence profile needed by successful teachers, according to the task-based approach. [21]

Does the Community of Foreign Language Practitioners Need Paradigms?

The radical expulsion of the mother tongue in the direct method, the uncritical widening of the use of key communicative concepts like authenticity and relevance for everyday life and the sidelining of the focus on form within the communicative approach are just three examples of sloganizing and overstretching concepts and procedures which, when transported via teacher training into the classroom, lead to a narrowing of the options available for practitioners. And this happens even though everybody would agree, on an abstract level, that the characteristics of the learners, their intended goals, institutional constraints, etc., would have to be carefully analyzed before statements could be made about how to proceed in any given situation.

Is this an unavoidable corollary of the way knowledge is created? Is it an expression of the hype cycle? Must it be seen as collateral damage in the context of general changes in the academic environment which favor ranking and marketing with their high-profile results and quick turnover to low-profile furthering of knowledge on complex issues? How would the community of practice, the theoreticians and practitioners Butzkamm and Caldwell referred to in the quote at the beginning of this chapter, have to proceed in order to minimize the side-effects of thinking, speaking and writing in approaches, turns and paradigms?

In his postscript to the second edition of *The Structure of Scientific Revolutions*, Kuhn (1970) refers to paradigms as shared examples:

> For it the term 'paradigm' would be entirely appropriate, both philologically and autobiographically; this is the component of a group's shared commitments which first led me to the choice of that word. Because the term has assumed a life of its own, however, I shall here substitute 'exemplars.' By it I mean, initially, the concrete problem-solutions that students encounter from the start of their scientific education ... To these shared examples should, however, be added at least some of the technical problem-solutions found in the periodical literature that scientists encounter during the post-educational research careers and that also show them by example how their job is to be done (...) All physicists, for example, begin by learning the same exemplars. (Kuhn, 1970: 186–187)

For someone who studied linguistics in the early 1970s, this quote conjures up the drawing of sentence trees, long discussions about the difference in deep-structure between 'John is eager to please' and 'John is easy to please', the exciting creativity of the colorless green ideas which sleep furiously[22] and the firm conviction that the structuralist approach missed out on what was really exciting about language. By the same token, novices on the way to becoming 'communicative' teachers of a foreign language nowadays are sometimes initiated by being shown examples of successful projects which allow learners to engage meaningfully with the target language. They do not encounter too much about focus on form, other than that it will turn up at the end of a task cycle.

Conclusion: Towards De-sloganizing Language Education Discourse

How and why certain examples and techniques are canonized, how concepts take hold in a community of practice and why they expire is for sociologists and other disciplines dealing with knowledge construction to find out. But communities of practice themselves have a responsibility to reflect on their own discourse. At the initial stages of entering a community of practice, it seems unavoidable, to a certain degree, that one tries to make sense of the complexity of the new environment by putting up a few dichotomous signposts. At that stage, the effects of sloganization do have a function by allowing novices to get a foothold and find a first safe ground. But to ensure that this remains just a feature of an initial stage of their professional development and does not become permanent knowledge, it is probably necessary for novice teachers to engage with the history and development of their own subject at a meta-level early on.

In this final section I will therefore briefly discuss five suggestions or tasks that could, in my opinion, contribute to avoiding or at least slowing down the process of sloganization and its side-effects:

- de-trivialization of the meaning of the term 'paradigm' and returning to how it was used by epistemologists like Kuhn;
- acknowledgment and appreciation of what has been added to the knowledge of foreign language learning by (often self-declared) new paradigms as augmentation of existing knowledge rather than revolutions;
- a vibrant (meta-)discussion about the points at which new ideas degenerate into slogans;
- accepting research which looks into the side-effects of self-proclaimed paradigm shifts as serious and relevant; and
- accepting the insight that there is rarely one single solution to any given challenge.

The first task requires a critical look at the use of concepts like 'approach', 'turn' or 'paradigm'. By juxtaposing the use of the term 'paradigm', e.g. in the history of science debate by Thomas Kuhn with its use by language education researchers, it could be shown that the developments the latter proposed are rather minor, compared to the ones discussed by the former. Claiming that changes such as the communicative approach, the constructivist approach, the dichotomy of interculturality versus transculturality in the course of the last 20 years and the naïve concept of autonomy constitute new paradigms illustrates the limited nature of scholarly debate in foreign language learning research.

Another task would be to look at the improvements brought about by what their authors claim to be paradigm shifts. Whatever enters academic discourse as a new 'paradigm' usually draws attention to a previously underestimated aspect of foreign language learning. It was justified that the direct method rebelled against a practice of foreign language teaching in which the target language was in danger of becoming an object of pure contemplation rather than a means of communication, and consequently focused on the use of the target language. It was justified that the communicative approach noticed that despite all the oral communication in the audiolingual approach, non-form focused and meaningful interaction in the target language was not at the center of classroom activities, and therefore focused on the negotiation of meaning, on project work that transcended the classroom, etc. These changes could and should be seen as contributions to the broadening of knowledge and the widening of options for language teachers and learners, while at the same time bearing in mind that this is only half of the story, due to the side-effects of regarding these improvements as paradigmatic changes.

A third task would therefore be to look at how and when these important new focal points degenerated into slogans[23] which dominated the debate and prevented a more differentiated discussion about how the new foci could be integrated into already existing knowledge. Knowledge about the complex processes of learning and teaching within educational contexts is not as advanced as it could be.

Another task would be to look at the side-effects of frequent announcements of new paradigm shifts on language education practice. The inflated use and announcement of 'new paradigms' are likely to lead teachers, who are confronted day by day with the complexity of teaching and learning, to get tired of 'yet another new approach' in professional development seminars and workshops. If they are independent enough, they may just shrug their shoulders in view of the latest academic craze and grumble about useless 'helicopter training'. If they are not, they might want to apply what has just been advertised to them as 'the right way' in their own context – and with a group of learners for whom it is anything but.

The fifth task, finally, is not confined to the field of language education but focuses on the fact that it is unlikely that there will ever be a single solution to any given problem. It may be eye-opening to scholars and practitioners alike if they turn towards a discussion of the social consequences of dogmatic value systems or philosophical texts or, at the very least, passages like the following by philosopher Odo Marquard:

> Gefährlich ist immer und mindestens der Monomythos; ungefährlich hingegen sind die Polymythen. Man muss viele Mythen – viele Geschichten – haben dürfen, darauf kommt es an; wer – zusammen mit allen anderen Menschen – nur einen Mythos – nur eine einzige Geschichte – hat und haben darf, ist schlimm dran. (Marquard, 1981: 98)[24]

Notes

(1) In his 2014 farewell lecture at Gießen University, Ulrich Horstmann compared the increasing production of turns to the dancing dervishes and described it polemically as the *Selbstpirouettisierung des Fachs* (self-pirouettization of the subject) (Horstmann, 2014: 6).
(2) This is not an unimportant consideration at a time when universities sometimes look as if they have shifted their *raison d'être* from the acquisition of knowledge to the acquisition of external third-party funding.

(3) Nonetheless, one can occasionally find the use of 'paradigm' or 'turn' as a reference in titles relating to aspects of language education research as well, e.g. *Language and Culture Pedagogy: From a National to a Transnational Paradigm* (Risager, 2007).
(4) In the German speaking area at that time it was established as an academic subject in East Germany only, notably in Leipzig under the stewardship of Gerhard Helbig.
(5) When a radical constructivism framework was postulated for language education by Wendt (2002) in the renowned German journal *Zeitschrift für Fremdsprachenforschung*, however, it triggered a heated debate in the following volume in which some of the more radical claims were rejected (cf. Bredella, 2002; Grotjahn, 2002; Hu, 2002; Wolff, 2002).
(6) Cf. titles like *Das konstruktivistische Lernparadigma und die neuen Medien* (The Constructivist Learning Paradigm and New Media) (Rinder, 2003).
(7) It is interesting that Butzkamm and Caldwell, who vehemently attack the dogma of monolingual foreign language teaching, use the word 'paradigm' in the title of their book: *The Bilingual Reform. A Paradigm Shift in Foreign Language Teaching* (2009).
(8) Cf. Rösler (1979). The fact that it had been shown that there is no best method unfortunately didn't bring a halt to thinking in and about global methods. Otherwise, there could be no explanation for the success of a book like Kumaravadivelu (2006), published more than a third of a century after Smith (1970).
(9) Cf., for example, Rösler (2008), Schmenk (2005).
(10) In this project, a group of high school students had to interact with 'real' people in a real airport, after having carefully prepared themselves for this communicative '*Ernstfall*' (the 'real thing'). The interviews carried out by small groups of students were the basis for classroom activities which led to texts (reports, posters) and presentations of these texts (cf. Legutke, 2006).
(11) 'Piepho's notion that ideal speech situations could be realized in EFL classes qua role playing seems – especially from today's perspective – too naive. The belief that egalitarian discourse could be simulated in language teaching, (...) has to be seen as an expression of the fact that the learning goal of communicative competence had gained utopian qualities. The transfer of Habermas' sociopolitical utopia to language teaching in schools had rather led to the creation of a foreign language teaching Arcadia. As seductive as these notions may have been, from today's point of view they seem too far away from the reality of foreign language teaching, like mythical transfigurations' (Schmenk, 2005: 71–72, my translation).
(12) 'As a result, a rather utilitarian concept of communicative competence gained currency, which was derived neither from Habermas' sociophilosophical concept nor from Hymes' ethnographic and sociolinguistic term: the description of communicative acts was reduced to a list of notions and functions, a manageable compilation of expressions that were included in FL in curricula to be "covered" in class' (Schmenk, 2005: 73, my translation).
(13) Cf. Rösler (2013b) for examples of how a beginners' textbook which takes the fact that learners are learning outside the target language area seriously can avoid focusing solely on everyday life in the target language area by introducing words for parts of the body in aesthetic contexts.
(14) 'The shift of the curricular emphasis away from focus on form and towards functionally appropriate use of the foreign language suggests to many observers that "communication" and "oral expression" make a formal view of language obsolete – this was neither intended nor is it expedient, but it evidently belongs to the phenomena which typically occur when paradigms are shifting and thus trigger pendulum swings in research which are prone to extremes' (Königs, 2011: 77, my translation).
(15) The weak version is satisfied to integrate communicative elements into an otherwise traditional, mostly form-focused classroom (Müller-Hartmann & Schocker-von Ditfurth, 2005: 4), while according to the strong version, students are encouraged to

use the target language to perform meaningful activities in the classroom and thus make learning possible (Müller-Hartmann & Schocker-von Ditfurth, 2005: 5).
(16) 'The so-called communicative turn in the 70s resulted in a shift away from mechanistic exercises designed according to the behaviorist model of thinking towards tasks that focused on the meaning-making potential of language and thus on using language in a way that allows for a connection of the various skills in an integrative manner' (Müller-Hartmann & Schocker-von Ditfurth, 2005: 4, my translation).
(17) '… with its too radical shift from learning techniques such as imitative practice of linguistic units and phrases or even pattern practice, the communicative turn has, in my view and upon analysis of plenty of teaching observations, virtually thrown these "babies" of behavioral learning concepts out "with the bath water": practicing is neglected in the interest of lively, thematically interesting classroom communication, which, however, happens to prevent communicative competence from being actually achieved' (Barkowski, 2004: 83–84, my translation).
(18) 'At the end of the task cycle there is a focus on form. This is different from a focus on language. Focus on form occurs when a teacher isolates particular forms for study and begins to work on those forms outside the context of a communicative activity' (Willis & Willis, 2007: 114, my translation).
(19) For a critique, see Rösler (2013a).
(20) 'Answers to the question of what forms of presentation, of cognitivization, of awareness raising, of practicing, etc. are (particularly) effective for building functional-communicative and structural linguistic skills can rarely be found by teachers, even in recent publications on the subject' (Schmelter, 2013: 75, my translation).
(21) Summarizing the analysis of research in Samuda and Bygate (2008), it could be said that research in this area 'konzentriert sich auf die beteiligten Personen, die Lernenden und die Lehrenden, auf die Interaktionen zwischen ihnen, auf die Kompetenzen, die die Lehrenden mitbringen müssen und die, die die Lernenden erwerben (sollen)' (focuses on the people involved, the learners and the teachers, on the interactions between them, on the skills that the teachers need to have and on those that the learners are (supposed) to acquire) (Rösler, 2013a: 47, my translation).
(22) The fact that Lewis Carroll's (1871) 'Jabberwocky' was not only written over nine decades before Chomsky's (1965) *Aspects* but was also a lot more fun, didn't get a mention.
(23) This is similar to the de-politicizing of communicative competence and its 'domestication' by breaking 'communication' down into notions and functions that could be compiled in lists.
(24) 'Dangerous is always and at least the monomyth; not dangerous, however, are polymyths. You have to be allowed to have many myths – lots of stories – that is the key; whoever – along with all the other people – only has (and is only allowed to have) one myth – just a single story – is in a bad place' (Marquard, 1981: 98, my translation).

References

Barkowski, H. (2004) Wie der Mensch seine Sprache(n) erwirbt und was daraus für die Förderung des Fremdsprachenunterrichts zu lernen ist – eine Zwischenbilanz. *DafWerkstatt* 3, 79–96.

Bredella, L. (2002) Die Entwertung der Welt und der Sprache in der radikal-konstruktivistischen Fremdsprachendidaktik. *Zeitschrift für Fremdsprachenforschung* 13 (2), 109–129.

Butzkamm, W. and Caldwell, J.A.W. (2009) *The Bilingual Reform. A Paradigm Shift in Foreign Language Teaching*. Tübingen: Narr.

Carroll, L. (1871) *Through the Looking Glass and what Alice Found There* (Illus. J. Tenniel). London: Macmillan.

Chomsky, N. (1965) *Aspects of the Theory of Syntax.* Cambridge, MA: MIT Press.
Feyerabend, P. (1975) *Against Method. Outline of an Anarchistic Theory of Knowledge.* London: Humanities Press.
Grotjahn, R. (2002) Informationsverarbeitungsparadigma und Radikaler Konstruktivismus: Kritische Anmerkungen zu Michael Wendt 'Kontext und Konstruktion'. *Zeitschrift für Fremdsprachenforschung* 13 (2), 139–163.
Habermas, J. (1971) Vorbereitende Bemerkungen zu einer Theorie der kommunikativen Kompetenz. In J. Habermas and N. Luhmann (eds) *Theorie der Gesellschaft oder Sozialtechnologie – Was leistet die Systemforschung?* (pp. 101–141). Frankfurt am Main: Suhrkamp.
Horstmann, U. (2014) *Über die Kleine Unsterblichkeit und wie man dahin kommt. Abschiedsvorlesung.* Gießen: Manuscript. See http://untier.de/abschiedsvorlesung-an-der-universitaet-giessen-2014-2/ (accessed 24 November 2017).
Hu, A. (2002) Skeptische Anmerkungen zu einer naturalisierten Erkenntnistheorie als Grundlage für das Lernen und Lehren von Sprachen: Eine Replik auf Michael Wendt (2002): Kontext und Konstruktion. *Zeitschrift für Fremdsprachenforschung* 13 (2), 165–180.
Königs, F. (2011) Verschollen im Bermuda-Dreieck? Anmerkungen und Beobachtungen zur Rolle der Grammatikvermittlung im Zeitalter von Kompetenzorientierung, Lernerautonomie und Neuen Medien. In B. Schmenk and N. Würffel (eds) *Drei Schritte vor und manchmal auch sechs zurück* (pp. 73–83). Tübingen: Narr.
Kuhn, T.S. (1970) *The Structure of Scientific Revolutions* (2nd edn). Chicago, IL: University of Chicago Press.
Kumaravadivelu, B. (2006) *Understanding Language Teaching. From Method to Postmethod.* Mahwah: NJ: Lawrence Erlbaum.
Legutke, M. (2006) Projekt Airport – revisited: Von der Aufgabe zum Szenario. In A. Küppers and J. Quetz (eds) *Motivation Revisited. Festschrift für Gert Solmecke* (pp. 71–81). Berlin: LIT.
Marquard, O. (1981) *Abschied vom Prinzipiellen.* Stuttgart: Reclam.
Müller-Hartmann, A. and Schocker-von Ditfurth, M. (2005) Aufgabenorientierung im Fremdsprachenunterricht: Entwicklungen, Forschung und Praxis, Perspektiven. In A. Müller-Hartmann and M. Schocker-von Ditfurth (eds) *Aufgabenorientierung im Fremdsprachenunterricht. Task-Based Language Learning and Teaching* (pp. 1–51). Tübingen: Narr.
Müller-Hartmann, A. and Schocker-von Ditfurth, M. (2013) Task-based teaching and assessment. In M. Byram and A. Hu (eds) *Routledge Encyclopedia of Language Teaching and Learning* (pp. 687–692). London: Routledge.
Piepho, H.-E. (1974) *Kommunikative Kompetenz als übergeordnetes Lernziel im Englischunterricht.* Dornburg-Frickhofen: Frankonius.
Rinder, A. (2003) Das konstruktivistische Lernparadigma und die neuen Medien. *Info DaF* 30 (1), 3–22.
Risager, K. (2007) *Language and Culture Pedagogy: From a National to a Transnational Paradigm.* Clevedon: Multilingual Matters.
Rösler, D. (1979) Feyerabend für die Sprachlehrforschung? In H. Heuer, H. Sauer and H. Kleineidam (eds) *Dortmunder Diskussionen zur Fremdsprachendidaktik* (pp. 151–155). Dortmund: Lensing.
Rösler, D. (2008) Lernziel kommunikative Kompetenz dreiunddreißig Jahre nach Piepho 1974 – ein kritischer Rückblick aus der Perspektive des Deutschlernens außerhalb des deutschsprachigen Raums. In H.E. Piepho and M. Legutke (eds) *Kommunikative Kompetenz als Fremdsprachendidaktische Vision* (pp. 115–129). Tübingen: Narr.
Rösler, D. (2013a) Erfüllen Aufgaben ihre Aufgabe? Ein Blick in den akademischen Diskurs. *Fremdsprachen lehren und lernen* 4 (2), 41–54.
Rösler, D. (2013b) Zu Risiken und Nebenwirkungen fragen Sie lieber nicht Ihren Theoretiker: Kommunikative Orientierung der Fremdsprachendidaktik und Deutsch

als Fremdsprache außerhalb des deutschsprachigen Raums. In J. Plews and B. Schmenk (eds) *Traditions and Transitions: Curricula for German Studies* (pp. 89–104). Waterloo, Ont.: Wilfrid Laurier University Press.

Samuda, V. and Bygate, M. (2008) *Tasks in Second Language Learning*. Basingstoke: Palgrave Macmillan.

Schmelter, L. (2013) Die 'dienende Funktion' der Grammatik im Französischunterricht. In L. Küster and U. Krämer (eds) *Mythos Grammatik?* (pp. 74–84). Seelze: Kallmeyer.

Schmenk, B. (2005) Mode, Mythos, Möglichkeiten oder: Ein Versuch, die Patina des Lernziels 'kommunikative Kompetenz' abzukratzen. *Zeitschrift für Fremdsprachenforschung* 16 (1), 57–87.

Schmenk, B. (2008) *Lernerautonomie: Karriere und Sloganisierung des Autonomiebegriffs*. Tübingen: Narr.

Smith, P. (1970) *A Comparison of the Cognitive and Audiolingual Approaches to Foreign Language Instruction. The Pennsylvania Foreign Language Project*. Philadelphia, PA: Center for Curriculum Development.

van Elek, T. and Oskarsson, M. (1975) *Comparative Method Experiments in Foreign Language Teaching*. Gothenburg: Department of Educational Research, School of Education, Sweden.

Wendt, M. (2002) Kontext und Konstruktion: Fremdsprachendidaktische Theorienbildung und ihre Implikationen für die Fremdsprachenforschung. *Zeitschrift für Fremdsprachenforschung* 13 (1), 1–62.

Wierlacher, A. (1980) Deutsch als Fremdsprache. Zum Paradigmawechsel internationaler Germanistik. Zugleich eine Einführung in Absicht und Funktion dieses Bandes. In A. Wierlacher (ed.) *Fremdsprache Deutsch I* (pp. 9–27). Munich: Fink.

Willis, D. and Willis, J. (2007) *Doing Task-Based Teaching*. Oxford: Oxford University Press.

Wolff, D. (1994) Der Konstruktivismus: Ein neues Paradigma in der Fremdsprachendidaktik? *Die Neueren Sprachen* 93 (5), 407–429.

Wolff, D. (2002) 'The proof of the pudding is in the eating' oder warum ich nicht als radikalkonstruktivistischer Mitstreiter von Michael Wendt verstanden werden möchte. *Zeitschrift für Fremdsprachenforschung* 13 (2), 181–186.

4 Slo(w)ganization. Against the Constant Need for Re-inventing the Discourse on Language Education: The Case of 'Multiple Intelligences'

Gerhard Bach

Since the communicative turn, foreign/second language teaching methodology has been highly responsive to innovation and change, mostly based on reflection and insight but at times also influenced by fads and fetishes. As a consequence of the latter, several slogans have mushroomed in language education discourse, covering up a lack of reflection and real innovation. Much like pop charts, hit lists of current slogans abound, in constant need of reinvention. This chapter argues that there would be little need for such reinventions (or, to use the appropriate slogan, 're-visions'), because much of what hides behind catch phrases turns out to be mere reinterpretations of well-established thoughts. A case in point is the term 'multiple intelligences', which was used to announce a paradigm shift in language education discourse after its propagation by Howard Gardner in the early 1980s. What was originally meant to be a wake-up call for medical research to expand its view of intelligence from the restricted cognitive domain to other domains quickly caught on in foreign language research and practice as a broadband remedy to meet the needs of individualizing learning processes. Armstrong (2017) neatly appropriated Gardner's model of educational practices by assigning to each particular 'intelligence' a plethora of learning designs and particular teaching options.

This chapter argues that the adaptation of the Gardner model adopted by Armstrong and modified further by German foreign language curriculum designers is little more than an all-too-ready reformulation of what used to be known as learning skills and learning strategies. Thus, the term 'intelligence' turns out to add little to our insight into what constitutes individual learning processes; it just sounds so much more serious and 'professional'. As a slogan, however, it has secured its position in German school curricula, mainly serving as a checklist for teachers to decide on how best to engage their students' individual 'intelligences'. In a nutshell, this chapter argues that, rather than propelling the discourse on language education into ever-new paradigms, slowing things down may turn out to have savory effects.

> He now had the courage to request that (...) impatience not be allowed, that his own pace be imposed on others for the good of all: 'I'm slow. Please adjust accordingly.' Sten Nadolny, *The Discovery of Slowness* (1987)

> Odd as it may seem, I am my remembering self, and the experiencing self, who does my living, is like a stranger to me. Daniel Kahneman, *Thinking, Fast and Slow* (2011)

Introduction

Postmodern life is in a constant mode of acceleration and no in-depth diagnosis is necessary to corroborate this. Fast food will be digested faster and more effectively if followed by a power nap, which in turn helps us to write more articles faster for immediate publication in ever-growing numbers of newly sprouting online journals, granting us higher hopes of a speedier climb up the professional ladder on our way to the next better paying and faster tenured job. The latest techno-media innovation of the global connectedness age helps us save time by organizing our multitasking challenges more efficiently. Slogans are the twittering lubricants in all of this, especially when they fit into the 140 characters text-messaging format.

Strange as it may seem, while the art of saving time reaches unprecedented heights through the introduction of ever-new technologies of communication and production, it nevertheless seems as though we are running out of time while we hasten to feed the needs and requests of our messaging services. Global connectedness demands of us that we run ever faster, not in order to get somewhere, but just to keep up with the pack – intellectual speed dating, so to speak. Slogans help us, if nothing else, to keep face, allowing us to pretend, for a fleeting moment, that we are ahead in this race.

There are numerous accounts, both academic and popular, outlining the dangers implicit in this race and suggesting that acceleration in the end leads to monstrous forms of alienation: from time and space, from objects and actions and from self and others. One byproduct of such constant acceleration is that under pressure we tend to make half-hearted decisions.

Another is that we tend to quickly fall in line with catchphrases and slogans. Slogans seduce us into thinking less, giving us (ironically) more time for seemingly quick-witted conclusions. Slogans are a neat way to camouflage our unwillingness, if not our incapability, to slow down when everyone else is speeding up.

I have two witnesses from different poles of the world – one artistic, the other academic – to substantiate this thesis. Their positions are briefly presented, and a first level of connectivity to the common topic, sloganization, is established. Each of these is presented as a prologue to the main exploration of the decline of complex issues into sloganized simplicity. As the reader doubtless realizes, this somewhat lengthy introduction is a strategy of slowing down the fast pace of academic turnaround, what might be called the strategy of *slow* or, in the terms of the business world, *lean* thought management.

Slow and Fast

Prologue 1

In his novel, *The Discovery of Slowness* (1983; first English language edition, 1987), novelist Sten Nadolny delineates John Franklin's (1786–1847) expeditions into the Arctic regions of what then came to be known as the Northwest Passage. Franklin's persistence in believing that there had to be a passage along the Arctic mainland coast, so Nadolny's (fictional) argument goes, is indebted to a 'defect', an impairment Franklin displayed from early boyhood onwards governing all his perceptions, decisions and insights, namely an apparently inborn force of slow movement, slowed down action and slow-motion thinking. Nadolny's presentation eventually leads the reader to the conviction that only because of this impairment could Franklin have achieved so much. This impairment was Franklin's *slowness* in everything he observed and did: 'John Franklin, always looking on with a friendly and faintly surprised expression, was an ideal listener for relentless thinkers. Therefore he heard many phrases no one else wanted to hear' (Nadolny, 1987: 88). At a time of diverse revolutions – industrial (transportation), social (communication technologies) and otherwise – where all movement accelerates at an ever-growing pace, Franklin's slowness became an invaluable strength: 'Slowness became honorable; speed became the servant. The large overview was not a good view, for it overlooked too much. Presence of mind, raised to a law, created neither a present moment nor a specific point of view' (Nadolny, 1987: 164). In this tale of time external (as given or determined) and time internal (as experienced), Nadolny shows how against all odds slowness prevails over speed (the acceleration of life in the industrial age). To the contemporary reader on a moral scale, it signals how important it is, in our late-modern and postmodern era, to determine and maintain our own speed when it comes to meaning-making and decision formation. Slowness, so Nadolny says, is an art which renders meaning to one's thoughts and actions. Gradually, over the course of several journeys into the Arctic, Nadolny's protagonist develops the 'Franklin system': 'If a slow person, against all predictions, had managed to survive in a fast profession, that was better than anything else.' (Nadolny, 1987: 179)

Prologue 2

In 2011, Daniel Kahneman, Nobel Prize recipient in Economics (2002), published *Thinking, Fast and Slow*. In this book, he summarizes his insights gathered over 30 years of empirical research in economics and sociopsychological theory. The field Kahneman staked out is called 'behavioral economics'. It deals with the question of why we make decisions against our better knowledge – be these our investments in the stock market or our spending habits in the supermarket – and then stick to them against all odds. The book's central thesis concerns the dichotomy between two modes of thought, i.e. the two different ways in which the brain generates thoughts and formulates these into decisions. Kahneman (2011: 20–21) calls these mental processes 'systems' (Table 4.1).

Kahneman describes a number of scientific experiments carried out over the past four decades that highlight the differences between these two thought systems, and how they influence decision makers to arrive at different results even when given the same input. These experiments, he claims, tell us a lot about ourselves – our coherence, attention, laziness, associations, how we jump to conclusions and how we form judgments.

Obviously, decisions based on either of these two systems have wide-ranging consequences, and Kahneman's intention is to reveal where we can trust our fast-paced intuitions and where we cannot, and what we need to do in order to tap into the benefits of slow thinking. He offers practical and enlightening insights into how choices are made in both our

Table 4.1 Two modes of mental systems

System 1	System 2
Fast	Slow
Automatic	Effortful
Frequent	Infrequent
Emotional	Logical
Stereotypical	Calculating
Subconscious	Conscious

Source: Kahneman (2011: 20–21).

business lives and our personal lives, and how we can use different techniques to guard against the mental glitches that often get us into trouble due to the consequences of the decisions we have made.

Convergence and overlap

Where, and more importantly how, do these two scenarios connect?

Fast thinkers will immediately recognize John Franklin's effortful and calculating procedure in charting the course of his own future. John Franklin's brain is a System 2 brain. Sounds logical? Great! Easy! Let's store it in our brains, catch phrase it, find a slogan; let's call it the 'K2-paradigm'. Done. Time to move on to the next issue. For Kahneman, the operating system behind such decision-making processes is what he characterizes as the WYSIATI paradigm: *What You See Is All There Is*. 'WYSIATI facilitates the achievement of coherence and of the cognitive ease that causes us to accept a statement as true. It explains why we can think fast, and how we are able to make sense of partial information in a complex world' (Kahneman, 2011: 87).

Slow thinkers will, in a matter of hours or days or weeks (years for John Franklin), remind the fast thinkers of Kahneman's (2011: 85–88) 'over-confidence' axiom, which the author identifies as the driving force behind fast thinkers' rationale: 'The confidence that individuals have in their beliefs depends mostly on the quality of the story they can tell about what they see, even if they see little' (Kahneman, 2011: 87).

In his analysis of these three prototypes of knowledge (shown in Table 4.2), Kahneman observes that when the mind makes decisions it deals primarily with *Known Knowns*, phenomena it has already observed and stored as conclusive. It rarely considers *Known Unknowns*, phenomena that it knows to be relevant but about which it has no information by which to provide closure. Finally, the mind appears oblivious to the possibility of *Unknown Unknowns*, unknown phenomena of unknown relevance. It is precisely John Franklin's gift of slowness, so Nadolny says, that allowed him to access and, if only to a certain extent, master the territory of the *Unknown Unknowns*. What Franklin saw was more than there was, and for that 'simple' reason he was able to discover the Northwest Passage.

Table 4.2 WYSIATI

Known Knowns	Phenomena the mind has already observed
Known Unknowns	Phenomena that the mind knows to be relevant but about which it has no information
Unknown Unknowns	Unknown phenomena of unknown relevance about which the mind is oblivious

Source: Kahneman (2011: 85–88).

In turning to language education discourse and the issue of sloganization, my conceptual argument of slo(w)ganization at this point converges with (1) the 'Franklin system' *and* (2) Kahneman's over-confidence axiom. With Nadolny/Kahneman, I argue that we, as teaching professionals, teacher-educators and researchers, have learned, by rule of the postmodern requirement, to think fast and furiously and to ignore complexity. Our understanding of the world (not merely that of language education) comprises sets or frames of observations, which may or may not allow for generalization and closure. Further, we have learned not to trust in the role of chance and therefore falsely assume that a future event, such as a plan for a lesson, a learning objective or an array of activities, will mirror a past event, such as the experience that a lesson has worked, i.e. the over-confidence of the Known Known, namely that the formulation of learning objectives carries relevance.

I will exemplify this by applying Kahneman's WYSIATI axiom to the sloganization process that has occurred in language education discourse concerning the impact of 'multiple intelligences' on language teaching practices. First, I present a brief overview of Howard Gardner's 'theory of multiple intelligences'. Then I analyze how Thomas Armstrong instrumentalizes these 'intelligences' for language education classroom practices. My general thesis is that 'multiple intelligences', when broken down to the level of learning and teaching, represent little more than what for decades we have known as 'learning styles' and 'learning strategies'.

Multiple Intelligences

Context

Lisa is a 10-year-old 5th grader in a German EFL classroom. Her school has decided to implement the foreign language portfolio as proposed by the European Commission (CEO, 2017). This is Lisa's entry in her personal language portfolio (transcript, German original, my translation):

> I love English because we get to go outside and play English games and sing songs. I like reading the stories in our book best. When I read I look at the pictures and this helps me say the words better. When we write I also think of the pictures. I think it's funny when I say 'hello, how are you' to my teacher in the hallway and she looks at me in surprise. I sometimes say funny words to myself. I hate doing math in English, the numbers sound funny: 'four*teen*', 'fif*teen*' and so on.

Lisa investigates her own learning processes and so she relates to us certain means or strategies that she employs in order to learn for and by herself and in order to communicate successfully with others. There are obvious connections that exist between what Lisa explains about her learning and what researchers suggest they know about language acquisition and learning. In particular, such knowledge bears remarkable connections to intelligence theory, learning styles and learner strategies. Lisa manages to express with clarity and distinction what language educators value greatly: language awareness, multi-channel learning strategies, context-specific communicative competence, low affective filter, etc.

The question arising from Lisa's entry in her language learning portfolio for the context of our investigation of issues concerning sloganization is the following. Contemporary interpretations of Lisa's learning behaviors suggest 'multiple intelligences' at work here, as identified and categorized by Howard Gardner (see next section). More traditional interpretations, less current but equally 'durable' in terms of validity, point to learning styles and strategies and their foundation in social-psychology (see the section on 'Multiple Intelligences Theory Sloganized and Labeled': 63). The question to be addressed, then, is not only which conceptual domain explains Lisa's learning more accurately, but also what ties exist between the two conceptual domains and to what extent they represent fast thinking or slow.

Howard Gardner's theory of multiple intelligences

Gardner's 'theory of multiple intelligences' (MI theory) has, for several decades now, challenged the traditional view of *intelligence* as a singular capacity which can be adequately measured by IQ tests. Gardner defines 'intelligence' as an ability to solve problems or create products that are valued in particular contexts. Interpreting the results of his brain surgery research conducted over several decades, Gardner isolated seven such 'intelligences', adding two more over the course of two decades (Table 4.3). According to Gardner,

- all human beings possess all nine intelligences in varying degrees;
- these intelligences are located in different areas of the brain and can work either independently or together;
- each person thus has a different intellectual composition and applies his/her intelligences according to a specific profile;
- as teachers, we can improve education by addressing the multiple intelligences of our students.

For Gardner, each 'intelligence' holds immediate learning potential. It is a small step for him to project, in very general terms, the possibilities inherent in his MI theory to the field of education. While empirical evidence has always displayed a diversity of agents to be active in individual learning processes, it has been considered an important step forward that with Gardner's 'intelligences' such agents have become tangible, i.e. they have become observable in the core operations learners are able to perform. For Gardner, a core operation is a basic information-processing

Table 4.3 Seven (plus two) Intelligences

Intelligence/Learner	Core operations/Application in learning
Logical-mathematical/'numbers smart'	Ability to detect patterns, reason deductively and think logically. This intelligence is most often associated with scientific and mathematical thinking.
Verbal-linguistic/'word smart'	Mastery of language. This intelligence includes the ability to effectively manipulate language to express oneself rhetorically or poetically. It also allows one to use language as a means to remember information.
Musical/'music smart'	Encompasses the capability to recognize and compose musical pitches, tones and rhythms. (Auditory functions are required for a person to develop this intelligence in relation to pitch and tone, but are not needed for the knowledge of rhythm.)
Visual-spatial/'art smart'	Involves the ability to manipulate and create mental images in order to solve problems. This intelligence is not limited to visual domains – Gardner notes that spatial intelligence also develops in blind children.
Bodily-kinesthetic/'body smart'	The ability to use one's mental abilities to coordinate one's own bodily movements. This intelligence challenges the popular belief that mental and physical activity are unrelated.
Interpersonal[a]/'people smart'	Capacity to detect and respond appropriately to the moods, motivations and desires of others.
Intrapersonal[a]/'self smart'	Capacity to be self-aware and in tune with inner feelings, values, beliefs and thinking processes.
Naturalist[b]/'nature smart'	Ability to recognize and categorize plants, animals and other objects in nature.
Existential[c]/'wondering smart'	Sensitivity and capacity to address and resolve questions about human existence, such as the meaning of life, birth, death, afterlife.

Notes: [a]Because of their close association in most cultures, they are often linked together. [b]Added in 1993. [c]Suggested for inclusion in 1999; reviewed in 2006.
Source: Adapted from Gardner (1993, 1999, 2006).

mechanism and it functions like a neural network in the brain that takes a particular kind of input or information and processes it. Educational researchers have used this concept of information-processing mechanisms to redefine the principles of teaching and learning, and educators have used them to redesign Gardner's *theory* into *taxonomies* as tools for detecting individual abilities, knowledge and skills. Gardner's core operations, when translated into learning activities (as performative actions), reflect the range of 'intelligent' operations an individual is able to perform. While MI theory was originally developed out of a response to and a sharp criticism of psychometric intelligence testing and had a clear objective in advancing therapeutic aid for people with certain brain malfunctions, Gardner soon recognized the general educational potential of what he himself termed a 'theory' (for others perhaps simply a 'model'), suggesting that we can improve education by addressing the multiple intelligences present but possibly unchartered and therefore inactive in our students. It has been a small step from classifying intelligent behaviors to transforming them into models of learning and applying them in specific learning situations. It needs to be clarified, therefore, how such transformations occur, and how the adaptation of a general theory benefits concrete learning.

Multiple intelligences theory applied in language education (Armstrong)

The most widely known application of MI theory reflecting individual learning styles and needs was presented by Thomas Armstrong in *Multiple Intelligences in the Classroom*. First published in 1994, the book's 4th edition (2017) is now hailed by the publisher as a 'bona fide education classic in its own right' (back cover blurb). The book projects the possibility of modelling learning activities along the lines of Gardner's 'intelligences'. Where Gardner vaguely suggested the educational potential of his MI theory, Armstrong steps in and develops a model for the implementation of individual intelligences in learning settings. Armstrong agrees with Gardner that although each child possesses all nine intelligences and can develop all of them to a fairly high level of competence, the individual child, from an early age onward, seems to show what Gardner (1999: 51) calls 'proclivities', i.e. inclinations and preferences in specific intelligences. By the time children begin school, they have established ways of learning that run more along the lines of some intelligences than others. Following Gardner's projections, Armstrong suggests ways to operationalize such intelligences, based on the theory that once we know how to address them specifically they will help make learning easier. Armstrong also cautions against the tendency to pigeonhole children's learning proclivities into single, observable styles. In general, students reveal individual strengths in *several* areas, at least two or three. *Mapping* Gardner's intelligences, Armstrong concludes that young learners revealing particular learning styles achieve best when they are supplied with learning aids that align with their proclivities, that is to say, with their likes and dislikes. From this concept Armstrong builds a model of the 'think-love-need' paradigm (Table 4.4).

When applied, for instance, to Lisa's description of her own language learning situation, Armstrong's model exemplifies the spectrum that characterizes her individual learning profile, and it reveals that in her learning she creates an amalgam of specific interconnected intelligences. Following the Armstrong model, and comparing it with conventional descriptors of (language) learning, Lisa's 'composition of learning' is shown in Table 4.5.

As a learner, Lisa applies diverse 'intelligences' in a spectrum of approaches based on concrete and imminent learning needs. She

Table 4.4 Eight ways of learning

Children who are highly	Think	Love	Need
Logical-mathematical	By reasoning	Experimenting, questioning, figuring out logical puzzles, calculating	Materials to experiment with, science materials, manipulatives, trips to the planetarium and science museum
Linguistic	In words	Reading, writing, telling stories, playing word games	Books, tapes, writing tools, paper, diaries, dialogue, discussion, debate, stories
Musical	Via rhythms and melodies	Singing, whistling, humming, tapping feet and hands, listening	Sing-along time, trips to concerts, music activities at home and school, musical instruments
Visual-spatial	In images and pictures	Designing, drawing, visualizing, doodling	Art, video, movies, slides, imagination games, mazes, puzzles, illustrated books
Bodily-kinesthetic	Through somatic sensations	Dancing, running, jumping, building, touching, gesturing	Role play, drama, movement, things to build, sports and physical games, tactile experiences, hands-on learning
Interpersonal	By bouncing ideas off other people	Leading, organizing, relating, manipulating, mediating, partying	Friends, group games, social gatherings, community events, mentors/apprenticeships
Intrapersonal	In relation to their needs, feelings and goals	Setting goals, meditating, dreaming, planning, reflecting	Secret places, time alone, self-paced projects, choices
Naturalist	Through nature and natural forms	Playing with pets, gardening, investigating nature, raising animals, caring for planet earth	Access to nature, opportunities for interacting with animals, tools (e.g. magnifying glass, binoculars)

Source: Adapted from Armstrong (2017).

illustrates an important factor both Gardner and Armstrong stress in their respective models, namely that the multiplicity of intelligences and the approaches applied do not reflect a hierarchy of lower and higher competences, such as that set out in Bloom's taxonomy of lower and higher order thinking skills (Bloom, 1956). While Bloom's concept, even in its revised form (Anderson *et al.*, 2001), relies on the notion of building cognitive competence on a scale from 'lower' to 'higher' order information-processing skills, Armstrong adheres to Gardner's equanimous view: 'By the time children begin school, they have probably established ways of learning that run more along the lines of some intelligences than others. … Keep in mind, however, that most students have strengths in several areas, so

Table 4.5 Lisa's 'composition of learning'

Lisa's portfolio entry	Conventional descriptors	Gardner/Armstrong 'intelligences'
I love English because (1) we get to go outside and play 'English' games and sing songs. I like reading the stories in our book best. (2) When I read I look at the pictures and this helps me say the words better. (3) When we write I also think of the pictures. I think it's funny (4) when I say 'hello, how are you' in English to my teacher in the hallway and she looks at me in surprise. (5) I sometimes say funny words to myself. (6) I hate doing math in English, the numbers sound crazy: 'fourteen', 'fifteen' and so on.	(1) Cultural dimension of language learning and creative interaction (2) Networking reading with visual signals (3) Networking writing with visual signals (4) Social dimension of communication and empowerment (5) Mental processing (6) Sense of language as emotion	(1) Bodily-kinesthetic, musical (2) Spatial-visual (3) Spatial-visual, bodily-kinesthetic (4) Interpersonal (5) Intrapersonal (6) Logical-mathematical, musical

you should avoid pigeon-holing a child in only one intelligence' (Armstrong, 2017: 32).

Multiple intelligences theory: Global and local perspectives

Whether we consider adopting the MI model for our assessment scale in the foreign language classroom or not, we need to remind ourselves that 'intelligence' is not a universally agreed upon concept. Gardner, however, quietly implies this, and Armstrong adopts the universalist notion in his model. I would argue, however, that any approach to discovering how learners learn is intrinsically culture- and context-bound. To my mind, the balance between importing 'global' advice and implanting it in local educational soil in order to grow a linguistically more capable 'product' has taken the course of the ever-growing need for speed outlined in the introduction above. Particularly in Germany, the shockwaves generated by PISA (Programme for International Student Assessment) have resulted in discrediting the 'local' and setting too great hopes in the 'global'. The results of the first test carried out on a worldwide scale were unsettling for Germany (OECD, 2001). Considering the nation's economic and political significance it was assumed that German schoolchildren would perform at the top of the league, which was not the case. In fact, scores were markedly below the OECD average level. Reforms were rapidly enacted, Finland and Japan being the new models for rethinking education in Germany. The reforms notwithstanding, a decade later the number of Germans scoring in the top category for literacy is still below the OECD average (OECD, 2013). Superimposing the global onto the local apparently has had little, if any, effect.

The case of 'multiple intelligences' is similar. MI theory has been prominently embedded in the internal US debate over measuring intelligence in traditional and non-traditional ways. The argument of MI theory in this debate is that textbooks, lectures and standardized tests are not sufficient to produce a level of understanding that goes beyond mere recognition and repetition, but that more is required to assure learning has occurred. Students need to involve their total selves, and this includes using their bodies, imagination, social sensibilities, emotions and naturalistic inclinations, as well as their verbal and reasoning skills in order to master new material.

Exporting this discourse and the resilient debate it has generated in the United States to other local contexts demands attention to different paradigms. Language learning is an activity highly influenced by locally defined cultural norms and collective practices, by local contexts and regional and/or national expectations. Because learners develop and implement their strategies inside such contexts, their strategies are culturally encoded, as are the models teachers use to teach. In other words, Lisa's strategies are what she describes them to be in the immediate context of her classroom, her immediate cultural group setting and her immediate local environment. Send her to Greece, Ghana or Hong Kong, and she will develop new intelligent learning behaviors as well as new notions of learning nurtured by her new environment. The outcome will be language learning practices characteristic of her previous language learning experiences, her new experiential setting, and the environmental instructional setting responsible for her learning.

Multiple Intelligences Theory Sloganized and Labeled

Multiple intelligences in the historical dimension

Theories as proposed by Gardner and adopted into learning models by educators such as Armstrong have generated concern among educators whose parameters of judgment are built on more conservative psychological and pedagogical insight and evidence. For example, at this point we have no empirical evidence from research conducted in the language learning sector to prove or disprove the validity and operability of the intelligences synergy as projected by MI theorists and MI educationists. Criticism focuses less on MI theory as such, and more on its practical applications in schools. Collins (1998: 95), one of the earliest critics of Gardner's theory's excursions into educational territory, argues that 'evidence for the specifics of Gardner's theory is weak, and there is no firm research showing that its practical applications have been effective' (Collins, 1998: 95).

An unbiased analysis of Lisa's 'proclivities' spectrum would associate her learning behaviors as exemplary of the three basic learning dispositions long identified in educational psychology, namely knowledge-based dispositions, social-affective dispositions and motor skills. In other words, the MI-based Armstrong model: (a) renames existing concepts; (b) it does not enhance our understanding of how learners learn, (c) but rather fosters a universalist understanding of learning behavior, (d) that is inappropriate because it is insensitive to social/cultural contexts; eventually, this (e) serves the current dynamic for the marketization of ideas (even those that are not new), a process that bears the label of 'sloganization'.

This is illustrated in the following examples: where MI theorists get excited over Lisa's 'multiple intelligences', more conservative analysts would remind us that we have been aware of such multiple strategic approaches since the 1970s; at the time, they were simply called learning *styles*, and were seen in close proximity to learning *strategies*. Still, 'multiple intelligences' sounds so much more advanced, in fact, so much more intelligent, that some curriculum planners have hastened to copy and paste Armstrong's taxonomy into their curriculum guidelines. This was the case in Germany, where the 'think-love-need' triad was assimilated into lesson plans and instructional scenarios as a scientifically proven approach to assure learning success for learners of all ages. Brunner and Rottensteiner (2014), for example, have developed interactive scenarios based on MI principles for elementary school pupils. Puchta *et al.* (2009) have collected a plethora of classroom activities for high school and adult learners in the area of German as a second/foreign language.

A similar Kahneman-inspired System 1 approach of overly fast thinking to resolve learning issues occurred in the 1960s with the implementation of immensely cost intensive, but in the long run inefficient language labs. Modeled on the behavioristic stimulus-response learning sequence, language lab activities were considered to be better suited to control learning processes and outcomes. In comparison, classroom interactive learning processes were considered slow and less controllable. Why, then, were language labs destined to fail, which they did rapidly after the 1970s language lab hype subsided? For Kahneman, language lab learning would represent System 1 mental operations; both implement the behavioristic cycle of repetition, punishment and reward. System 1 educationists were overly excited and jumped to conclusions, thus making irrational choices about the effectiveness of a learning model already on its way out, because behaviorism was gradually giving way to developmental learning models (Piaget, Vygotski).

More recently, another similar System 1 fast-thinking default has been threatening instructional advancement, namely John Hattie's *Visible Learning* (2008), which, despite its many helpful insights, at least in Germany has been sloganized to resurrect 'teacher-centered instruction', the 'chalk and talk' approach thought to have gone extinct from the educational landscape. Thinking fast *or* slow – what goes around, comes around.

The feel-good quality of 'smart'

Telling every child that she or he is 'smart' might well be considered a smart device of MI theory for selling its product. As spelled out in the Introduction to this book, education in the past rarely ever considered itself as merchandise to be marketed. Twenty-first century changes in the professional habitus of educationists and educational stakeholders has modified this view, and the impetus to reinvent oneself in order to adapt to ever-changing economic and social conditions has become an accepted norm in most educators' professional worlds. Branding, labeling and sloganizing have become accepted selling devices in a world in which constant innovation is in demand. Much like other slogans (see 'autonomy' in the Introduction to this volume), 'MI theory' has been mainstreamed, not so much by its 'inventor' himself (Gardner), but by its educational proponents such as Armstrong, who recognized its selling power by adding suitable labels.

Telling every child that she or he is smart creates, as critics have repeatedly stressed, an artificial classroom atmosphere where learning is seen in the light of attitude rather than that of skills, competences and knowledge acquisition. Barnett, Ceci and Williams (2006), in a direct response to Gardner's claims, write: '[M]ere relabeling may not have a permanent curative effect. ... Focusing on the label rather than on meaningful performances that demonstrate skill may lead children to become further disillusioned once the first blush passes'; and the authors conclude that 'the focus must be on displaying meaningful skills and competencies, not simply on feeling that one is smart' (Barnett *et al.*, 2006: 101).

Despite such cautionary words, there is general agreement that we need to see intelligences, styles and needs operating on a continuum. Polarizing observable behavior in binaries such as 'the spatial-visual versus the logical-mathematical' or 'cognitive versus affective-emotional' turns out to be counterproductive and, in view of neurological research and empirical studies in EFL pedagogy, inaccurate and inadequate. What it tends to do, for System 1 thinkers and System 2 thinkers alike, is to force a one-dimensional cause-and-effect logic upon an originally multidimensional concept.

What is the logic inherent in the 'think-love-need' triad suggested by Armstrong for teachers to use as a planning and assessment tool for 'intelligent' classroom activities? Is it a valid premise to assume that children 'need' more of what they already possess in intellectual abilities ('think') and what they already 'love' to do in particular? Or would they actually be better off with an enriched learning environment in those areas in which they perform *less* 'intelligently'? Broad-band 'intelligence' as a tool (a theory?) with seven or more discrete functions is a remedy readily available for the fast-brain System 1 educators for whom learning is reduced to a cause-and-effect relationship. Multiple intelligences theory light and lean, bite-sized, quickly digested. Hopefully, few will choke on the slogan.

References

Anderson, L.W., Krathwohl, D.R., Airasian, P.W., Cruikshank, K.A., Mayer, R.E., Pintrich, P.R., Raths, J. and Wittrock, M.C. (2001) *A Taxonomy for Learning, Teaching, and Assessing: A Revision of Bloom's Taxonomy of Educational Objectives*. New York: Pearson, Allyn & Bacon.

Armstrong, T. (2017 [1994]) *Multiple Intelligences in the Classroom* (4th edn). Alexandria, VA: Association for Supervision and Curriculum Development.

Barnett, S.M., Ceci, S.J. and Williams, W.M. (2006) Is the ability to make a bacon sandwich a mark of intelligence? and other issues: Some reflections on Gardner's theory of multiple intelligences. In J.A. Schaler (ed.) *Howard Gardner Under Fire: The Rebel Psychologist Faces His Critics* (pp. 95–114). Chicago, IL: Open Court.

Bloom, B.S. (ed.) (1956) *Taxonomy of Educational Objectives, Handbook I: The Cognitive Domain*. New York: David McKay.

Brunner, I. and Rottensteiner, E. (2014) *Mit multiplen Intelligenzen Begabungen fördern und Kompetenzen entwickeln: Praxisbeispiele für erfolgreiches Unterrichten in der Grundschule und Sekundarstufe I*. Baltmannsweiler: Schneider Verlag Hohengehren.

CEO (2017) *European Language Portfolio (ELP)*. Strasbourg: Council of Europe. See https://www.coe.int/en/web/portfolio (accessed 29 November 2017).

Collins, J. (1998) Seven kinds of smart. *Time*, 19 October, pp. 94–96.

Gardner, H. (1993) *Multiple Intelligences: The Theory in Practice*. New York: Basic Books.

Gardner, H. (1999) *Intelligence Reframed: Multiple Intelligences for the 21st Century*. New York: Basic Books.

Gardner, H. (2006) *Multiple Intelligences: New Horizons in Theory and Practice*. New York: Basic Books.

Hattie, J. (2008) *Visible Learning. A Synthesis of Over 800 Meta-Analyses Relating to Achievement*. New York: Routledge.

Kahneman, D. (2011) *Thinking, Fast and Slow*. New York: Farrar, Straus & Giroux.

Nadolny, S. (1987) *The Discovery of Slowness* (trans. R. Freedman). New York: Viking.

OECD (2001) *Knowledge and Skills for Life: First Results from PISA 2000*. Paris: OECD iLibrary. See http://dx.doi.org/10.1787/9789264195905-en (accessed 23 November 2017).

OECD (2013) *PISA 2012 Results: What Makes Schools Successful? Resources, Policies and Practices, Volume IV*. Paris: OECD iLibrary. See http://dx.doi.org/10.1787/9789264201156-en (accessed 23 November 2017).

Puchta, H., Krenn, W. and Rinvolucri, M. (2009) *Intelligenzen im DaF-Unterricht: Aktivitäten für die Sekundarstufe und den Erwachsenenunterricht. Deutsch als Fremdsprache*. Stuttgart: Klett.

5 Just Another Prefix? From Inter- to Transcultural Foreign Language Learning and Beyond

Britta Viebrock

Since the early 1980s, 'intercultural learning' has been one of the central concepts in the German discourse on foreign language education, employed by different stakeholders (scholars, education policy makers, members of the teaching profession) – although this does not mean that it has gone undisputed. 'Intercultural learning' was followed by the notion of 'transcultural learning' in the late 1990s; the proliferation and popularization of both concepts within and across the different domains of language education discourse have been characterized by instances of sloganization. Slogans are created – deliberately or not – by taking concepts or parts of texts out of their textual or historical context and subsequently working with a reduced version. This reduction results in definitional and conceptual inaccuracy, or simplification and trivialization. The purpose of this paper is to examine these processes of sloganization by tracing the emergence and historical contextualization of the notions of inter- and transcultural learning, and by analyzing how they are used by different stakeholders in the field of foreign language education. I will begin my argument with a brief historical contextualization of intercultural learning in the German discourse. I then analyze influential definitions of this concept. Similarly, I analyze the notion of transcultural learning. A systematic comparison of both concepts shows many similarities in their expansion and regression; at the same time, it reveals each concept's potentials and limitations. Next, I reflect on the resonance of the concept of intercultural learning and to a lesser extent transcultural learning, and how they have been appropriated in selected education policy papers. I will show that this genre is particularly prone to sloganization because education policy papers often rely on academic concepts and key terms but without making explicit their definitions or expanding on underlying assumptions. Lastly, I look at the significance and acceptance of both concepts in the teaching profession.

Introduction: A Historical Contextualization of the 'Intercultural' in the German Discourse on Foreign Language Education

In the field of foreign language education, the term 'intercultural' occurs in many different combinations: intercultural learning, intercultural communication, intercultural education (in German, alternatively *Erziehung* or *Bildung*) or, reflecting a more recent paradigm shift, intercultural competences (Council of Europe, 2001: 102–105). Moreover, a plurality of disciplines makes use of the notion of the 'intercultural'; for example, psychology, linguistics, various philological strands of literary and cultural studies, sociology, education and pedagogy. This makes it difficult to pinpoint the origin of the term and trace its development within one particular academic field. With regard to foreign language education, Krumm (2007: 138) refers to a publication by Lado, who as early as 1967 pointed out the necessity of learning and using a foreign language within its cultural context. However, the cultural contextualization of language learning and use was fostered neither in the structure-oriented audio-lingual/audio-visual approach of the 1960s nor in the early communicative approaches of the 1970s. Therefore, it is usually agreed that the 1980s mark the onset of the general discussion and mainstreaming process of intercultural learning. In the German discourse on foreign language education, the concept was widely accepted by the mid-1990s (cf. Byram, 1995, 1997; Edmondson & House, 1998; Hu, 1999, 2000; Vollmer, 1995).

In comparison with international approaches (such as 'teaching culture' in the Anglophone world or *civilisation* in French), the German discourse shows a number of peculiarities rooted in the specific history of education in Germany. *Fremdsprachendidaktik*, the discipline concerned with foreign language education in the German academic system, has no direct equivalent in other languages. In English, for example, its fields of study might be covered by applied linguistics, second language acquisition or curriculum development (cf. Schmenk, 2015; also Viebrock, 2016). Consequently, the terms used in the German discourse cannot simply be translated into English or inscribed into an international discourse without additional explanations. In the field of teaching culture, for instance, the concepts of inter- and transcultural learning chronologically follow a line initiated by *Realienkunde*, then continued by *Kulturkunde* and *Landeskunde*. The *Realienkunde* of the late 19th and early 20th centuries focused on the aspects of geography, climate, history, infrastructure and the transport system of the target language's nation (cf. Leupold, 2007: 128–129). Communication was seen as part of *Realienkunde*, as were political and social structures. Engerman (2005: n. p.) stresses that 'Realien outlasted ephemera like ideology and even political systems'. He also points out that there is no appropriate English equivalent to the term: 'The English "realities" doesn't suggest the word's resonance in 18th Century German philosophy.' *Kulturkunde*, which developed during the Weimar Republic, aimed at extending the objectives of *Realienkunde* by 'delving into the study of a foreign people' and 'penetrating the foreign cultural world' (Apelt, 1967: 12, my translation). The central approach of *Kulturkunde* was cultural comparison, which was in itself neither value free nor innocent. Apelt has documented numerous positions that show how *Kulturkunde* was instrumentalized in the 1930s and in Nazi Germany for ideological purposes by being used to demonstrate a presumed 'superiority of German culture': 'The task of language learning and studying foreign cultures was "to make the educated German aware of the values of the culture of his fatherland by contrasting them with foreign countries"' (Apelt, 1967: 21, my translation). In contrast, the *Landeskunde* approach aimed at the advancement of international understanding: instead of focusing on rather isolated *Realien*, it aspired to a more in-depth insight into a 'target' community and its cultural assets. This differentiated it from *Kulturkunde*, which was hardly ever concerned with 'the other culture' in its own right; *Landeskunde* clearly bore humanist traces, and aimed at understanding 'the other' (cf. Schrey, 1979 [1968]: 260). Even though factual and institutional knowledge retained great importance, the *Landeskunde* approach also comprised contrastive cultural studies, relating – but not necessarily critically evaluating – 'one's own' and 'the foreign' perspectives.

The chronology of approaches to teaching culture in the foreign language classroom seems to display a lacuna in the postwar years, when attempts to continue the *Landeskunde* methodology of the 1920s were overlaid by the more structural approaches to foreign language teaching of the 1960s (cf. Leupold, 2007: 129). The concept of intercultural learning, which in the German discourse is inseparably linked to Byram's model of 'intercultural communicative competence' (cf. Byram, 1997), became increasingly important after the communicative approach had emerged in the 1970s, and prospered particularly in the 1990s. In order to facilitate real communication with speakers of a foreign language in other countries, there was a growing interest in how to behave and what to say in these encounters and in everyday situations in general. This paradigm envisioned foreign language speakers as a clearly definable, rather homogeneous group, who would benefit from profound behavioral knowledge and a (mutual) change of perspective.

Terminological Considerations and Definitions

Despite the lively discussion of the concept of intercultural learning in Germany over two or three decades – a discussion that has oscillated between euphoria and harsh criticism – no congruent understanding has been reached. Even in 2009, Hu and Byram (2009: xi) state: 'the concept remains as fuzzy as ever and is at risk of not being realized in concrete ways.' Bach (1998: 194) has expressed disapproval of the 'inflationary' use of the term, an observation that implies criticism of its imprecision and definitional inaccuracy. However, early calls (for example, by Edmondson & House, 1998) to do away with the term altogether due to its fuzziness and ambivalence stirred up controversies. Hu (1999: 299), for example, maintained that controversial discussions hardly ever lead to simple, unambiguous solutions, and that phases of intellectual as well as practical experimenting in language classrooms and beyond are necessary and have to be endured. Interestingly, a similar debate seems to have emerged with respect to the concept of transcultural learning (see next section, 'From Inter- to Transcultural Foreign Language Learning – and Back?').

A definition of intercultural learning proposed by Vollmer (1995: 105) comprises three main dimensions: cognition/knowledge, emotion/attitude and reflexivity. The cognitive dimension aims at the expansion of knowledge about the sociocultural reality of a community of speakers, which – according to Vollmer – could be either a foreign nation or a minority community within one's own country. The affective dimension aims at open-mindedness and tolerance of otherness, as well as the reduction of stereotypes, prejudices and discrimination. The third dimension stresses the necessity of reflecting on one's own perspective and sociocultural background, and on how they influence one's thinking and acting. The dimensions of Vollmer's definition are not necessarily bound to a specific context, and could be applied to any kind of collective or individual encounter; his description of what makes a community of speakers, however, relies on a rather static, homogeneous notion of culture and its collective values, defined linguistically and territorially, perhaps even ethnically.

In a similar fashion, Byram (1995, 1997) bases his concept of 'intercultural communicative competence'[1] on four dimensions: knowledge, skills, attitudes and values. In a publication prior to his often-cited model of 1997, he describes four components of intercultural competence, which relate to cognitive/analytical and affective/emotional domains (cf. Byram, 1995: 270ff.). The first constituent competence (*savoir être*) is the affective ability to distance oneself from ethnocentric attitudes and perceptions, and to build up and maintain a stable relationship between 'one's own' and 'a foreign' culture: 'In order to relativize and understand the relationship of one culture to another, learners need to "decentre," to gain distance from their own culture and cultural identity by both analytic approaches to new phenomena and experiential acceptance of otherness' (Byram, 1995: 271). The second constituent competence (*savoir apprendre*) aims at enabling the learner to examine und understand unknown cultural phenomena, and to integrate cultural meaning 'into their existing understanding of self and other' (Byram, 1995: 271). As a third constituent competence (*savoirs*), the learner needs 'a system of cultural references' (Byram, 1995: 271) to structure and relate new knowledge and experiences. This includes a general knowledge of the structure of social groups, processes and identities. The fourth constituent competence (*savoir faire*) denotes the ability to integrate and apply the previous competences in concrete encounters: the significance of cultural practices has to be perceived, discovered and possibly relativized. This ability requires skills of contextualization and interpretation (Byram, 1995: 272).

Byram has further developed his ideas into the widely acknowledged model of 'intercultural communicative competence' (ICC; Byram, 1997), which is structured somewhat differently. First, s*avoir apprendre* and *savoir faire* have been integrated into 'skills of discovery and interaction'. Secondly, the dimension of *savoir comprendre* as 'skills of interpreting and relating' rather static material, such as texts, has been made explicit. Thirdly, the dimension of *savoir s'engager*, or critical cultural awareness, which includes the ability to substantially evaluate cultural practices, perspectives and products, has been added. The ICC model has influenced many academic papers as well as documents issued by education authorities (e.g. the CEFR, the German national core curriculum for foreign languages, etc.). It has recently been taken up in a publication by Blell and Doff (2014), who attempt to revise and complement Byram's model with a transcultural dimension (cf. discussion below). What is interesting, however, is that Byram refuses to provide an explicit definition of the notion of 'culture'. Instead, he claims that any definition would have 'to suit the purposes of the foreign language teacher' (Byram, 1997: 39), and would thus mainly focus on elements that are represented in oral and written language. Instead of 'culture', he prefers to speak of 'beliefs, meanings and behaviours' (Byram, 1997: 39) that include the values shared by a social group. While this elaboration arguably implies the notion of collectivity as decisive, it simultaneously denies expressions of performativity, i.e. the interactive negotiation or production of meaning within or across different groups. Byram accepts criticism of his understanding of culture as 'too static' (Byram, 1997: 39); he nonetheless insists that his concept is feasible in the context of foreign language teaching, which aims at preparing learners for mobility or short-term residence abroad. At this point, 'the country' also comes in as a definitional factor, which can again be related to a nation-oriented understanding of culture.

The need for a critical reading of Byram's notion of culture is further reinforced when one considers material for classroom use based on his model. *The Autobiography of Intercultural Encounters* (cf. Council of Europe, 2008), for example, a tool for documenting and reflecting on what is called 'intercultural encounters', makes clear that nationality and the ability to speak a national language remain the most important points of reference for defining cultural affiliation. In this document, an intercultural encounter is defined as an experience in one's own country 'with someone from a different country' or 'with someone from another cultural background', marked by a different language, religion or ethnicity (Council of Europe, 2008: 3). One of the examples provided for the learners' orientation depicts the arrival in France of a university student who is amazed at the French bus driver's friendliness. This example bears traces of stereotyping, and is highly suggestive of a notion of culture that is clearly definable, static and territorially bound. It does not leave much room for the learners to bring in more varied experiences that do not meet the established categories.

The example shows that Byram's appropriation of the notion of culture in his model of intercultural competence undoubtedly includes reduction and simplification, which are indicative of sloganization. This might be an expression of the attempt to narrow down the definition of a concept used widely in various disciplines to a single, specific context – foreign language education. However, in Byram's work, processes of sloganization occur only partly because concepts are taken out of their textual/historical contexts, likely because its orientation towards functionality, practicality and methodical applicability in foreign language education interferes with the conceptual clarity derived from merely theoretical considerations. The cart is put before the horse, so to speak, when theoretical concepts and technical terminology are justified on the basis of their assumed practicality in foreign language education – or, more precisely, in foreign language education that is predominantly functional. Feasibility and practicality are certainly important criteria when preparing a particular topic for educational use, a process that might entail a certain amount of simplification for the sake of clarification. When it comes to academic discourse, however, such criteria risk acting as thought-terminating clichés, curtailing conceptual and terminological advancements right from the start. I would consider Byram's model, highly influential though it has been, a case in point.

The previous analysis has shown that the definitions formulated by both Vollmer (1995) and Byram (1995, 1997) start from learners' national, geographic or ethnic backgrounds, and are based on the assumption of a more or less homogeneous cultural collective, territorially, nationally or ethnically defined; this entails a certain amount of simplification, and consequently sloganization. By contrast, Hu (1999: 298–299) has proposed an alternative definition that classifies intercultural learning as a function of the contents negotiated, and thus of the quality of interaction. Starting from the assumption that learners might still feel the need for clear-cut cultural distinctions and adhere to a common-sense understanding of culture, Hu claims that these distinctions need to be challenged in the light of contemporary conditions of life. From her point of view, intercultural learning in the FL classroom is possible when awareness of the following is raised:

- interdependence of language and cultural meaning/significance;
- beliefs about values and norms held in the region(s) where the foreign language is spoken;
- learners' own individual norms;
- their own perspective on the world;
- stereotypes and prejudices;
- different notions of culture.

In contrast to the previous definitions, Hu's understanding of intercultural learning is neither related to the speakers' ethnic or national background, nor bound to a collective perspective. Intercultural learning can take place even among individual speakers of the same language, according to Hu, as long as each of them expresses their own cultural interpretations, i.e. their assumptions of cultural specifics, mentalities, stereotypes, their perceptions and perspectives. What is important is that the learners become aware of their cultural attributions. Hu's definition would also allow for different methodological applications from those based on the above-mentioned model of ICC. Although it still employs the notion of the *inter*cultural, many aspects of Hu's definition anticipate and overlap with the discussion of the *trans*cultural paradigm, which will be explained in the following section.

From Inter- to Transcultural Foreign Language Learning – and Back?

The notion of transculturality

The changing circumstances of our world and its social constellations have fostered the transition from intercultural to transcultural concepts. Transculturality is seen as a more flexible concept that meets the challenges of a globalized modernity: instead of proclaiming some kind of cultural homogeneity, notions of hybridity are recognized and appreciated. The understanding of transculturality in the German discourse on foreign language education was originally based on the works of the philosopher Wolfgang Welsch (e.g. 1999). Welsch developed the notion of the transcultural on the basis of a terminological analysis of the intercultural and its underlying binary perceptions of culture. In brief, his argument puts forward the idea that an *inter*cultural understanding of culture is based on a clearly defined, homogeneous and undifferentiated society. Reaching back to Herder's concept of the nation as the dominant model in the 19th and (early) 20th centuries, cultures appear as autonomous islands, characterized by 'internal uniformity and clear separation from what is outside' (Delanoy, 2013: 158). Even though the focus of *inter*culturality might be on the relationships between individual cultures, the notion has a clearly separatist character. These spheres can only clash with each other; they cannot integrate or understand each other. Doff and Schulze-Engler (2011: 1) reinforce this understanding:

> [I]f more or less absolute cultural difference is posited as the starting point for processes of 'intercultural learning,' and essentialist binary oppositions between one's own culture and 'strange,' 'alien' or 'other cultures' are set up, the well-meant pedagogical objective of 'intercultural understanding' actually reproduces stereotyped notions of cultural difference that are hard to reconcile with the social and cultural realities that teachers and learners are faced with in an increasingly globalised world.

Welsch continues to point out that the description of contemporary cultures as islands or spheres is questionable in the age of globalization, since cultures are no longer homogeneous and separate. Rather, they are characterized by mixing and fusing, or – in Pennycook's (2007: 47) words – by 'borrowing, bending and blending'. For this reason, Welsch favors the term 'transculturality', which in his eyes most accurately describes the close connections and interpenetrations of contemporary cultures. To give an example: the way of life of a scientist, a journalist or a professional football player can no longer be described as being German or French; rather, it has become European, or even global. What is more, the profession is only one of several possible modes of life by means of which individuals can link up with others. Represented graphically, the notion of transculturality resembles a complex network structure, with individuals interconnected in different territorial and de-territorial or virtual social groupings. From the perspective of social network analysis, such a structure might rather be called 'networked individualism' (Wellman, 2001).

In the German context, Welsch's understanding of transculturality has been taken up by scholars in the field of postcolonial studies and *Neue Englischsprachige Literaturen und Kulturen* (new English literatures and cultures) (Antor, 2006; Antor *et al.*, 2010; Delanoy & Volkmann, 2006; Schulze-Engler & Helff, 2008), as well as in other humanities disciplines mentioned above (e.g. in education: Göhlich *et al.*, 2006). An important international proponent of the concept is Pennycook (2007). In the field of foreign language education, the concept of transculturality has been adopted as 'transcultural learning', and promoted as an advancement of intercultural learning by Doff and Schulze-Engler (2011), Eckerth and Wendt (2003), Eisenmann *et al.* (2010), Freitag-Hild (2010) and Matz *et al.* (2014). While intercultural learning foregrounds communication with ('native') speakers of other languages, transcultural learning focuses more explicitly on heterogeneous societies, hybrid identities, and how these are reflected in literature, film and other art forms. In this respect, transcultural approaches have particularly focused on materials that reflect postcolonial discourses, for example in the field of *Neue Englischsprachige Literaturen und Kulturen* (cf. Doff & Schulze-Engler, 2011; Eisenmann *et al.*, 2010) or in fictions of migration (cf. Freitag-Hild, 2010).

Critical voices

A more critical discussion of the term has been provided by Delanoy (2006, 2013, 2014). He observes that the notion of transcultural learning quite deliberately does not altogether abandon the concept of culture; only monolithic or binary forms of culture are rejected: more generally, '(...) trans-theories do not remove basic categories such as culture or difference but offer specific perspectives on them' (Delanoy, 2013: 159). Whether this makes transcultural learning truly different from intercultural learning remains to be seen. Somewhat ironically, Welsch himself makes use of a binary opposition: 'inter' versus 'trans'. In addition, the concept of transculturality has been accused of employing a 'celebratory rhetoric' (by Delanoy, 2014: 21; drawing on a statement by Wachinger, 2003: 149). Certainly, Welsch treats transculturality as an affirmative concept – one that understands mixing, fusing and hybridization as important steps towards a more advanced notion of culture and cultural awareness. This approach bears a striking resemblance to '[t]he celebration of increased heterogeneity of Western cities' in the notion of 'superdiversity' critically investigated by Pavlenko (in this volume). At the same time, an affirmative concept of transculturality denies any positive aspects one might find in delineation or separation. It becomes clear that Welsch's notion comprises both a descriptive and a normative dimension (cf. Volkmann, 2011: 113–114), which are not always clearly distinguished. While the concept is useful in describing current social constellations and developments, it tends to be applied in a prescriptive manner, and fails to acknowledge the power dimensions in international relationships. In particular, the 'shop-shelf mentality' (an expression used by Schulze-Engler in an oral conversation) inherent in Welsch's understanding of transculturality – as if everyone could simply pick and choose their cultural building blocks – has been critically discussed. Even though Welsch (2009), in a later publication, restricts the individual's cultural choices and extends his concept to include approaches that critically reflect dimensions of power (such as postcolonial, global and feminist studies), he does not develop his thoughts consistently. In a way, he still appears to equate globalization with cultural advancement. For this reason, Delanoy (2014: 25) critiques Welsch's notion of transculturality, arguing that it mainly serves a capitalist economy as the driving force of globalization.

Future perspectives

When asking which direction such notions as inter- and transcultural learning should take in foreign language education, the different suggestions that have been made reiterate the dispute over intercultural learning between Edmondson and House (1998) and Hu (1999, 2000), mentioned earlier in this chapter. Plikat (2017) favors abolishing the terms altogether. In contrast, he supports an alternative concept, which has only gained minor recognition in the field of foreign language education so far (cf. Plikat, 2017: 197): 'discourse awareness'. Plikat does not provide a distinct definition of the term but, relying on the explication of the notion of discourse by Foucault (1971) and Fairclough (1989), stresses its potential for reflecting and negotiating power dimensions and making visible plurality without having to rely on a misleading and ambiguous notion of culture.

While this differentiation could be interpreted as a de-sloganizing strategy for academic discourse, i.e. in the interests of conceptual clarity and definitional accuracy, it is questionable whether the notion of culture can be banned by 'prescription'.[2] Alternatively, Antor (2006), while keeping the notions of inter- and transcultural studies, has suggested the delineation of specific competences in order to equip learners with appropriate tools for reflecting on the cultural complexities of our world. The learners would need to have knowledge about cultural theories, an awareness of the notion of alterity[3], a reflective attitude and the ability to relativize their perspectives. The dimensions Antor suggests mainly conform to the cognitive dimension of the notion of competence, omitting any motivational, volitional, emotional and non-linguistic domains, which makes them applicable to more advanced and cognitively mature learners. The significance of the existence of a counterpart for individual transformation (as a definitional aspect of alterity) has been reinforced by Delanoy (2014), who also sticks with the notion of the transcultural. He favors the term 'hermeneutic transcultural foreign language teaching', which he explicitly dissociates from the concept introduced by Welsch. Delanoy's concept stresses the importance of dialogue and reflexivity, which have already been prominent in the intercultural debate. However, his deliberate dissociation of a term from one of his most influential precursors could be blamed for contributing to its sloganization.

A different approach is pursued by Blell and Doff (2014), who take up Byram's influential model of ICC and try to complement it with a transcultural dimension. They argue: 'Transcultural learning, the development of transcultural competence (...) is complementary to intercultural learning and aims at the successful understanding of people in dynamized inter- and transcultural processes, in either face-to-face or text-conducted (e.g. literature, film, music) encounters' (Blell & Doff, 2014: 83). In order to equip today's learners with the ability to reflect on the dynamics, plurality and hybridity of modern societies, they add four aspects to Byram's model (cf. Table 5.1).

- 'global knowledge', which denotes knowledge of the complexity of global processes and asymmetrical power relations;
- 'multiple literacies', which includes language competences/intercomprehension skills in several languages as well as the ability to deal with multimodal texts;

Table 5.1 Model of inter-transcultural communicative competence by Blell and Doff (2014)

Knowledge	Skills of interpreting and relating	Education	Attitudes
Knowledge Of social groups and their products and practices in familiar and new cultural contexts, and the general processes of societal and individual interaction	*Skills of interpreting and relating* An ability to interpret a document or event from various cultures, to explain and relate it to familiar documents or events	*Education* Critical cultural awareness/political education: an ability to evaluate critically and on the basis of explicit criteria, perspectives, practices and products in familiar and new cultures and countries	*Attitudes* Curiosity and openness, readiness to suspend disbelief about different cultures and dynamic or mobile cultural situations and familiar beliefs (maybe 'floating' in between)
Plus ▶ Global knowledge Of social groups and their products and practices **beyond** the self/other, and knowledge about asymmetrical and disputed global cultural processes		*Plus ▶ Critical transcultural awareness* An ability to evaluate critically and flexibly on the basis of manifold perspectives and perspective changes, practices and products **beyond** the self/other (perspective consciousness); to be aware of cultural synergies and dissents/perspective consciousness	
Plus ▶ Multiple literacies E.g. basic multilingual knowledge/media knowledge/visual knowledge to interpret various modes of presentation		*Plus ▶ Border literacies* An ability to interpret cultural processes in which the insider/outsider status is replaced by blurring the boundaries and recognizing multiplicities or identity and group affiliation	
		Skills of discovery and interaction An ability to acquire new knowledge of a culture and cultural practices and the ability to operate knowledge, attitudes and skills under the constraints of real-time communication and interaction (listen carefully, ask/ask for clarification, moderate, explain, mediate, etc.)	

Source: Blell and Doff (2014: 86).

- 'critical transcultural awareness', which focuses on the coordination of different perspectives and a reflection of their influences on ongoing individual processes of identity formation;
- 'border literacies', which denotes the ability to manage dynamic boundaries in different domains (e.g. the understanding of gender or culture).

While Byram's main categories – knowledge, attitudes, skills and values – clearly relate to a nationally and territorially defined cultural collective, Blell and Doff's extensions reach beyond a static understanding of culture and focus particularly on dynamic and performative processes. They demand as follows:

> Co-ordinating perspectives and perspective consciousness seem to be most important in managing transcultural situations in which the insider and outsider status is constantly being replaced by 'blurring the boundaries' (for example: race, class, gender, culture, disablement) and recognizing and evaluating changing identities or group affiliations. Transcultural learners must be competent in recognizing, analyzing and successfully managing 'borders' and 'border situations' of all kinds (not only geographic ones). (Blell & Doff, 2014: 87)

In their use of terminology, the notion of culture is deliberately detached from a merely territorial or national understanding and projected mainly onto group affiliations, whether self-imposed or attributed by others.

In the first instance, Blell and Doff's model may be criticized for its inconsistent, and possibly incompatible, underlying notions of culture, availing itself of different theoretical foundations in disparate discourses: as argued above, the elements of Byram's model of ICC depend upon a rather static, nation-oriented, clearly definable notion of culture. The transcultural extensions added by Bell and Doff challenge exactly these certainties and focus on processual qualities, dynamics and performativity, which seem to be at odds with the characteristics previously mentioned. However, a complementary understanding of both extensions of cultural learning (inter- and trans-) seems to have the potential to bridge the gap between highly abstract theoretical considerations and the common-sense use of concepts in different contexts (cf. Hu, 1999). A complementary concept acknowledges the existence of nations and countries as social, political or geographical constructs, which can be made topical in the foreign language classroom, but at the same time demands an increasing differentiation and thorough reflection of any aspect that is talked about as well as a general awareness of the complexities of contemporary societies and individual identities.

To conclude, the overview given in this section shows that, despite the many attempts to clarify the notions of interculturality and transculturality, the situation remains complex, ambiguous and possibly as 'fuzzy as ever'. The lack of precision in definitions of intercultural learning and their underlying notions of culture prompts one to wonder whether the concept was ever anything but a slogan in the first place. The development of transcultural learning, which comprises more advanced terminological and conceptual reflections, may have the potential to de-sloganize the 'intercultural', given that it explicitly aims at a higher degree of clarity and exactitude. However, by differing only in the prefix, and keeping the basic category of culture, transculturality can also be understood as a continuation of the existing conceptual difficulties. The complementary model suggested by Blell and Doff (2014) is somewhat Solomonic in nature, but also retains the use of the term culture. This might become problematic when such academic terminology is appropriated in different contexts, or by different stakeholders, as will be explained in the next section.

The Appropriation of Inter- and Transcultural Learning in Education Policy Papers

In the field of foreign language education, theoretical concepts are used by different stakeholders for different purposes. The notions of both inter- and transcultural learning are not only used in academic discourse; they also resonate in formal guidelines and national education policy papers. Reflecting the development towards competence-based teaching, the German national educational standards for foreign languages at lower intermediate level (KMK, 2003) and upper intermediate level (KMK, 2012) distinguish among communicative competences, methodological or media competences and intercultural competences to be achieved in the foreign language classroom. The definition of the latter relies on Byram's (1997) model of ICC. Obviously, some of the criticisms leveled by Welsch would apply here, since Byram's notion of culture is conceived as mainly national or territorial. What is even more interesting, however, is the case of the federal state of Hesse, where the educational standards explicitly make use of the notion of *trans*cultural competence, rather than intercultural competence. The following definition is given:

> Transcultural competence includes the ability and willingness to appreciate and respect different cultural perspectives and to learn from them. An understanding that thinking, action and behavior are shaped by one's own culture, but can be modified, is part of this [transcultural competence]. (HKM, 2011: 16, my translation)

In addition, according to the document, transcultural competence comprises knowledge about one's own culture and other cultures. It facilitates a differentiated view on ecological and economic aspects of a globalized world. A self-confident, open-minded and appreciative attitude towards other cultures becomes apparent in thinking, feeling and action (HKM, 2011: 11f.).

The understanding of transcultural competence displayed here blends elements associated with *inter*cultural competence (e.g. a clear binary and collective distinction between 'one's own' and 'the foreign') and a more specific notion of *trans*cultural competence (e.g. a more differentiated view of aspects of a globalized world). Looking at the general definition only, the specific choice of terminology certainly displays typical elements of sloganization processes, such as decontextualization and simplification.

If one also takes into consideration the objectives specified in the Hessian core curriculum for Years 9 and 10 (HKM, 2011: 21), a clear attribution of the notion of culture to a national or territorial dimension is much less distinct or explicit. A notion of 'the other' is not necessarily used in opposition to 'one's own' on a collective level, but possibly rather in the sense of alterity, as demanded by Antor (2006). Individual qualifications and conditions (such as plurilingual competences) are accentuated, as well as the ability to take over and coordinate perspectives. Tolerance of ambiguity is also included in the competence dimensions, which stipulate that the learners are able to:

- apply cultural knowledge to provide direction in communicative situations;
- tolerate uncertainties in understanding;
- search for means to compensate for comprehension gaps;
- take over different cultural perspectives;
- show sensitivity towards other values, attitudes, norms and customs in an appropriate way;
- explain their point of view in an age-appropriate way and according to their foreign language competence, as well as respond to criticism;
- apply their plurilingual competence successfully. (HKM, 2011: 21, my translation)

The function of curricula and other education policy papers is to define intended learning outcomes, competence domains and proficiency levels, as well as to suggest topics to be dealt with, methods to be applied or materials to be used. As such, they provide teachers with orientation and formal safeguards for the educational decisions they make. Curricula are important stakeholders in the teaching profession; they can be understood to function as a mediator between academic discourse, teachers' mindsets and classroom practice. In accordance with this function, curricula utilize academic concepts so as to facilitate a more abstract description of/reflection on individual teaching approaches, procedures and objectives. It goes without saying that they should strive for terminological clarity. At the same time, however, curricula are subject to more practical considerations, as can be seen in the example of the core curriculum of Hesse. They are usually much shorter than academic elaborations; they appeal to a much broader readership that is not necessarily familiar with the intricacies of the academic discourse in the particular field of interest. Education policy papers almost inevitably remove concepts from their original context and work with a reduced or common-sense version in order to disseminate academic concepts and appeal to a broad audience. In this respect, education policy papers may be the very genre where generalization and sloganized expressions are to be expected.

In view of these assumptions, one could say that while the core curriculum of Hesse displays the expected instances of sloganization, it also reflects the general difficulties of coming to terms with these concepts. It attempts to relate its considerations to the academic discourse by using up-to-date terminology and elaborate concepts, yet the need to make education policy papers accessible to the majority of foreign language teachers almost inevitably involves resorting to less abstract and less academic expressions, as well as simplification and context reduction. In conclusion, processes of sloganization are almost inevitable in a field with different stakeholders. In particular, they appear at points of transition between the different domains of the language education profession. This will be illustrated further in the following section, which looks at yet another stakeholder: the perspectives of practitioners in the field.

Teachers' Appropriations of Inter- and Transcultural Learning

Starting from the assumption that, in foreign language education, academic concepts exercise a greater influence if they are acknowledged and adopted or appropriated by practitioners, a group of students and I were interested in the following questions: What significance do EFL teachers assign to the concepts of inter- and transcultural learning? What meanings do they attach to them? How do they employ them in their teaching? We carried out an interview study with 20 teachers; from this study, 16 transcript analyses could be used for this paper. In class, we developed an interview manual with an initial visual focus that problematized the notion of cultural attribution and mechanisms of stereotyping (http://www.ohio.edu/orgs/stars/Poster_campaign.html). The manual covered 10 topical areas, ranging from personal experiences through classroom scenarios, appropriate materials, the representation of the topic in textbooks, personal significance of both the topic and the core curriculum, and finally to individual definitions and reflections of the concepts of intercultural and transcultural competence. Each interviewer tried to take a non-directive attitude, aiming at understanding and reconstructing, but not judging, the teachers' positions. In line with the principles of qualitative research studies, we did not proceed from any hypotheses but we certainly had prior assumptions: in terms of distinguishing between the concepts of inter- and transcultural learning we expected to find a general personal relevance, but very little distinction in the use of the two terms.

The analyses (content, argument and metaphor analyses; cf. Viebrock, 2007) yielded some very interesting results. Although in general our assumptions were confirmed, the overall picture appears more complex. A few teachers who marked inter- and/or transcultural learning as an area of personal interest were able to provide quite elaborate explanations of the concepts. However, their choice of words included the use of many tentative pronouns and adverbs ('somehow', 'somewhat', and the like), as well as a lot of false starts and attempts to rephrase, indicating the difficulty of coming to terms with the concepts. Despite being able to provide comparatively elaborate definitions, one teacher described the terminological differences as 'vague' and 'difficult to grasp for teachers who do not predominantly study theories' (my translations; the original quotations are in German). Accordingly, other interviewees claimed that they do not distinguish between the terms at all. They also reconstructed their meanings in very individualistic ways. We repeatedly found objectives such as 'the appreciation of otherness', 'tolerance', 'empathy' and 'interpersonal skills' in our sample. Occasionally, a need for 'global education' was mentioned. In addition, the term 'diversity' was used frequently; however, it was not necessarily applied to any cultural dimension. In general, it is probably safe to say that the practitioners we interviewed are concerned about their learners' attitudes towards other people or cultures, but they use their own terms and apply their own definitions, which are not necessarily related to the way the concepts are defined and used in academic discourse.

When explicitly asked about the concept of intercultural learning, most of the teachers applied a rather monolithic understanding of culture, similar to the one criticized by Welsch. When asked about any differences between inter- and transcultural learning, the teachers were either unable to specify any, or tried to deduce meaning from the different prefixes, which led to rather idiosyncratic definitions, e.g. '"trans" means "across" and "inter" is "between", hence I would understand inter as stressing a connection, similarities and learning together, whereas I would understand transcultural as learning about something *different*'; or

> I would understand transcultural in a way that I take my culture as a starting point for getting to know another culture, (that I) observe, review, compare and build a bridge to. I would see this on a one-to-one basis: my culture in contrast to *one* other culture, not necessarily *many* others. (…) Interculturality means plurality, that there are several cultures, and my culture, my point of reference is only one of many. (My translations; underscores indicate particular emphasis)

Generally, the teachers we interviewed adhered to a common-sense understanding of terminology. Their arguments were often rather sweeping. Their explanations of the terms were inspired by general pedagogical principles, and with a concrete group of learners in mind. While some demonstrated a rather critical view of how cultural diversity is presented in textbooks, and complained about both the prescriptive approach and the oversimplified depiction of cultural elements, others reported to strongly rely on the textbook. Many of our interviewees assumed that the textbooks take up and reflect recent educational and political developments and present them to teachers in ready-made portions for consumption. A critical attitude along the lines of Leung's (2009) 'independent professionalism', where teachers display a more critical attitude and a great amount of autonomy, is not considered necessary by these teachers. At this point, several imperatives of the teaching profession also came to the surface: for example, the notion that a teacher has to 'finish' the textbook during the course of the school year, in order to prepare the ground for the subsequent teacher, was repeatedly mentioned.

To sum up the results of our interview study: dimensions of inter- and transcultural learning play a role for the teachers interviewed, but they can take on very personal meanings and are usually reinterpreted and reshaped depending on the actual context. The teachers' concepts and choice of words are characterized by a lower degree of theorization and by a common-sense use of terminology. With this conclusion, I do not mean to say that knowledge and concept transfer should work only in a one-directional and top-down manner (from academic discourse to education policy to classroom practice); rather, teachers' perceptions and actions are strongly influenced by their individual environments. In a field such as foreign language education, with its different stakeholders and a noticeable theory-practice divide, an integrative strategy is necessary to motivate teachers to adopt concepts considered important in academic discourse or education policy. Conversely, theoretical works and educational policy papers ought to take teachers' perspectives and needs into consideration so as to 'translate' theories more appropriately and thus help bridge the gap between theory and practice (cf. Viebrock, 2010). This suggestion confirms research results regarding teacher professionalism. Commonly, teachers who must respond to pedagogical or educational innovations 'prescribed' by academic discourse and/or education policy are often not or are only partly familiar with abstract theoretical concepts or official policy papers; they display idiosyncratic reconstructions of the terms, approaches and functions suggested there (cf. Viebrock, 2014: 77–79). Since it is also known that a certain degree of acceptance of concepts is an essential prerequisite for the successful implementation of any kind of innovation, the results of our interview study can be used to show how the different stakeholders in the language teaching profession (teachers, education policy writers, scholars) approach the respective concepts from specific perspectives and with specific objectives or needs for action, which have to be integrated in order to advance the means to reflect upon classroom practice. To avoid any confusion or misunderstanding at this point, I would like to stress that I do not regard one of the domains and their perspectives as superior to the others; rather, each of their frameworks of reference should be taken into consideration when reflecting on aspects such as definitional inaccuracy, simplification or trivialization.

Conclusion and Outlook

In this chapter, I have examined the notions of intercultural and transcultural learning and how three different groups concerned with the teaching profession approach and conceptualize them: scholars, education policy writers and the experiences of practitioners. While it might seem natural that the scholarly discourse offers the most elaborate and also the most abstract reflection of terms, any application in more practical contexts almost inevitably involves reduction, simplification and homogenization. This is particularly salient in the case of 'culture'. In the academic discourse there are a multitude of definitions of culture, which can be systematized in different ways. In line with Plikat (2017: 45ff.), four understandings of culture can be distinguished: (i) a normative understanding in the sense of Eagleton's (2000) 'Culture with a capital "C"'; (ii) a totalizing understanding of culture, which also lies at the core of Welsch's (2005) criticism; (iii) culture as a societal subsystem (science, arts, humanities) reflecting specific interpretations of the world; and (iv) a semiotic understanding of culture as a web of significance (Geertz, 1973), whose meaning has to be analyzed. Plikat convincingly claims that in scholarly discourse this fourth notion of culture is most prominent, but that instances of 'falling back' on totalizing notions can be found when these complex theoretical concepts are projected onto practical scenarios and applied in research projects or in the foreign language classroom. Whereas in academic discourse different dimensions of the notion of culture (e.g. territorial versus deterritorial, static versus dynamic, inherited versus performative, collective versus individual, homogeneous versus heterogeneous, pure versus hybrid, to name but a few) have been thoroughly examined in the process of elaborating the theoretical concepts, in the field of education policy and the practical teaching profession a totalizing notion, which has been related in this paper to a common-sense understanding, proves to be powerful and more resistant to critical reflection. The restrictive elements of this notion seem to guarantee a manageable situation in the classroom, devoid of unwanted ambiguity and confusion.

The continuing differentiation of terms in academic discourse (including Plikat's notion of 'discourse awareness') will certainly contribute to conceptual clarity; however, it will probably not make it any easier to adopt these even more diverse concepts into education policy papers or foreign language classrooms.

The very nature of foreign language education, which is understood here as a discipline with different stakeholders involved, and the necessary transitions between academic discourse, education policy and classroom practice, inevitably include moving back and forth between more abstract considerations and practical necessities, and might thus reinforce processes of sloganization. From my point of view, this is a risk that must be taken if we want to develop meaningful concepts for all stakeholders alike.

Notes

(1) Byram employs the notion of 'competence' instead of 'learning', which has implications for the discussion of these concepts (see also Hu & Byram, 2009). In this chapter, the distinction between *learning* and *competence* will not be a primary focus. It is important to keep in mind, however, that a paradigm shift can be observed in both domains: from *Realien-* and *Landes-* to *inter-* and *transcultural*, as well as from *-kunde* to *learning* and *competence*.
(2) This is particularly salient in view of the different stakeholders involved in language education that are considered in this chapter. Especially for teachers, an abstract concept such as 'discourse awareness', which Plikat (2017: 230) himself regards an 'intellectual tool', may be even more dissociated from their everyday language use than academic notions of 'intercultural' or 'transcultural' learning or competence, and may thus widen the notorious gap between academic discourse and classroom practice even further.
(3) The concept of alterity is closely linked with the works of Levinas (1999 [1970]) in the phenomenological tradition. It describes the ability to distinguish between self/not-self and appreciates the other as an alternative viewpoint, necessary in the process of identity construction. While the concept in itself is affirmative, appropriations for processes like 'othering', i.e. the active construction of the other for the purpose of reinforcing one's own position as normality, reveal an imbalance inherent in any kind of thinking in binary oppositions, for it privileges one domain and conceptualizes the other as a negative version of the first.

References

Antor, H. (2006) *Inter- und Transkulturelle Studien: Theoretische Grundlagen und Interdisziplinäre Praxis*. Heidelberg: Universitätsverlag Winter.
Antor, H., Merkl, M., Stierstorfer, K. and Volkmann, L. (2010) *From Interculturalism to Transculturalism: Mediating Encounters in Cosmopolitan Contexts*. Heidelberg: Universitätsverlag Winter.
Apelt, W. (1967) *Die kulturkundliche Bewegung im Unterricht der neueren Sprachen in Deutschland in den Jahren 1886 bis 1945. Ein Irrweg deutscher Philologen*. Berlin: Volk und Wissen.
Bach, G. (1998) Interkulturelles Lernen. In J. Timm (ed.) *Englisch lehren und lernen. Didaktik des Englischunterrichts* (pp. 192–200). Berlin: Cornelsen.
Blell, G. and Doff, S. (2014) It takes more than two for this tango: Moving beyond the self/other-binary in teaching about culture in the global EFL-classroom. *Zeitschrift für interkulturellen Fremdsprachenunterricht* 19 (1), 77–96. See http://tujournals.ulb.tu-darmstadt.de/index.php/zif/article/view/17/14 (accessed 23 November 2017).
Byram, M. (1995) Reflecting on 'intercultural competence' in foreign language learning. In L. Bredella (ed.) *Verstehen und Verständigung durch Sprachenlernen?* (pp. 269–275). Bochum: Brockmeyer.
Byram, M. (1997) *Teaching and Assessing Intercultural Communicative Competence*. Clevedon: Multilingual Matters.

Council of Europe (2001) *Common European Framework of Reference for Languages: Learning, Teaching and Assessment*. Cambridge: Cambridge University Press.
Council of Europe (2008) *Autobiography of Intercultural Encounters*. Strasbourg: Council of Europe. See http://www.coe.int/t/DG4/AUTOBIOGRAPHY/AutobiographyTool_en.asp (accessed 23 November 2017).
Delanoy, W. (2006) Transculturality and (inter)-cultural learning in the EFL classroom. In W. Delanoy and L. Volkmann (eds) *Cultural Studies in the EFL Classroom* (pp. 233–248). Heidelberg: Universitätsverlag Winter.
Delanoy, W. (2013) From 'inter' to 'trans'? Or: Quo vadis cultural learning? In M. Eisenmann and T. Summer (eds) *Basic Issues in EFL Teaching and Learning* (pp. 157–167). Heidelberg: Universitätsverlag Winter.
Delanoy, W. (2014) Transkulturalität als begriffliche und konzeptuelle Herausforderung an die Fremdsprachendidaktik? In F. Matz, M. Rogge and P. Siepmann (eds) *Transkulturelles Lernen im Fremdsprachenunterricht: Theorie und Praxis* (pp. 19–35). Frankfurt am Main: Lang.
Delanoy, W. and Volkmann, L. (eds) (2006) *Cultural Studies in the EFL Classroom*. Heidelberg: Universitätsverlag Winter.
Doff, S. and Schulze-Engler, F. (eds) (2011) *Beyond 'Other Cultures'. Transcultural Perspectives on Teaching the New Literatures in English*. Trier: WVT.
Eagleton, T. (2000) *The Idea of Culture*. Oxford: Blackwell.
Eckerth, J. and Wendt, M. (eds) (2003) *Interkulturelles und transkulturelles Lernen im Fremdsprachenunterricht*. Frankfurt am Main: Lang.
Edmondson, W. and House, J. (1998) Interkulturelles Lernen: Ein überflüssiger Begriff. *Zeitschrift für Fremdsprachenforschung* 9 (2), 161–188.
Eisenmann, M., Grimm, N. and Volkmann, L. (eds) (2010) *Teaching New English Literatures and Cultures*. Heidelberg: Universitätsverlag Winter.
Engerman, D. (2005) George Kennan, a conservative's conservative American diplomat did more than any other envoy to shape U.S. policy during the Cold War. *Chicago Tribune News*, 22 March. See http://articles.chicagotribune.com/2005-03-22/news/0503220317_1_george-frost-kennan-cold-war-18th-century (accessed 23 November 2017).
Fairclough, N. (1989) *Language and Power*. London: Longman.
Foucault, M. (1971) *L'ordre du discours: Leçon inaugurale au Collège de France prononcée le 2 décembre 1970*. Paris: Gallimard.
Freitag-Hild, B. (2010) *Theorie, Aufgabentypologie und Unterrichtspraxis inter- und transkultureller Literaturdidaktik. 'British Fictions of Migration' im Fremdsprachenunterricht*. Trier: WVT.
Geertz, C. (1973) *The Interpretation of Culture. Selected Essays*. New York: Basic Books.
Göhlich, M., Leonhard, H., Liebau, E. and Zierfas, J. (eds) (2006) *Transkulturalität und Pädagogik: Interdisziplinäre Annäherungen an ein kulturwissenschaftliches Konzept und seine pädagogische Relevanz*. Weinheim and Munich: Juventa.
HKM (2011) *Bildungsstandards und Inhaltsfelder. Das neue Kerncurriculum für Hessen. Sekundarstufe I – Gymnasium. Moderne Fremdsprachen*.Wiesbaden: Hessisches Kultusministerium. See https://kultusministerium.hessen.de/sites/default/files/media/kerncurriculum_moderne_fremdsprachen_gymnasium.pdf (accessed 23 November 2017).
Hu, A. (1999) Interkulturelles Lernen. Eine Auseinandersetzung mit der Kritik an einem umstrittenen Konzept. *Zeitschrift für Fremdsprachenforschung* 10 (2), 277–303.
Hu, A. (2000) Begrifflichkeit und Interkulturelles Lernen. Eine Replik auf Edmondson & House 1999. *Zeitschrift für Fremdsprachenforschung* 11 (1), 130–136.
Hu, A. and Byram, M. (2009) Introduction. In A. Hu and M. Byram (eds) *Intercultural Competence and Foreign Language Learning: Models, Empiricism, Assessment* (pp. vii–xxv). Tübingen: Narr.

KMK (Kultusministerkonferenz) (2003) *Bildungsstandards für die erste Fremdsprache (Englisch/Französisch) für den Mittleren Schulabschluss*. Munich: Wolters Kluwer Deutschland. See http://www.kmk.org/fileadmin/veroeffentlichungen_beschluesse/2003/2003_12_04-BS-erste-Fremdsprache.pdf (accessed 23 November 2017).

KMK (Kultusministerkonferenz) (2012) *Bildungsstandards für die fortgeführte Fremdsprache (Englisch/Französisch) für die Allgemeine Hochschulreife*. Bonn and Berlin: Wolters Kluwer Deutschland. See http://www.kmk.org/fileadmin/veroeffentlichungen_beschluesse/2012/2012_10_18-Bildungsstandards-Fortgef-FS-Abi.pdf (accessed 23 November 2017).

Krumm, H. (2007) Curriculare Aspekte des interkulturellen Lernens und der interkulturellen Kommunikation. In K. Bausch, H. Christ and H. Krumm (eds) *Handbuch Fremdsprachenunterricht* (pp. 138–144). Tübingen: Francke UTB.

Lado, R. (1967) *Moderner Sprachunterricht. Eine Einführung auf wissenschaftlicher Grundlage*. Munich: Hueber.

Leung, C. (2009) Second language teacher professionalism. In A. Burns and J. Richards (eds) *The Cambridge Guide to Second Language Teacher Education* (pp. 49–58). Cambridge: Cambridge University Press.

Leupold, E. (2007) Landeskundliches Curriculum. In K. Bausch, H. Christ and H. Krumm (eds) *Handbuch Fremdsprachenunterricht* (5th edn, pp. 127–133). Tübingen: Francke UTB.

Levinas, E. (1999 [1970]) *Alterity and Transcendence* (trans. M.B. Smith). New York: Columbia University Press.

Matz, F., Rogge, M. and Siepmann, P. (eds) (2014) *Transkulturelles Lernen im Fremdsprachenunterricht*. Frankfurt am Main: Lang.

Pennycook, A. (2007) *Global Englishes and Transcultural Flows*. London and New York: Routledge.

Plikat, J. (2017) *Fremdsprachliche Diskursbewusstheit als Zielkonstrukt des Fremdsprachenunterrichts. Eine kritische Auseinandersetzung mit der Interkulturellen Kompetenz*. Frankfurt am Main: Lang.

Schmenk, B. (2015) Eine sonderbare Spezies: Fremdsprachendidaktik. Eine(?) Disziplin(?) an den Schnittstellen von akademischen, bildungspolitischen, gesellschaftlichen und erzieherischen Forschungs- und Wirkungsfeldern. In S. Doff and A. Grünewald (eds) *Wechsel-Jahre? Wandel und Wirken in der Fremdsprachendidaktik* (pp. 5–15). Trier: WVT.

Schrey, H. (1979 [1968]) Englischunterricht und Englandkunde. Überlegungen zu einer zeitgemäßen landeskundlichen Didaktik. In W. Hüllen (ed.) *Didaktik des Englischunterrichts* (pp. 253–268). Darmstadt: Wissenschaftliche Buchgesellschaft.

Schulze-Engler, F. and Helff, S. (eds) (2008) *Transcultural English Studies: Theories, Fictions, Realities*. Amsterdam and New York: Rodopi.

Viebrock, B. (2007) *Bilingualer Erdkundeunterricht. Subjektive didaktische Theorien von Lehrerinnen und Lehrern*. Frankfurt am Main: Lang.

Viebrock, B. (2010) Alltagstheorien, methodisches Wissen und unterrichtliches Handeln. In S. Doff (ed.) *Bilingualer Sachfachunterricht in der Sekundarstufe. Eine Einführung* (pp. 107–123). Tübingen: Narr.

Viebrock, B. (2014) Zur Professionalisierung von Lehrkräften im bilingualen Erdkundeunterricht. *Zeitschrift für interpretative Schul- und Unterrichtsforschung* 3, 75–82.

Viebrock, B. (2016) *Fremdsprachendidaktik* – a female domain? In D. Elsner and V. Lohe (eds) *Gender Awareness in the Foreign Language Classroom* (pp. 53–69). Tübingen: Narr.

Volkmann, L. (2011) The 'Transcultural Moment' in English as a Foreign Language. In S. Doff and F. Schulze-Engler (eds) *Beyond 'Other Cultures': Transcultural Perspectives on Teaching the New Literatures in English* (pp. 113–128). Trier: WVT.

Vollmer, H. (1995) Diskurslernen und interkulturelle Kommunikationsfähigkeit: Der Beitrag der Pragmalinguistik und der Diskursanalyse zu einem erweiterten Sprachlernkonzept. In L. Bredella (ed.) *Verstehen und Verständigung durch Sprachenlernen?* (pp. 104–127). Bochum: Brockmeyer.

Wachinger, T. (2003) *Posing In-Between: Postcolonial Englishness and the Commodification of Cultural Hybridity.* Frankfurt am Main: Lang.

Wellman, B. (2001) *Little Boxes, Glocalization, and Networked Individualism. Manuscript, Centre for Urban & Community Studies.* University of Toronto. See http://calchong.tripod.com/sitebuildercontent/sitebuilderfiles/LittleBoxes.pdf (accessed 23 November 2017).

Welsch, W. (1999) Transculturality – the puzzling forms of cultures today. In M. Featherstone and S. Lash (eds) *Spaces of Culture: City, Nation, World* (pp. 194–213). London: Sage.

Welsch, W. (2005) Auf dem Weg zu transkulturellen Gesellschaften. In L. Allolio-Näcke, B. Kalscheuer and A. Manzeschke (eds) *Differenzen anders denken. Bausteine zu einer Kulturtheorie der Transdifferenz* (pp. 314–341). Frankfurt am Main and New York: Campus.

Welsch, W. (2009) *Was ist eigentlich Transkulturalität?* See http://www2.uni-jena.de/welsch/papers/W_Welsch_Was_ist_Transkulturalit%C3%A4t.pdf (accessed 23 November 2017).

6 On Common 'Exposure' and Expert 'Input' in Second Language Education and Study Abroad

John L. Plews

Drawing on a process exemplified in Williams' (1985) Keywords, *this chapter investigates second language acquisition (SLA) scholarship and study abroad data to explore the terms 'exposure' and 'input'. It traces how 'exposure' – as in* exposure to a language in a country where it is spoken *– has largely fallen out of favour among SLA experts despite its continuing currency in general discourse. The chapter reveals how academics have produced contrasting meanings for the term – setting, time, type of language, etc. – as they have oriented more to the alternate slogan 'input' to describe more or less the same phenomenon; this variability and contestation can provide a fertile ground for exploring what the term has to offer. The chapter also suggests that the ungovernability of 'exposure' in popular discourse drove scholars to replace it with the seemingly more school-bound, hypothesized and governable 'input'. Brief study abroad data provide an important emic perspective and further layer of meanings that resemble both academic and popular discussions as well as drawing attention again to the human vulnerability in language acquisition. The chapter explores this network of terms, people and position-takings not simply to elevate 'exposure' but to understand its situation and bring to light a range of meanings.*

Introduction

Having taught languages for some time in schools, universities and study abroad programs, I have become curious about how students who are used to teacher-facilitated language learning take advantage of the ostensibly greater abundance and diversity of language available to them when fortunate enough also to experience foreign immersion. That is, I wonder how they deal with this 'exposure'. Certainly, personal difficulties and intercultural misunderstandings can lead to study abroad participants orienting away from interactions in the target language (e.g. DeKeyser, 2010; Isabelli-García, 2006; Wilkinson, 1998). But even in study abroad courses that include assignments requiring students to explore local sites of interest for peer presentation in the target language or to reflect analytically on their individual experiences of hearing and using the target language during everyday encounters, some students' attention to situation-specific language can be less than judicious. While study abroad research shows variation in participants' development of language abilities and is beginning to map how the environment, interactions and psychological orientation contribute to or hinder learning (for an overview, see Kinginger, 2009), it is less well documented what students do, don't do or think they do with all that language. In wondering about study abroad participants' 'exposure' to language, I also got thinking about the word 'exposure'. How is this word used in research in second language acquisition (SLA), second language education (SLE) and study abroad? While I often hear the word 'exposure' in general conversation about language learning – '*The only way to really learn another language is to be exposed to it in a country where it is spoken*' – it seems to be less in favor in expert circles: it is not indexed in recently published, authoritative SLA readers such as those by Hinkel (2005), Mitchell *et al.* (2013) or Ortega (2009) (see also Ranta & Meckelborg, 2013: 3). If applied linguists choose not to use this term, what other words are used to describe the phenomenon? The word 'input' springs to mind, but is it the same as 'exposure'? And as 'exposure' persists in common discussion, can it still have something to contribute to academic discourse? Motivated by such questions and inspired by an analytical process illustrated by Raymond Williams (1985) in his book *Keywords*, I undertake here an investigation of 'exposure' as a common phrase and as it has occurred in SLA and SLE research in order not to restore the word 'exposure' to an elevated position but rather to understand its situation and to bring to light its meanings, ultimately especially regarding understanding study abroad participants.

Investigative Process as Methodology

In his book *Keywords*, originally published in 1976, Williams (1985) describes a process for analyzing certain words that are used by people who speak the same language and yet do not; that is, single items of vocabulary in one language that are used differently by or have developed different values across different social groups historically. Noting that a word can take on specialized meanings across particular disciplines, Williams was attracted rather to words that he heard 'being used in general discussion in what seemed to [him] interesting and difficult ways' (Williams, 1985: 14); his interest lay in the variations of the usage of words, especially within contemporary popular discourse, that were relational and also particular. Williams set to work tracing 'the available and developing meanings of known words (...) and the explicit but as often implicit connections which people were making, in what seemed to [him], again and again, particular formations of meaning – ways not only of discussing but at another level of seeing many of our central experiences' (Williams, 1985: 15). The keywords he chose to explore in his work were ones he believed were used to generally understand certain activities and at the same time through their variability were representative of 'certain forms of thought', and that to him seemed 'to open up issues and problems (...) of which we all needed to be very much more conscious'. For Williams, the words themselves are 'elements of the problems' (Williams, 1985: 16). In his method of investigation, any one use of a word by any one group is neither wrong nor more right than its use by any other, although a powerful group will claim their use is the right one (Williams, 1985: 11). Rather, in Williams' process of investigation, it is 'the range that matters' (Williams, 1985: 17) and differences and 'changes are not always either simple or final. Earlier and later senses coexist, or become actual alternatives in which problems of contemporary belief and affiliation are contested' (Williams, 1985: 22). Thus, he 'emphasize[s] interconnections' or 'actual contexts' but also especially the words' 'own internal developments and structures' (Williams, 1985: 23) and considers 'the present – present meanings, implications and relationships – as history'. Williams' investigative process is not ideological or transformative; he does not claim that understanding the meanings of a particular word will lead to solving the issues with which it is associated. Rather, his prime objective is to provide 'an extra edge of consciousness', to show 'variations (...) just because they embody different experiences and readings of experience, and this will continue to be true, in active relationships and conflicts, over and above the clarifying exercises of scholars or committees' (Williams, 1985: 24). Yet this consciousness is also critical in the sense that it will enable speakers of this vocabulary not to take it so much for granted as part of 'a *tradition* to be learned [or] a *consensus* to be accepted' and having a 'natural authority', but also to shape and use it in new ways.

My intention in reconsidering 'exposure' – a word that is used meaningfully and possibly variably between general and disciplinary discourse for explaining language learning – is to draw new attention to the persistence of the popular meaning of the word and to compare that with its development and possible replacement in academic writing, thereby tracing a context in which to make available a range of meanings to consider. To me, 'exposure' is a keyword that is used in general discussion to represent a certain understanding of best practice in language learning; it is embedded in a longer phrase that functions as a folk slogan with considerable popular authority: *The only way to learn a language is to be exposed to it in a country where the language is spoken.* Not being indexed in synoptic readers suggests that 'exposure' entails a form of thought that is not so popular among academic authorities.

Admittedly, while motivated by the endurance of the term 'exposure' in general discourse, I focus more on academic uses and developments. Following Williams' investigative process, I trace the available and developing meanings of 'exposure' in general discussion, in an online dictionary, in academic discourse, and finally in a research interview with a study abroad participant. I offer close readings of research publications in order to discover the various connections and claims scholars are making with the word and its alternatives representing beliefs about language learning. As a social group, language education scholars will need to deal with this word, scrutinize it, put it to their own use or confront it with other terms. I thus provide a level of consciousness about the use, contestability and ongoing viability of the keyword. I include an analysis of interview data in order to challenge the sloganization of alternate terms from an often-overlooked emic perspective. What is ultimately at stake is our potential and self-permission to use 'exposure' to shape our discussion of the activity of learning more consciously and insightfully.

'Exposure' in Second Language Acquisition and Second Language Education Research

Critical dilemma

I begin with the way in which 'exposure' is used in general discussion related to second language study abroad. I am struck by how frequently I am told in the domestic arena – by students, their parents, and colleagues both inside and outside modern languages departments, not to mention the popular media, university international office homepages or the private language teaching industry – that the best way to learn a language is *to go to a country where the language is spoken* (see also Ferguson, 1995). This blanket statement seems to me like something akin to *the best way to eat is to go to a restaurant*. It is promising, lacks subtle yet important details or alternatives and assumes consistency in the quality of experience. But whenever I have asked why this is so, I have learned that this popular belief usually means that optimal language learning necessarily takes place, once having got to a country where the target language is spoken, through 'exposure' to the omnipresent second language by an osmosis-like mechanism of hearing and presumably interacting with lots of perfectly proficient native speakers going about their natural business. Apparently, popular belief maintains that language learning does not optimally take place through language instruction and awareness activities guided by a teacher, responding to corrective interaction with a teacher, and study specifically in a domestic class. What is served up in the domestic classroom seems to lack nutritional value, while abroad you are barely shown a menu and you turn into Brillat-Savarin or Egon Ronay or Wolfram Siebeck with a full stomach and never a thought of indigestion. 'Exposure' is the way to learn a language, *to be where it is spoken for natural purposes*, and according to general discussion you cannot get that in a domestic foreign language classroom. But since the domestic classroom is the province of most second language educators and scholars, you can imagine how much that word 'exposure' must grate. All-crucial, full-meal-deal 'exposure' is popularly deemed beyond their domain and implies their limitation at best, and redundancy at worst.

Dictionary basics

A search on Google (which uses the *Oxford Dictionary*) defines the noun 'ex·po·sure' first in terms of physical experience as 'the state of being exposed to contact with something' and 'a physical condition resulting from being outside in severe weather conditions without adequate protection'. All the initial examples of the word in use are negative, conveying the meaning of 'deadliness': 'the dangers posed by **exposure to** asbestos'; '**exposure to** harmful chemicals'; 'he died of **exposure** at 8,000 feet'; 'suffering from exposure'. Clearly, the primary order of 'exposure' is human vulnerability. The next definition in the first set is more about intellectual experience, as shown by the synonyms 'introduction to, experience of/with, contact with, familiarity with, acquaintance with, awareness of'. The examples are linked to the knowledge of cultural discourses: 'his **exposure to** the banking system' and '**exposure to** great literature'. The final definitions in the first set are scientific and economic, with both implying change, one creating a technical negative and the other assuming a potential monetary negative: 'the action of exposing a photographic film to light or other radiation'; 'the action of placing oneself at risk of financial losses, e.g. through making loans, granting credit, or underwriting insurance'. The second set of definitions and synonyms continue the negative theme: 'the revelation of an identity or fact, esp. one that is concealed or likely to arouse disapproval' and 'uncovering, revelation, disclosure, unveiling, unmasking, discovery, detection; denunciation, condemnation'. The accompanying examples indicate that 'exposure' is something some would rather avoid: 'she took her life for fear of exposure as a spy' and 'the exposure of a banking scandal' – the meanings of danger and vulnerability are thus conveyed again. The next definition is 'publicizing' as exemplified by 'scientific findings receive regular exposure in the media' and 'we're getting a lot of exposure'. The third and final definition concerns 'the direction in which a building faces' as in the synonyms 'outlook, aspect, view; position, setting, location' and the example 'a southern exposure'.

In sum, the dictionary explains that 'exposure' is largely done *to* someone and that, beforehand, they are unsuspecting, unprepared, unaware or have reason to fear. But it can also be more conscious as *the action of*. Either way, there is a personal risk or the drawing of unwanted or even wanted attention to oneself. 'Exposure' to another language is not given as an example here, yet another school subject is used to illustrate one of the definitions of the related verb: 'introduce someone to (a subject or area of knowledge). "students were exposed to probability and statistics in high school."' This again underscores the passivity (in learning): there is no action by the students. There is also no mention of the grammatical actor: a teacher. Yet there must surely be somebody to introduce somebody else to a subject.

Second language acquisition and second language education research

Perhaps it is because of the meaning of *unschooled osmosis* or the *withdrawal from educational structures* implied by 'exposure' in popular discourse that I rarely hear the term in expert circles. Nonetheless, 'exposure' has been used across several lines of SLA and SLE research. To trace the use and contestability of 'exposure', I searched for the term in scholarly databases, choosing articles by influential scholars from various domains within the field. For example, in his study of language forgetting, Cohen (1975) uses the phrases 'non-exposure to [the L2]' and 'exposure time' when describing what happens to learners' language abilities after instruction has finished. Second language exposure is connected especially with *time spent in contact* with the target language while learning it specifically in the classroom. This is not surprising given that the point of Cohen's research relies on a shift from a period of instruction to some time after instruction. Phrases such as 'second language contact' and 'immersed' are used interchangeably with 'exposure', while 'non-exposure' and 'contact' also refer to out-of-school conditions. Here, 'exposure' implies a *state of being in time*, meaning to receive language instruction or to spend part of one's life in a certain linguistic community.

In SLA theory, Bialystok (1978) includes 'exposure' as a key element in the model of second language learning she proposes to explain differences in achievement between learners as well as across aspects of language for an individual learner. In her theory, 'exposure' is a descriptive category under the umbrella term 'input': 'The model outlines aspects of the input of information through various kinds of exposure to the language' (Bialystok, 1978: 69). 'Input' is language to 'be experienced or encountered' (Bialystok, 1978: 70) and the 'undifferentiated context in which exposure to language occurs' (Bialystok, 1978: 71). 'Input' is the broad and necessary experiential phenomenon of *language-in-the-world* that encompasses without distinction both the language instruction and language community that we see in Cohen. Bialystok somewhat cumbersomely uses upper-case 'Language Exposure' as an alternate general collective term for 'various settings' (Bialystok, 1978: 78), while lowercase 'exposure' and 'language exposure' refer to three 'specialized kind[s] of exposure' classifiable by their 'nature' (Bialystok, 1978: 75): the (uppercase) 'Language Classroom', 'books' and 'immersion in the native culture'. While 'input' is synonymous with collective 'Language Exposure' and means the occurrence of language to be experienced, 'exposure' is one of three specific sociolinguistic or textual *settings* that, according to the model, differently affect the way the learner is witness to – by unconsciously processing or consciously strategizing through – the necessary 'input'. Bialystok then introduces the phrase 'communicative exposure' (Bialystok, 1978: 77), which she contrasts with the 'formal presentation of the system'. These parallel 'acquisition' and 'learning', and the learner can 'deliberately arrange for such [communicative] exposure' to enable acquisition. Here, 'exposure' is used not only to connote the *setting* of 'input' but also the *type*, the way language occurs in a given setting to be experienced by the learner (i.e. meaningful conversation versus grammar explanation). Bialystok intimates that learners can take an active role in their language development, adopting strategies in an acquisition-oriented communicative type of 'exposure'. This is noteworthy because it shows that learners have agency in the otherwise receptive language ecology conveyed by 'exposure' and 'input'. The variation and inconstant synonymousness of meaning of 'exposure' and 'input' indicates that the value of one or the other as well as the mechanism they describe is contested.

Pica's (1983) article on adult acquisition of English as a second language cites Bialystok's work and uses the extended phrase 'different conditions of exposure' in the title, twice in the abstract and twice in the text. Her use of 'exposure' at first combines and slightly modifies Bialystok's meaning of categories of *settings* with her meaning of *types of input-as-language-occurring*: 'three different conditions of exposure to English L2: (1) Instruction Only, (2) Naturalistic, and (3) Mixed (a combination of 1 and 2)' (Pica, 1983: 465). She also names (1) 'formal lessons' and (2) 'naturalistic experiences'. But Pica separates settings and types when stating that 'These conditions allow for differences in the kinds of L2 exposure available'; 'conditions' now denotes settings that are understood independently of language (i.e. the classroom, outside the classroom) while 'kinds of L2 exposure' signals sameness with *types of input-as-language-occurring*. Indeed, Pica (1983: 466) contrastingly defines 'formal classroom and naturalistic contexts' as learning through the presentation of rules and error feedback for the former and acquisition not through the presentation of rules but the communication of meaning for the latter. She even uses the phrase 'naturalistic input'. In Pica, the academic usage of 'exposure' has shifted or spread from the *state of being or time spent in contact*, including instruction, to sociolinguistic *settings* as distinct from the overall *language made available*, which is called 'input', to either form-focused or meaning-focused *types of language made available*, that is, types of 'input'.

However, Pica is not consistent. For example, while 'input' means *language made available*, 'exposure' does not always mean the *type* and can mean *receptively put into contact*, as in the following: 'The first group [of study participants] was exposed to naturalistic input' (Pica, 1983: 468). Elsewhere, 'exposure' is synonymous with naturalistic settings in contrast to the classroom: 'in studies in which formal instruction has been shown to be more efficient than exposure to second language development (...), "exposure" was not clearly defined.' Pica's sincere assertion of the ungovernability of 'exposure' is notable. Yet she too vacillates between turns of phrase, making the exact meaning of 'exposure' unclear or variable, with other terms serving just as well: we read about 'distinctly different language contexts' (Pica, 1983: 468), where 'context' suffices for *settings*; 'conditions of target language exposure', where 'conditions' and 'exposure' refer to *settings* and *type(s)*, respectively; then the phrase 'the effect of different *emphases* in L2 exposure on [an adult classroom] population' (Pica, 1983: 469) emphasizes where the meaning of *types* lies, but 'exposure' here represents *time spent in contact* rather than *setting*, or maybe '*emphases*' means degrees of time or intensity and 'exposure' means *types*; the phrase 'degrees of exposure to naturalistic input' (Pica, 1983: 470) certainly indicates *time spent in contact*. So, on reading Pica's (1983: 471) research question – 'Does the production of adult acquirers of English as a second language differ according to the conditions of exposure to linguistic input?' – we may presume either 'conditions' or 'exposure' to mean the *types* of language made available, or 'conditions' to mean *setting* and 'exposure' to mean *contact*. Perhaps I am splitting hairs, since the question makes the same sense either way, but when Pica next describes the subjects in her study, the word 'exposure' evidently comes to mean *receptive or non-interactive contact* **as opposed to** reactive or interactive contact *either* in the classroom or out of the classroom, with interaction marked off by 'conversation with': 'Instruction Only. (...) With the exception of minimal input from films, television, music, newspapers, and magazines, their only exposure to and conversation with English speakers came through classroom and textbook instruction. (...) Naturalistic. (...) Subjects' exposure to and conversation with English speakers came from residence in the English-speaking community' (Pica, 1983: 472). Later, Pica refers to 'the three language exposure conditions' (Pica, 1983: 476), returning to *all types* of language made available in different settings, and not only receptive non-interactive. 'Exposure' in Pica is *not clearly defined* and its meanings vary.

Genesee's (1983) review of bilingual immersion programs uses 'exposure' when describing the different kinds of programs and their theoretical justification. When discussing early immersion programs, he remarks that 'all three perspectives [neuropsychological, psycholinguistic, and social psychological] favoured early intensive exposure to French' (Genesee, 1983: 6), and that evidence shows 'adolescents and adults can achieve levels of second-language proficiency that are as high as or even higher than those of children who receive the same amount of second-language exposure, if exposure is of a short duration' (Genesee, 1983: 6–7). Here, 'exposure' means *time spent in contact*, and especially in the classroom, but when presenting other research Genesee's use of the word embraces the *type of language available* since the idea of time is captured by 'long-term' and the type is introduced as 'naturalistic': 'individuals who begin second-language learning early (…) are more likely than those who begin later to achieve native-like levels of proficiency if given long-term natural or naturalistic exposure' (Genesee, 1983: 7). This *time spent in contact* is like Cohen's (1975) and perhaps Pica's (1983) 'exposure' since it concerns *receptive classroom language* and *instruction* as seen when Genesee describes the particulars of early immersion – 'pupils are not required to use French with the teacher or with one another even though the teachers are instructed to address all of their comments to the students in French' – and when he discusses language achievement: 'students do not acquire native-like mastery of French syntax [because] the only native speaker model they have extensive exposure to in school is the teacher' (Genesee, 1983: 15). Although, following this, *reactive or interactive out-of-class contact* is also intended: 'Surveys of the students' French language use outside school indicate that they have little extensive extracurricular exposure' and 'the lack of native French-speaking peer models in Immersion programs along with the very nature of school-talk in general means that Immersion students are not exposed to the informal register used commonly by their French-speaking age mates.'

When reviewing studies comparing kinds of immersion, academic achievement or double immersion, Genesee again uses expressions such as 'amount of exposure', 'additional exposure', 'intensity of exposure' (Genesee, 1983: 17), 'early exposure and extended exposure', 'cumulative second-language exposure' (Genesee, 1983: 20), 'limited exposure' (Genesee, 1983: 21) or 'limited prior exposure' (Genesee, 1983: 22), 'more (…) exposure' (Genesee, 1983: 24) and 'initial exposure' signifying *time spent in contact*. Nonetheless, he shifts to a meaning that includes *type of language available*, meaning code (perhaps associated with *setting*), especially when providing a contrast to classroom instruction, and likely both *receptive* and *interactive or reactive* as conveyed by the word 'use': 'results indicate there is an advantage associated with early second-language instruction, namely the opportunity it affords for more instruction and/or second-language exposure'; 'The possibility of extracurricular use of the second language (…) in bilingual communities where real possibilities to use the language exist. This type of exposure is likely to be important' (Genesee, 1983: 19); and 'less English language instruction and exposure' (Genesee, 1983: 24). The coupling of 'exposure' with 'extracurricular use' shows again the learner's possible agentive role in relation to 'exposure'. Indeed, Genesee expounds on the implication of students' active control of and reactive response to the use of language (see Genesee, 1983: 38). In many respects, his critical point is close to the popular belief of *being exposed to a target language community*.

When later theorizing differentiated language development in bilingual children, Genesee (1989) again uses 'exposure' to mean *time spent in contact*, including with different *types of language* by code: 'it is necessary to study the language models to which bilingual children are exposed' (Genesee, 1989: 163); 'rates of mixing are difficult to interpret or compare across studies owing to (...) differential exposure to the languages in question' (Genesee, 1989: 164); and 'one would expect children exposed to frequent and general mixing to mix frequently' (Genesee, 1989: 169). These few instances of a word Genesee has used widely before are surpassed by the abundant mobilization of 'input', which has replaced 'exposure' for one of its earlier meanings. Genesee uses 'input' here not in Bialystok's sense as the *undifferentiated context in which exposure to language occurs* – which is now rather just 'exposure' – but with the meaning of *type of language made available* or presented. In this article, *type* also means language code: 'bilingual children's mixed utterances are modeled on mixed input produced by others' (Genesee, 1989: 169) and 'It is difficult, however, to ascertain the exact relationship between input and rate or type of mixing from the available research, since descriptions of the language-input conditions are either totally lacking (...), or, at best, are general and impressionistic' (Genesee, 1989: 170, see also 171, 174) – here 'conditions' refers to who is speaking, for how much of the time and whether they are mixing codes.

The flipped meanings of 'exposure' and 'input' between Genesee's two works can be explained by the intervening influence of Krashen's (1985) 'Input Hypothesis' (see also 1982). Krashen distinguishes the two terms, promoting 'comprehensible input' as the hero and epoch-making slogan of his theory of language acquisition. In that theory, 'exposure' refers to the presence and use of language in the learner's environment – the experiential phenomenon of *language-in-the-world*, which Bialystok called 'input' – and is differentiated from 'comprehensible input' as the following example explains: 'in cases where "exposure" really entails comprehensible input, as in some school situations, we see a relationship [between exposure and proficiency]. Where exposure does not entail comprehensible input, e.g. an immigrant in a situation in which he can use his first language and uses the second language very little, we see a much weaker or no relationship' (Krashen, 1985: 14). The discursive shift occurs in that definition where 'exposure' is and is not the same as 'comprehensible input'. 'Input' is now a specific *type of language made available*, such as the modified version of the target language used by teachers when interacting with students in class. It is not language in the environment that might not even be attended to or used by the L2 speaker, as in Krashen's example of immigrants working in their mother tongue.

In Krashen's theory, the language of 'exposure' can be refined scientifically and socio-affectively to make 'comprehensible input', and wherever it is not refined it will not lead to acquisition. He states, 'The Input Hypothesis claims that humans acquire language in only one way – by understanding messages, or by receiving "comprehensible input"' (Krashen, 1985: 4). 'Input' is a message, an amount of appropriately managed and optimally contextualized language, that is thereby understood among all the noise of 'exposure'; he continues:

> We are able to understand language containing unacquired grammar with the help of context, which includes extra-linguistic information, our knowledge of the world, and previously acquired linguistic competence. The caretaker provides extra-linguistic context by limiting speech to the child to the 'here and now.' The beginner-language teacher provides context via visual aids (pictures and objects) and discussion of familiar topics. (…) To be more precise, input is the essential environmental ingredient. (Krashen, 1985: 4)

With Krashen, 'exposure' is deemphasized while 'input' is advanced as refined language that is managed for the sake of comprehensibility – an essence of language distilled by teachers for learners. Indeed, we see Krashen's influence and the crisis for 'exposure' already in Schmidt (1983: 138), who aligns 'exposure' in informal environments and 'natural exposure' with informal interaction and distinguishes it from 'formal instruction'; he recalls Krashen when asserting that, even in informal environments, 'exposure' is not the same as 'active involvement' in conveying messages. Here, 'exposure' is reserved for a sociolinguistic *setting* as well as a *receptive and non-interactive relation to language*. The meaning of the keyword 'exposure' is clearly different from what we know from general discussion and scholarship up to now; in contrast to 'exposure', meaning *setting without active contact*, the (inter)*active contact of the learner* has become the cause célèbre of SLA, and 'input' the slogan behind which experts rally.

Taking on Krashen's theory, 'input' is one of many scientific-sounding terms that Swain (1985) mobilizes in her article about input–output relationships in learners' interaction with native-speaker teachers and, in a sign that discourse has changed, she does not use the keyword 'exposure'. Her terms include 'foreigner talk', 'learner talk' or 'learner input', 'peer talk' or 'peer input', 'teacher talk', 'intake', 'output', 'negative input', 'feedback', 'conversational turns', 'negotiating meaning', and so forth. In their derivation and effect each term is surely indebted to Krashen's (pseudo-)scientific slogan 'input' and jostles as a slogan-in-the-making or at least as a supporting-cast mini-slogan. 'Learner input' (Swain, 1985: 235) refers to *language made available* to learners in the delimited classroom scenario termed 'interactional events'. In fact, Swain provides a precise definition halfway through her discussion that echoes Krashen: 'Comprehensible input I take to mean language directed to the learner that contains some new element in it but that is nevertheless understood by the learner because of linguistic, paralinguistic, or situational clues, or world knowledge backup' (Swain, 1985: 245). Swain distinguishes 'comprehensible input' from 'negative input': the latter shows failed communication and does not necessarily contain the new element. She argues that 'the nature of the [comprehensible] input received' (Swain, 1985: 236) is important but not enough for grammatical development; she proposes 'comprehensible output' in interaction as necessary for communicative competence. That is, she emphasizes the importance of 'input that occurs in interaction where meaning is negotiated' (Swain, 1985: 246), or 'where the learner has received some negative input – and (...) is pushed to use alternate means to get across his or her message' (Swain, 1985: 248). In such interactions, the learner and the more proficient interlocutor characteristically modify their language through paraphrasing and expansions to make the 'input' comprehensible, presumably by emphasizing the new element among the many clues. Swain consistently uses 'contributions' to refer to the learner's speech, while reserving 'input' for their exchange partners – who, here, are native-speaker teachers – and offering the field the new mini-slogan 'comprehensible output', defined as 'Being "pushed" in output' (Swain, 1985: 249) to produce messages that are not only understood but also precise and appropriate. Swain contends that the classrooms she observed have plenty of 'comprehensible input', but few opportunities for 'comprehensible output'. It is also clear that in the absence of 'exposure' the field can mobilize many terms as colluding mini-slogans to govern the knowledge of SLA.

The diminishing returns of 'exposure' as influenced by Krashen and others continue especially where it is differentiated from 'interaction'. Pica and Doughty (1985: 123) define 'exposure' as 'input' that is 'not negotiated through direct interaction or unattended to by participants'. This is Krashen's 'exposure' that is not 'comprehensible input' as opposed to the one that is. It is *non-interactive* and *receptive* language that washes over learners. This 'exposure' does not contribute optimally to language development because the student does not turn it into modified 'input': 'conversational adjustments were more abundant in the teacher-fronted activity but served only as a form of exposure to class members who listened while their teacher interacted with others' (Pica & Doughty, 1985: 131). 'Input', for which both teachers and students serve 'as sources' (Pica & Doughty, 1985: 118), is the umbrella term and throughout indicates *language made available* ('available', Pica & Doughty, 1985: 123) as discrete points – 'T-units, fragments, and interjections' (Pica & Doughty, 1985: 123) – and as *type* – 'non-native input'. The language made available acts as linguistic data for learners: 'selected students received 12 percent of the total input among group participants, but only 3 percent of the input in the teacher-fronted activity' (Pica & Doughty, 1985: 129). Scholars are indeed turning

Krashen's 'school-situation' 'exposure [that] really entails comprehensible input' into precise and appropriate *aspects of language made available*, and not the 'immigrant-situation' type of *language-in-the-world* that might wash over learners.

Spada's (1986) study of the effects of the amount and type of informal second language contact also contrasts 'mere exposure' with 'conversational interaction': 'If (...) negotiation of meaning is the key to getting comprehensible input, which in turn is thought to aid the second-language acquisition process, then conversational interaction in English can be viewed as contact which is more beneficial to the learner than mere exposure to linguistic input via the radio, television, etc.' (Spada, 1986: 186). 'Exposure' is marked as the *receptive* and *non-interactive experience of language*, and 'input' refers to *aspects of language to be learned*. 'Exposure' is diminished by the word 'mere' since only 'conversational interaction' requires the learner to negotiate meaning and improve the 'input' received to make it 'comprehensible' for learning, but 'input' is nonetheless a component of both 'mere exposure' and 'conversational interaction'. In the second of only two instances of 'exposure', this experience of language is measurable in terms of time and/or aspects of language: 'more exposure to a greater variety of contexts for language use and register variation outside the classroom' (Spada, 1986: 191). 'Input' or 'linguistic input' and 'comprehensible linguistic input' consistently refer to *language made available* specifically for learning. Significantly, 'contact' appears 196 times in this article. It is used in terms of *setting* ('out-of-class contact'), *quantity* ('*amount* of contact', 'high contact', 'low contact', 'less contact', 'greater contact', 'more contact'), and *type* ('informal contact', '*type* of contact', 'difference in contact', 'quality of [learners'] contact'). As the article's title indicates, 'contact' functions as the opposite of instruction, subsuming both 'mere exposure' and 'conversational interaction' and embracing what elsewhere is deemed 'exposure' in natural settings such as television and conversation. Curiously, in-class interaction is not 'contact' here, as it is 'instruction'.

Also studying second language instruction, Doughty (1991) first distinguishes between 'exposure' and 'instruction'. The latter is concerned with the classroom as one and the same as her experimental treatment, while the former initially refers to a general *state of being* or *experience* ('exposed to informal contexts', Doughty, 1991: 440) but comes to mean the (frequency of) *presentation* of, or *opportunity* to experience, aspects of language (Doughty, 1991: 442, 447, 457, 459, 460). In her experimental design, the control group 'received no instruction' and is referred to as 'exposure-only' (Doughty, 1991: 446), while the two experimental groups received instruction 'in addition to exposure' (Doughty, 1991: 442). In effect, 'exposure' slides between domains as the *experience of language*: 'both instructed [experimental] groups also experienced the same artificially high and marked exposure to sentences containing relative clauses as did controls'

(Doughty, 1991: 459). Thus, 'exposure' is all things here: *informal/natural setting, opportunity to experience* and *language made available*. 'Input' is mobilized in relation to comprehension and as a 'set' of 'data' (Doughty, 1991: 440) but is secondary to the focus on instruction.

These scholars have been helpful to advancing the fundamental knowledge of SLA and SLE. They also attest to what we might consider an ongoing manoeuvre in the professional literature which wrests knowledge of optimal SLE away from the popular discussions of time spent in another country supported by the keyword 'exposure' – where that knowledge would remain professionally ungoverned. Instead such knowledge generation is kept for the classroom domain of second language educators and scholars. I would never suggest that there is any consciously willed and explicit assertion of power by any of these scholars; their words are part of a growing professional discourse. Yet the staunch use of 'input' – as well as of the surge in associated scientific mini-slogans – along with the removal of 'exposure', at the same time as 'input' is coming to mean the *language made available*, is an expression of a profession's discomfort with the ungovernability of the knowledge it professes to govern. Common 'exposure' is too indecent for the field of SLE. It cannot be observed easily as a controlled, classroom environment. This drive to a more experimental perspective might entail a narrowing of possible meanings. Meanwhile, the governability of 'input', of making available specific language, provides an exchange value for scholars' and teachers' work and dedication.

Across other lines of SLA and SLE inquiry, 'exposure' persists but is contained by association with code and 'contact' and not with 'input' in interaction. Spada and Lightbown's (1989) report on the language development of intensive learners uses 'exposure' to refer to a *quantifiable experience* of a code including in a classroom setting: for example, 'approximately 1000 hours of exposure to French' (Spada & Lightbown, 1989: 12); 'had been exposed to ESL under the "new" programme' (Spada & Lightbown, 1989: 15). There are no instances of 'input', but there are 26 instances of 'contact', which are distinguished from 'Classroom interaction patterns' (i.e. instructional choices). Here, 'contact' includes both conversation and media, that is, the out-of-class and non-interactional 'exposure' of Spada (1986). 'Contact' seems also to operate synonymously with 'exposure': 'both intensive and regular programme students reported more contact with English (...). The considerably greater exposure to English is seen for both grade 5 and grade 6 intensive students with the greatest increase in contact shown by grade 5' (Spada & Lightbown, 1989: 19).

Loschky (1994) uses 'exposure', meaning *source of language* (i.e. source of 'input') – as in 'exposed to large doses of L2 input' (Loschky, 1994: 305) – and/or *linguistic environment, mode, or setting* – as in 'TV provides their only exposure to L2 German'. 'Input' refers to the *language made available* – 'daily TV watching was his only source [i.e. exposure] of English input'. Here, the language made available is a code. Loschky uses 'input' extensively, as such or in combination with qualifying terms that multiply its taken-for-granted value in the manner of a slogan ('input hypothesis', 'unmodified input', 'premodified input', 'input types', 'input comprehension', 'second language input', 'comprehensible input', 'incomprehensible input'), and he cites Krashen and Long. This 'input' relies on how it is performed in relation to interaction: whether it is unmodified or premodified. But 'exposure' is mobilized again to mean *time spent in contact* as in 'exposure to L2 input outside the experiment' (Loschky, 1994: 308), 'the input learners are exposed to during the experiment' and 'childhood L2 exposure' (Loschky, 1994: 309). The sense of 'exposure' as *source of language* and as *amount of time/frequency* of such sources is further underlined: 'exposed to new words' (Loschky, 1994: 312), 'exposed to a new vocabulary item' (Loschky, 1994: 313) and 'the multiple exposures to new vocabulary items'. In Loschky, 'exposure' is again the general phenomenon of *language in the world*, known by place and time, and always unmodified, or ungoverned. Meanwhile, input is what we work with; it is defined by having precise linguistic characteristics (e.g. containing 'repetitions', a number of 'words per utterance', 'syntax complexity', Loschky, 1994: 319) or refined by modification or governed through interaction especially by teachers.

The promotion and refinement of 'input' as the foundation of the knowledge of the field and disciplinary slogan continue with ever more marginalization of 'exposure', giving the impression that our keyword is somehow less suitable or precise, that is, just not academic enough. VanPatten's (2002) review of processing instruction (PI) refers to Gass's (1997) work on 'input' and 'interaction' in which she declares 'input' to be 'the single most important concept of second language acquisition' (VanPatten, 2002: 756). VanPatten still uses 'exposure' to mean *state of being* or *time spent in contact*, either in instruction or otherwise: 'Learners may not need to be told that Spanish inverts subject and verb in yes/no questions because this is immediately evident in simple questions that learners hear from the first day of exposure' (VanPatten, 2002: 761). 'Exposure' as the general experience of language is connected to but also contrasts with the active processing of data ('input'): 'Any theory that would suggest that acquisition does not happen as a result of exposure to and processing of input in some way has yet to establish what the learning mechanism is' (VanPatten, 2002: 763). Compared to these brief mentions of 'exposure' are 134 instances of 'input', which is not surprising since PI is a model of 'input processing' (IP) in which 'input' is structured in order to help learners make form-meaning connections – but it also goes to show how far the alternate has come. VanPatten (2002: 756) states that it is important not 'to speak of "input" in general terms' – for which there is presumably 'exposure' – but of 'learning mechanisms that act upon "input"' and that are concerned with how 'intake' is derived from 'input', whether instructed or natural. Thus, 'input' is *all types of language made available* at the precise moment language is to be acquired and it is distinguished from 'intake', which is the language the learner has acquired: 'Intake is defined as the linguistic data actually processed from the input and held in working memory' (VanPatten, 2002: 757) and 'Intake is that subset of filtered input that the learner actually processes and holds in working memory' (VanPatten, 2002: 761). Here, 'intake' is processed or 'filtered input', making unprocessed and unfiltered 'input' *linguistic data-in-the-world*, such as in the expression 'input utterance' (VanPatten, 2002: 760); it is not the linguistic data once taken in: 'Input provides the data, IP makes (certain) data available for acquisition' (VanPatten, 2002: 762). Remarkably close in meaning to 'exposure' (*being in contact with language as a general yet essential phenomenon*), 'input' (*the single most important concept of unfiltered data-in-the-world and its provision*) nonetheless has replaced 'exposure', for it is the discursive branding process of 'input' alone – its reiteration that sets it apart from 'exposure' – that allows scholars and teachers to take charge of second language development in theory, the governing denied them by the *general terms* or *common discussion* of 'exposure'. Indeed, VanPatten (2002: 763) asserts: 'input is fundamental for acquisition and is needed for the creation of an underlying mental representation of the linguistic system. The point of research over the last 20 years has been to determine just what the links are between the developing system and input.'

In describing their interaction hypothesis, another model of second language learning, Gass and Mackey (2006) use 'exposure' only twice, while 'input' occurs frequently along with 'interaction' and 'output'. In the first instance, 'exposure' is used in an overview of the model: 'In simple terms, the interaction approach considers exposure to language (input), production of language (output), and feedback on production (through interaction) as constructs that are important for understanding how second language learning takes place' (Gass & Mackey, 2006: 3–4). Evidently, 'exposure to language' is now the plain English (*in simple terms*) equivalent and definition of the scientific 'input' – they are synonymous and divided only by discourse membership. There is no attention to whether 'exposure' or 'input' convey exactly *time, setting* or *type*; we can only surmise, given the presence of 'output' and 'interaction', that 'exposure' or 'input' must be *receptive* since 'output' and 'interaction' entail being *active* and *reactive*. 'Input' is next defined as 'language that is available to the learner through any medium (listening, reading, or gestural in the case of sign language)' and 'raw data' (Gass & Mackey, 2006: 5), which sounds like Bialystok's *undifferentiated context in which exposure to language occurs* as well as her *various settings* (Bialystok is not cited; Krashen, Swain and Ellis are). In the second instance, 'exposure' is used when discussing the role of the frequency of input: 'language constructions are learned "through using language, engaging in communication" (…) – in other words, through language use as well as exposure to input.'

Now 'exposure' and 'input' are separate, with the former meaning the *opportunities to receive* (not necessarily duration) and the latter solely conveying *raw linguistic data*. In Gass and Mackey, 'exposure' means *language made available* and *time* and *setting*. Meanwhile, 'input' takes on *language made available* only: 'input forms the positive evidence that learners use as they construct their second language grammars.' In Gass and Mackey's approach, 'interaction' includes confirmation checks, clarification requests, recasts, that is, feedback, yet none of this is designated 'input' despite surely being *linguistic data made available*, nor is it 'exposure' despite also being *opportunities to receive*. This is despite the pivotal role played by learners' attention to feedback in their model, which in their own words resembles 'exposure': 'it is necessary for learners to notice the relationships between their initially erroneous forms, the feedback they receive, and their [modified] output' (Gass & Mackey, 2006: 14). On close inspection, Gass and Mackey essentially say – if put *in simple terms* – that *we learn from our mistakes if we dare to study and correct them once they have been made available to us (i.e. once we have had the opportunity to receive them as negative data, or been exposed to them)*. Despite the undoubtedly thoughtful mobilization, scientification and sloganization of a number of terms by scholarly discourse – among them especially 'input' – we might forgive ourselves if we were to pause for a while to wonder whether 'exposure' is just as adequate an expression in helping to describe the situation and if it has served us well to have more or less banished it from professional discourse.

Leow (2007) provides an inclusive – albeit confusing – definition of 'exposure', meaning both instructional and non-instructional grammar presentation: 'the term *exposure* refers to both formal grammatical explanation/presentation (which (…) will be subsumed under the generic term *information*) and formal exposure, given that learners may be *exposed* to, and not necessarily *instructed* on grammatical information with the expectation that they will somehow pay attention to targeted L2 forms or structures during exposure' (Leow, 2007: 44). Likewise, 'input' is defined as 'the L2 data (form-based and/or meaning-based) that learners receive either in the formal classroom or in a naturalistic setting' (Leow, 2007: 21). Thus, Leow makes a difference between 'exposure' as presentation, as the *act or opportunity in time for the provision of information* (we often read 'during exposure' and 'after exposure'), and 'input' as *data received*, as a thing (we read 'data in the input'). In Leow, it is again possible to have 'exposure to L2 input' (Leow, 2007: 25, 26, etc.; or 'to the linguistic data', Leow, 2007: 29; 'to the targeted forms', Leow, 2007: 30; 'to the structured input', Leow, 2007: 40), which reveals that 'input' is not language per se but specifically *discrete items of grammar*. Clearly, there is still a role for 'exposure' as directly or indirectly instructional presentation in the classroom, but scholarly discourse has put the focus on learner attention to 'input' – on the student who dares to study. Indeed, the academic publications reviewed in this section have mobilized the slogan 'input' not only to capture necessary data in learning language, but to position and rally scholars, teachers and conscientious learners as guardians of this professional knowledge. Yet, common 'exposure' persists as a meaningful keyword that is either roughly synonymous with or distinct from 'input'.

Study Abroad Research

'Exposure' in study abroad research

What is the situation, beyond the domestic language classroom, in study abroad? Segalowitz et al.'s (2004) comparison of linguistic gains in study abroad and domestic classroom contexts uses 'exposure' to mean a *state of being in time* that is naturalistic and related to the code: '[students'] exposure to the presumably rich linguistic environment' (Segalowitz et al., 2004: 2); 'exposure to Spanish outside of class' (Segalowitz et al., 2004: 11). This experience is quantifiable: 'how much exposure to the target language students have'; 'amount of exposure to the language' (Segalowitz et al., 2004: 15). There is only one instance of 'input', which clearly indicates a focus on a *discrete aspect of language*: 'new input (for example, new vocabulary)' (Segalowitz et al., 2004: 15). In a similarly comparative work on oral performance gains, Segalowitz and Freed (2004) use 'exposure' to indicate *state of being in contact* – '[learners] are regularly exposed to the L2 more intensively through the local media than they would be "at home"' (Segalowitz & Freed, 2004: 174) – and this can be both beyond and in the classroom: compare 'few L2 extracurricular exposure opportunities' (Segalowitz & Freed, 2004: 193) and 'differences in classroom-based exposure' (Segalowitz & Freed, 2004: 193). 'Input' appears twice and necessitates learner attention that was not mentioned in the examples of 'exposure': 'metacognitive strategies to attend to input in particular ways' (Segalowitz & Freed, 2004: 176) and 'to make use of language input the learner has to be able to process that input well' (Segalowitz & Freed, 2004: 177). While 'exposure' is the more general *experience of language in the natural or instructional environment*, 'input' is that *language made available specifically for learning*. 'Contact' appears frequently, defined as 'to interact with NSs' (Segalowitz & Freed, 2004: 177), and combined with several qualifiers indicating one setting or another and so making it practically synonymous with 'exposure': 'out-of-class contact', 'home-stay family contact', 'extracurricular contact', 'classroom-based language contact', 'in-class contact', 'classroom instructional contact', 'classroom-based contact'.

But 'exposure' becomes contested or replaced in this scholarly domain too. DeKeyser (2007) uses the word 'exposure' once in his chapter about students' language practice while studying abroad, while 'input' appears

11 times, either alone or as 'comprehensible input'. The preference reflects a discourse spurred by Krashen, who is cited. DeKeyser pairs 'exposure' with 'interaction' and relates 'input' to them both when explaining advanced learners' progress on study abroad: 'They interact more (...), they take more frequent advantage of "extracurricular listening" (e.g. to radio, films, television) (...), and they are "more adept at managing the ceaseless flow of TL [target language] input" (...) during such exposure and interaction' (DeKeyser, 2007: 211). The word 'such' refers 'exposure' back to the example of 'extracurricular' genres of 'radio, films, television' accessible in study abroad contexts in the second section of the sentence and, obviously, 'interaction' back to 'They interact more' in the first section. We thus understand 'exposure and interaction' as mutually exclusive, as passive and active. 'Exposure' encompasses the *receptive, general state of being in the language environment* or *various modes/settings*, but which excludes 'interaction'. Also, 'input' is a specific element occurring 'during' both the passive experience of the linguistic environment and the activity of interaction; it is the *language made available* in the environment and through activity or, more precisely, *language made available that is just right for skillful 'managing'* as data to be processed for acquisition. But 'input' in 'exposure' ('situations'), as distinct from 'input' in 'interaction', is soon disregarded by DeKeyser exactly because it is not interactive or manageable: 'listening to university lectures, watching television, listening to tour guides, eavesdropping on conversations (...). Situations like these obviously do not provide practice in output/interaction and are severely limited even in terms of input because it may be either very repetitive or very hard to comprehend. In neither case does the student get good comprehensible input' (DeKeyser, 2007: 213). 'Input' in 'interaction' fares little better: 'even when practice is truly interactive, it may do little to stretch the limits of the student's interlanguage because it is almost formulaic in nature.' Here, preferable 'input' is inherently tasked 'to stretch', resembling Swain's 'pushed'. Putting aside the sweeping nature of both assertions (each softened by 'it may') in order to return to the issue of 'exposure', academic discourse is again intent on obscuring 'exposure' with 'input', for not only does DeKeyser place it below 'interaction' in importance, but his refined usage of 'input' as signifying *language optimally made available for processing* is ultimately also even dropped so that 'input' again holds a meaning that is indistinguishable from earlier meanings of 'exposure': DeKeyser laments that students' re-creation of formulaic classroom-like interactions in study abroad contexts 'makes them miss many opportunities to learn from input *provided* overseas' (DeKeyser, 2007: 214, emphasis added).

Pérez-Vidal and Juan-Grau's (2011) article on the effects of the various environments of study abroad on language development uses 'exposure' and 'input' in overlapping ways and combined in 'input exposure' (Pérez-Vidal & Juan-Grau, 2011: 157, 161). The terms are first considered synonymously and both are initially received, but 'exposure' is subsequently actively obtained and becomes the quantifiable and classifiable access to 'input' – they are now separate – with the latter being one of three forms of *linguistic data*: 'whereas in formal instruction (FI) the classroom is most generally the sole source of exposure and input to the target language, [study abroad] constitutes a context in which learners can avail themselves of massive and varied exposure to input, interaction, and feedback in natural, authentic exchanges' (Pérez-Vidal & Juan-Grau, 2011: 158). Overall, 'exposure' means the general *phenomenon of language* – 'high quality exposure environments such as [study abroad]' (Pérez-Vidal & Juan-Grau, 2011: 158) – or *time spent in contact* with the code – 'learners may be exposed to massive amounts of target language input in a variety of situations' (Pérez-Vidal & Juan-Grau, 2011: 161); 'during this period, exposure to the TL was limited to the classroom' (Pérez-Vidal & Juan-Grau, 2011: 168); 'Exposure to the target language was massive, sociolinguistically varied and authentic' (Pérez-Vidal & Juan-Grau, 2011: 169). 'Exposure' is the phenomenon in which 'input' as *linguistic data* is located – 'in a FI context, input exposure is restricted to the classroom' (Pérez-Vidal & Juan-Grau, 2011: 161) – and yet also synonymous with 'input' – 'greater opportunities for exposure and interaction' (Pérez-Vidal & Juan-Grau, 2011: 165). While 'input' is generally synonymous with 'exposure' – 'different input conditions', 'the role of input while abroad' (Pérez-Vidal & Juan-Grau, 2011: 158) – it is also used exclusively to refer to the specific *manner of utterance or activity providing linguistic data* to learn – 'input and output are fashioned by teachers to attend to form'; 'via input and feedback' (Pérez-Vidal & Juan-Grau, 2011: 161); 'the kind of input that most benefits different types of learners' is exemplified by 'outdoor communication' and 'academic work' (Pérez-Vidal & Juan-Grau, 2011: 165). Finally, it is located again within 'exposure' as the *linguistic data made available* in the experience of language: 'more contact opportunities with [exposure to?] the input available while abroad' (Pérez-Vidal & Juan-Grau, 2011: 161); 'the extent to which learners draw on the context and input learning environment conditions [input exposure?]' (Pérez-Vidal & Juan-Grau, 2011: 167). The fluidity of the terms in Pérez-Vidal and Juan-Grau is again an expression of the discursive struggle taking place.

Ranta and Meckelborg's (2013) article on international students' use of English explicitly engages with the term 'exposure'. They use it first in the sense of *time spent in contact* with a code and differentiated from 'interaction': 'opportunities for exposure to the target language and interaction with native-speakers' (Ranta & Meckelborg, 2013: 1). This receptive meaning occurs later in the article – 'learners need to be exposed to a language to learn it' (Ranta & Meckelborg, 2013: 2) – but is not consistent, as seen by the expression 'interactive exposure' (Ranta

& Meckelborg, 2013: 5) and the phrase 'much less high-quality exposure', which is equated with 'amount of interaction' (Ranta & Meckelborg, 2013: 22). 'Experience' is not a synonym for 'exposure', as evidenced by the instance of 'quantity and quality of exposure experienced' (Ranta & Meckelborg, 2013: 1), where *phenomenon of language* or *language made available* are likely meanings. This *time spent* or *phenomenon of language* can be broken down: 'Exposure was measured using a computerized log' that included a range of 'receptive' and 'interactive' uses of English and 'considerable variation [in] amount and type' (Ranta & Meckelborg, 2013: 1). Following Spada and Lightbown (1989), Ranta and Meckelborg use the expression 'out-of-classroom contact' (Ranta & Meckelborg, 2013: 4), which is interchangeable with 'exposure' (Ranta & Meckelborg, 2013: 26). But while Spada and Lightbown's (1989) 'contact' excludes 'instruction', their 'exposure' includes the classroom, and Ranta and Meckelborg's 'exposure'/'contact' includes 'instruction' *in* English when not *of* English. Another expression used by Ranta and Meckelborg (2013: 4, 21) is 'exposure data'. These data are not the *linguistic data made available* as in 'input' in other works, but rather the *measured time spent in contact*. This meaning recurs when reviewing Ginsberg and Miller's (2000) article in order to refer to the *time spent* with Russians speaking Russian: 'the L2 exposure experienced by American students in Russia' (Ranta & Meckelborg, 2013: 5).

The first use of 'input' seems interchangeable with 'exposure' in that it is *quantifiable and classifiable available language*: '[a naturalistic] environment provides access to input that is both ample in quantity and diverse in quality' (Ranta & Meckelborg, 2013: 2). Indeed, Ranta and Meckelborg (2013: 3) quote Lightbown and Spada's (2006) definition of 'input' as 'the language that the learner is exposed to (either written or spoken) in the environment', which makes 'input' as all-encompassing as the *phenomenon of language-in-the-world* that is 'exposure'. They maintain that '*exposure* is often used as a synonym for input' (Ranta & Meckelborg, 2013: 3, original emphasis) and claim that 'exposure (...) can cover both input and (...) output' (Ranta & Meckelborg, 2013: 3) as well as being 'associated with (...) *interaction*' (Ranta & Meckelborg, 2013: 4, original emphasis); later we read 'a range of activities that (...) provide the learner with input and/or output opportunities' (Ranta & Meckelborg, 2013: 15), which sounds like 'exposure', and sure enough 'input-oriented' and 'output-oriented variables' (Ranta & Meckelborg, 2013: 16) are exclusive sets that together make 'exposure variables' (Ranta & Meckelborg, 2013: 16). These activities (input, output and exposure variables) are also referred to as 'type of contact' (Ranta & Meckelborg, 2013: 6), 'type of exposure' (Ranta & Meckelborg, 2013: 7, 22, 24), 'types of L2 use' (Ranta & Meckelborg, 2013: 15), 'language use behaviour' (Ranta & Meckelborg, 2013: 21), 'language practice' (Ranta & Meckelborg, 2013: 21) or 'kind of exposure' (Ranta & Meckelborg, 2013: 21, 22). The all-encompassing definition of 'input' taken from Lightbown and Spada (2006) differs from their own use of the term in their earlier works (Spada, 1986; Spada & Lightbown, 1989) examined above. Further, Ranta and Meckelborg's claim of the synonymousness of the terms 'exposure' and 'input' in academic literature – while also showing one to be an umbrella term – has not been entirely borne out in my examination and is certainly not the case in Spada and Lightbown.

I have shown that there is overlap and back and forth between the terms as well as a tendency in academic literature to distinguish between 'exposure' and other terms such as 'input', 'interaction', 'instruction', and so forth, and with notable variation. The trend has been mostly to diminish the common keyword 'exposure' and advance the theoretical, hypothesized and scientific-sounding – and consequently authoritative – 'input'.

Study abroad data

Recalling DeKeyser (2007), the language that students hear on study abroad might well be repetitive or difficult and their interactions might be formulaic. Nonetheless, this unabridged target language and the formulas of students' interlanguage and guest–host relations contribute to the many opportunities in study abroad for students to hear, pay attention to and use – and acquire – the target language should they be motivated to do so. In this section I draw on interview data with one so motivated Canadian student, Daria,[1] to explore how she, as a non-expert participant, discusses what it is like to *learn a language [German] in the country where it is spoken*. Including such data adds an important and often overlooked emic perspective with its own meanings. Without using the word 'exposure', or 'input', 'interaction', and so forth, she immediately identifies the situation of second language learning that such terms have been mobilized in professional literature to capture.

Excerpt 6.1

It's just a different mindset (…) when you are actually in a place where people naturally speak the language than there is going to be in a classroom, because in a classroom, particularly in a place where you aren't surrounded by the language you aren't used to that habit of actually speaking it, I think that there is more of a mindset that it's actually more like a game and you feel a bit more foolish when you are actually doing the speaking, because it would actually be so much easier in English (…) this is the first time that I've ever really been in another country speaking another language and it's a different feeling that way. (…) Here it's an entirely different context. As soon as you get off the plane everyone is speaking it and it makes you feel like you're the odd one out when you're not. (…) It's not a game. You're surrounded by people it would be rude not to try and speak the language.

In the first excerpt, Daria summons what is commonly understood as 'exposure' to the code: 'you are actually in a place where people naturally speak the language'. She also expresses the meanings of naturalistic *setting* ('actually in a place where', 'another country', 'context'), *language-in-the-world* ('surrounded by the language'), and *time in contact* ('habit of actually speaking it', 'As soon as you get off the plane') that we have encountered in the foregoing as 'exposure' and sometimes as 'input'. In keeping with popular discourse, she distinguishes this situation from the domestic language classroom, which she considers 'a game' in which one is 'foolish' not to communicate in the first language. Significantly, Daria understands these two situations as a matter of 'mindset', that is, fixed ways of thinking that predetermine a person's behaviour. In the classroom, a successful student must suspend linguistic reality and abide by a collective linguistic fantasy no matter how silly that might feel. (Is that fantasy the filtering of language made available?) In study abroad, the student must conform to a new reality for risk of becoming isolated ('odd one out') or being 'rude' to one's hosts. (Is this risky reality human vulnerability and the danger of contact?) These mutually exclusive attitudes predetermining the circumstance of language education – of *suspending reality to play the fool* versus *conforming to a new reality or duty to be polite* – provide a different take on 'exposure' and 'input' from the literature where the emphasis has been on formal explanation and informal conversation, types of language as data, and negotiation of meaning – but they are definitive for Daria.

In the second excerpt, Daria tells an anecdote that conjures both common and professional understandings of optimal SLA:

Excerpt 6.2

[My host mother's brother] told me at the very beginning, 'I'm going to try to speak entirely in German', he said this in German, 'because that's the best way to learn'. And I was saying, 'Yeah, of course.' So (...) we had an entire conversation where we spoke about such topics as, he told me the history of the place, he told me about various architectural terminology and things like that and I understood pretty much everything he was saying and it felt like such an accomplishment to be able to do that and another time when I was with the family, with miming and with making up words out of other words (...) I was able to tell the family about the fact that I had lived on a fire tower when I was younger (...) and done homeschooling, which are things that they don't teach you the terminology for in the basic levels, but with miming and making things up, making words up, I was able to communicate the concept and again it feels like such an accomplishment when you manage to get something across.

In keeping with common knowledge, Daria agrees with her non-expert native-speaker host that total immersion is 'the best way to learn' ('Yeah, of course'). The two conversations described are also in keeping with disciplinary theory. Although she most celebrates managing 'to get something across', she indicates that the conversations were thematically meaningful enough and difficult enough to push her beyond her given interlanguage ('things that they don't teach you the terminology for in the basic levels'). In doing so, she uses paralinguistic and linguistic clues ('miming', 'making up words') to make 'input' and 'output' comprehensible. Significantly, her 'contact' with the target language is not only receptive ('he told me (...) and I understood') but also interactive ('we spoke') and output-oriented ('I was able to tell', 'I was able to communicate').

This best-way-to-learn certainly requires the student to act. As seen again in the third excerpt, Daria knows that her current proficiency is insufficient for her purposes while abroad and so she draws on paralinguistic and linguistic ('miming', 'intimation') strategies and especially her imagination ('creativity') and a sense of self-responsibility ('I have to find', 'you have to make') to communicate what she wants to:

Excerpt 6.3
[Study abroad] has made my miming skills perhaps a bit better. [Laughter.] And it has perhaps opened up certain other levels of creativity that I would not otherwise have to employ. I don't like having only a limited vocabulary and only being able to communicate some things and I don't like changing my opinion because I have to which means that I have to find some other way of, perhaps intimation or something like that, to get that same message across! (...) It feels sometimes as though you have just a handful of very basic building blocks and you have to make a skyscraper or something like that! [Laughter.]

The interview with Daria provides insight into those circumstances we would generally and professionally refer to as 'exposure' and perhaps also as 'input'. While the literature has keenly manoeuvred from one to the other to more precisely describe the mechanism of optimally supplying language to learners, Daria's understanding focuses primarily on the predetermining attitudes of foolery and potential risk of the classroom and immersion. The professional tendency has been towards receptivity albeit with negotiation and attention as key, but action, imagination and agency are Daria's concern. Given her acknowledgment of the discrepancy between her 'handful of very basic building blocks' and the 'skyscraper' she wants to build, one wonders whether the disciplinary manoeuvring of 'exposure' to *undifferentiated language* and 'input' to *language made available* by interaction has obscured the *language solicited* corresponding with students' agency (and opposed to the kind of negotiation that appeases the proficient speaker standard) and desire to express their thoughts fully. Daria's 'exposure' is not just a *state of being* but, rather, *being intentionally present with language-in-the-world*.

Conclusion

Using Williams' investigative process into keywords has been productive both in raising consciousness of the various readings of experience embodied in the use of 'exposure' and in capturing the development of related slogans with which a particular social group has asserted the validity of its understanding of the same phenomenon. 'Exposure' – as in 'exposure to language' – is a keyword that has largely fallen out of favour in academic discourse on SLE. This has occurred despite or possibly because of the term's continued currency in popular discussion. The meaning and value of 'exposure' is taken for granted in folk discourse thanks to its being a key part of the saying: *The only way to learn a language is to be exposed to it in a country where it is spoken.* But scholars have taken issue with this implicitness of 'exposure' and made it their business to break down and know its components, even if this has meant diminishing the role of this vocabulary item. The word scholars prefer now is 'input'. Made salient by Krashen, this alternate term has been hypothesized and modelled; its fundamental scientific importance as precise data – for instance, in school situations in contrast to immigrant situations – makes more general 'exposure' practically indecent in language education circles. Perhaps it is because of the ungovernable popularity of 'exposure' that scholars have obscured it, whereas providing valuable 'input' has enabled them to control language acquisition knowledge and recognize their own value in that process. That is, in trying to make more precise meaning of 'exposure', they have largely abandoned the keyword for a slogan of their making. Indeed, 'input' is one of several terms – albeit the most favoured and most discussed of them all – that have been deployed to contest and take over the meaningful implicitness of 'exposure'. Yet this recent academic or sociocultural history of 'exposure' – its contestation, replacement, migration and persistence – has produced a range of contrasting and fluid meanings that provide fertile ground for ongoing explorations of what the term offers. Certainly, in adding the emic perspective of one exemplary study abroad student's experience of 'exposure', we see that 'exposure' is not so much time spent mostly passively in the presence of undifferentiated *language-in-the-world* (although it could be) but, rather, it might just be about *laying oneself bare* to the target language, being vulnerable to its dangers and taking risks, feeling obliged to communicate in and gain experience of, and confidence with, the language. 'Exposure' is a contested term, as either receptivity or a conscious activity requiring an active learner; its contestation has taken the form of the disciplinary branding process of the more governable 'input'.

Note

(1) For further details of this study, see Plews (2015).

References

Bialystok, E. (1978) A theoretical model of second language learning. *Language Learning* 28 (1), 69–83.
Cohen, A.D. (1975) Forgetting a second language. *Language Learning* 25 (1), 127–138.
DeKeyser, R.M. (2007) Study abroad as foreign language practice. In R.M. DeKeyser (ed.) *Practicing a Second Language: Perspectives from Applied Linguistics and Cognitive Psychology* (pp. 208–226). New York: Cambridge University Press.
DeKeyser, R. (2010) Monitoring processes in Spanish as a second language during a study abroad program. *Foreign Language Annals* 4, 80–92.
Doughty, C.J. (1991) Second language instruction does make a difference: Evidence from an empirical study of ESL relativization. *Studies in Second Language Acquisition* 13, 431–469.
Ferguson, C.A. (1995) Foreword. In B. Freed (ed.) *Second Language Acquisition in a Study Abroad Context* (pp. xi–xvi). Amsterdam: John Benjamins.
Gass, S.M. (1997) *Input and Interaction in Second Language Acquisition*. Mahwah, NJ: Lawrence Erlbaum.
Gass, S. and Mackey, A. (2006) Input, interaction and output: An overview. *AILA Review* 19, 3–17.
Genesee, F. (1983) Bilingual education of majority-language children: The immersion experiments in review. *Applied Psycholinguistics* 4, 1–46.
Genesee, F. (1989) Early bilingual development: One language or two? *Journal of Child Language* 16, 161–179.
Ginsberg, R.B. and Miller, L. (2000) What do they do? Activities of students during study abroad. In R.D. Lambert and E. Shohamy (eds) *Language Policy and Pedagogy: Essays in Honor of A. Ronald Walton* (pp. 237–261). Philadelphia: John Benjamins.
Google 'Exposure': definition. See https://www.google.ca/?gws_rd=ssl#q=exposure+definition (accessed 24 November 2017).
Hinkel, E. (ed.) (2005) *Handbook of Research in Second Language Teaching and Learning*. Mahwah, NJ: Lawrence Erlbaum.
Isabelli-García, C.L. (2006) Study abroad social networks, motivation, and attitudes: Implications for SLA. In M.A. DuFon and E. Churchill (eds) *Language Learners in Study Abroad Contexts* (pp. 231–258). Clevedon: Multilingual Matters.
Kinginger, C. (2009) *Language Learning and Study Abroad. A Critical Reading of Research*. Basingstoke: Palgrave Macmillan.
Krashen, S. (1982) *Principles and Practice in Second Language Acquisition*. Englewood Cliffs, NJ: Prentice-Hall.
Krashen, S. (1985) *The Input Hypothesis*. London: Longman.
Leow, R.P. (2007) Input in the L2 classroom: An attentional perspective on receptive practice. In R.M. DeKeyser (ed.) *Practicing a Second Language: Perspectives from Applied Linguistics and Cognitive Psychology* (pp. 21–50). New York: Cambridge University Press.
Lightbown, P.M. and Spada, N. (2006) *How Languages are Learned* (3rd edn). Oxford: Oxford University Press.
Loschky, L. (1994) Comprehensible input and second language acquisition: What is the relationship? *Studies in Second Language Acquisition* 16, 303–323.
Mitchell, R., Myles, F. and Marsden, E. (2013) *Second Language Learning Theories* (3rd edn). London: Routledge.
Ortega, L. (2009) *Understanding Second Language Acquisition*. New York: Routledge.
Pérez-Vidal, C. and Juan-Garau, M. (2011) The effect of context and input conditions on oral and written development: A study abroad perspective. *International Review of Applied Linguistics in Language Teaching* 49 (2), 157–185.
Pica, T. (1983) Adult acquisition of English as a second language under different conditions of exposure. *Language Learning* 33 (4), 465–497.

Pica, T. and Doughty, C. (1985) Input and interaction in the communicative language classroom: A comparison of teacher-fronted and group activities. In S.M. Gass and C.G. Madden (eds) *Input in Second Language Acquisition* (pp. 115–132). Rowley, MA: Newbury House.

Plews, J.L. (2015) Intercultural identity-alignment in second language study abroad, or the more-or-less Canadians. In R. Mitchell, N. Tracy-Ventura and K. McManus (eds) *Social Interaction, Identity and Language Learning during Residence Abroad* (pp. 281–304). EUROSLA Monographs Series 4. See http://www.eurosla.org/monographs/EM04/Plews.pdf (accessed 24 November 2017).

Ranta, L. and Meckelborg, A. (2013) How much exposure to English do international graduate students really get? Measuring language use in a naturalistic setting. *Canadian Modern Language Review* 69 (1), 1–33.

Schmidt, R. (1983) Interaction, acculturation, and the acquisition of communicative competence. In N. Wolfson and E. Judd (eds) *Sociolinguistics and Language Acquisition* (pp. 137–174). Rowley, MA: Newbury House.

Segalowitz, N. and Freed, B. (2004) Context, contact, and cognition in oral fluency acquisition: Learning Spanish in at home and study abroad contexts. *Studies in Second Language Acquisition* 26 (2), 173–199.

Segalowitz, N., Freed, B., Collentine, J., Lafford, B., Lazar, N. and Diaz-Campos, M. (2004) A comparison of Spanish second language acquisition in two different learning contexts: Study abroad and the domestic classroom. *Frontiers* 10, 1–18.

Spada, N. (1986) The interaction between type of contact and type of instruction: Some effects of the L2 proficiency of adult learners. *Studies in Second Language Acquisition* 8 (2), 181–200.

Spada, N. and Lightbown, P.M. (1989) Intensive ESL programmes in Quebec primary schools. *TESL Canada Journal* 7, 11–32.

Swain, M. (1985) Communicative competence: Some roles of comprehensible input and comprehensible output in its development. In S.M. Gass and C.G. Madden (eds) *Input in Second Language Acquisition* (pp. 235–253). Rowley, MA: Newbury House.

VanPatten, B. (2002) Processing instruction: An update. *Language Learning* 52, 755–803.

Wilkinson, S. (1998) Study abroad from the participants' perspective: A challenge to common beliefs. *Foreign Language Annals* 31 (1), 23–39.

Williams, R. (1985) *Keywords: A Vocabulary of Culture and Society* (revised edn). New York: Oxford University Press.

7 What on Earth is 'Language Commodification'?[1]

David Block

In recent years the term 'commodification' has entered the sociolinguistic lexicon, used not only with reference to changing orientations to (or epistemologies of) language in society, but also with reference to changing ontologies of language, that is, how language exists and occurs in the real world. Those who use the term usually draw on a baseline understanding that commodification is a process by and through which objects that were previously unsellable become sellable. In addition, they see it as a fairly recent phenomenon: the transformation of language and identity over the past 40 years in many parts of the world, which has been mediated and shaped by neoliberal economic policies and practices during the same time period. But what is 'commodification' and what does it mean to say that a language has become 'commodified'? In the literature on language commodification, Marx's views on the commodity form would seem to be a logical base, but are the ways in which commodification is used by many sociolinguists actually consistent with Marxist thought? Do they need to be? What are some of the theoretical bases that actually do support the validity of language commodification in a convincing way? And finally, is the use of 'language commodification' or 'linguistic commodification' or the 'commodification of language' (all three forms are used seemingly interchangeably) usually accompanied by conceptual clarification, or is it in danger of becoming a popular, often-used and taken-for-granted buzzword which is, in general, undertheorized and therefore in danger of becoming an empty slogan? In this chapter, my aim is to engage in a thinking process around these and other questions about language commodification and to suggest, at the end of this process, some ways forward.

Introduction

In recent years the term 'commodification' has entered the sociolinguistic lexicon, used not only with reference to changing orientations to (or epistemologies of) language in society, but also with reference to changing ontologies of language, that is, how language exists as a real-world phenomenon.[2] Thus, there have been edited collections with commodification at their center (Duchêne & Heller, 2013; Duchêne *et al.*, 2014; Flubacher & Del Percio, 2017; Pietikainen & Kelly-Holmes, 2013; Rubdy & Tan, 2008), to say nothing of survey pieces (Heller, 2003, 2010a, 2010b; Urciuoli & LaDousa, 2013), special issues in journals (e.g. Heller *et al.*, 2014) and panels and talks at sociolinguistics conferences. Those who use the term usually draw on a baseline understanding that commodification is a process by and through which objects that were previously unsellable become sellable, although as we shall see as this paper unfolds there is far more to it than just this. It has been used in reference to 'language' in an attempt to capture what Monica Heller (2002, 2003, 2010a, 2010b) and others see as a fairly recent phenomenon: the transformation of language and identity over the past 40 years in many parts of the world, which has been mediated and shaped by what Heller and Duchêne (2013: 9) term the 'tertiarization' of the economy[3] and what others see more generally as the enactment of neoliberal economic policies and practices during the same time period.

But what is 'commodification', and what does it mean to say that a language has become 'commodified'? In the literature on language commodification, Marx's views on the commodity form would seem to be a logical base, but are the ways in which commodification is used by many sociolinguists actually consistent with Marxist thought? Do they need to be? What are some of the theoretical bases which support the validity of language commodification in a convincing way? And finally, is the use of 'language commodification' or 'linguistic commodification' or the 'commodification of language' (all three forms are used seemingly interchangeably) usually accompanied by conceptual clarification, or are we in the realm of 'sloganization'? In other words, has 'language commodification' moved from being based on solid theoretical ground in its beginnings to being a popular, often-used and taken-for-granted buzzword which is, in general, undertheorized and therefore in danger of becoming an empty slogan?

In this chapter, I will not attempt to provide answers to these questions by singling out for criticism specific uses of commodification with reference to language, leaving such an exercise to the reader. Instead, I propose to engage in a more positive way with this topic around the previous questions, first going back to the basics of Marxist thought before considering notions such as the materiality of language, which may be seen as foundational to what Heller and others understand language commodification to be about. My aim, therefore, is to engage in a thinking process around the notion of language commodification and to propose, at the end of this process, some ways forward. In the remainder of this chapter, language commodification, in acronym form as LC, will be used to cover a range of similar terms such as 'commodification of language' and 'linguistic commodification' which, as far as I can tell, are all used with the same semantic intention.

Commodification: A Marxist Angle

A few years back, in an article focusing on the branding of English (more on this below), I wrote that LC was about a move 'from the valuing of a particular language for its basic communicative function and more emotive associations – national identity, cultural identity, the authentic spirit of a people, and so on – to valuing it for what it means in the globalized, deregulated, hyper-competitive, postindustrial "new work order" in which we now live ...' (Block, 2010: 294). Elsewhere, Park and Wee (2012) have written in similar terms about 'a transformation in the relationship between language and identity', contrasting a past, in which 'language is supposed to be a reflection or marker of one's social identity and therefore not something subject to exchange' with a present in which 'language (...) [has lost] that association' (Park & Wee, 2012: 125). They suggest that the latter position 'opens up the possibility of treating language as an economic resource to be cultivated for material profit, or acquired as a skill to be offered on the market' (Park & Wee, 2012: 125). These two definitions draw directly on the work of Monica Heller over the past 15 years (e.g. Heller, 2002, 2003, 2010a, 2010b), and it is Heller *et al.* (2014) who provide the following very helpful definition of 'commodification' as a base for their discussion of LC in the tourist industry in Catalonia, Switzerland and Francophone Canada:

> 'Commodification' is the expression we use to describe how a specific object or process is rendered available for conventional exchange in the market. Although the concept harks back to Marx's idea that capitalism was founded on the notion of turning work into a commodity, the word 'commodification' itself is recent, dating from the mid-1970s. Thus, although capitalism is centrally about producing and distributing commodities, and has historically and characteristically expanded the scope of what can be turned into one, the concept as a nominalized process does not seem to appear until the process affects areas of life hitherto treated as 'public' goods and not as profit-making ventures. (Heller *et al.*, 2014: 545–546)

In explanations of this type, we see how Heller and others (including Park & Wee and this author) have written with what I would call a degree of poetic licence, using LC to refer to an epochal shift in many societies in the world with regard to the value of languages – the move from primarily use value to exchange value in addition to use value. The notions of use value and exchange value are taken from Marxist theory, although in publications focusing on LC there is generally no in-depth engagement with Marx's lengthy treatments of the commodity form, and often there is no mention of Marx at all. The Heller *et al.* definition above, as well as another found in Duchêne and Heller (2012) are something of an exception, as they actually cite Marx, albeit only in passing. Thus, Duchêne and Heller (2012) state that '[c]ommodities are in fact things that have value' before adding that 'Marx pinpoints the fact that, in the end, the structure of work is determined by the market and by the interplay between useful and exchangeable products, both of which are linked to time, availability of labor and the consumption of goods' (Duchêne & Heller, 2012: 371). It should be noted that Duchêne and Heller do acknowledge that what they have written constitutes a '(too) short digression on the Marxist view of commodities' (Duchêne & Heller, 2012: 371).

However, given the Marxist overtones of these and other uses of LC, I am left to ask myself about how, in very general political economy terms, LC as a process may be conceptualized as a shift from language as use value to language as exchange value. It might be useful at this point to go back to the originator of the use value/exchange value distinction in political economy, which means going back, not to Marx, but to Adam Smith. In Book 1 of his classic political economy opus, the seldom-read but often-cited *The Wealth of Nations*, Smith wrote that '[t]he word value, it is to be observed, has two different meanings, and sometimes expresses the utility of some particular object, and sometimes the power of purchasing other goods which the possession of that object conveys. The one may be called "value in use"; the other, "value in exchange"' (Smith, 2012 [1776]: 32). A century later, Marx elaborated considerably on Smith's baseline definition of value with reference to 'commodities', not 'objects', as follows:

> As a use-value, every commodity owes its usefulness to itself. Wheat, e.g., serves as an article of food. A machine saves labor to a certain extent. This function of a commodity by virtue of which it serves only as use-value, as an article of consumption, may be called its service, the service which it renders as use value. But as an exchange value, a commodity is always regarded as a result; the question in this case is not as to the service which it renders, but as to the service which it has been rendered in its production. Thus, the exchange value of a machine is determined not by the quantity of labor-time which it saves, but by the quantity of labor-time which has been expended on its own production and which is, therefore, required to produce a new machine of the same kind. (Marx, 1904 [1859]: 34–35)

The mention of labor and production here is neither trivial nor banal, as it is essential to Marx's intention to avoid the 'vulgar economics' that he so often attributed to those he critiqued, moving beyond the surface level of commodity relations to a deeper and broader understanding of how capitalism works in practice, from production to distribution, to exchange, to consumption. As Marx explains,

> [p]roduction creates the objects which correspond to the given needs; distribution divides them up according to social laws; exchange further parcels out the already divided shares in accord with individual needs; and finally, in consumption, the product steps outside this social movement and becomes a direct object and servant of individual need, and satisfies it in being consumed. (Marx, 1973 [1858]: 89)

To understand capitalism is to understand how these four processes interrelate.

In Marx's view, commodities are embedded in this four-part process, but it is the commodity as a product of human labor, initially and at the most basic level with value for the uses that can be made of it, which is foundational to his analysis. This use value is reflected in how, for example, treated animal skins can be used to shelter the human body from the elements, a knife can be used to cut food, a pen can be used to write, and so on. All such objects mediate the satisfaction of basic biological and ideational needs and wants. From commodity production for such basic qualitative value, there is a shift as markets (and market-based economies) arise as sites in which individuals can acquire what they need or want, but which they cannot or simply do not produce themselves. In markets, commodities have exchange value, which means that they can be exchanged for other commodities as would be the case in a barter economy. Crucially, with the beginnings of capitalist economies came money-based exchange and the consequent separation between the social relationship of the individual in the production of a commodity and the act of its exchange. The acquirer of a commodity only comes into contact with the finished product but not the socially necessary labor time expended by the person who produced it, where socially necessary labor time refers to 'the labour-time required to produce any use-value under the condition of production normal for a given society and with the average degree of skill and intensity of labour prevalent in that society' (Marx, 1990 [1867]: 129). This is the beginning of a disconnection between the social relationship of production processes and end-products. In this progression, the alienation of labor occurs, as the production of commodities escapes the control of the laborers/producers.

The alienation of labor, that is, the ceding of labor to those who control the means of production, begins in production processes, in which the labor expended by workers is 'external' to them, 'not voluntary but coerced (...) [and] *forced*', separated from their 'essential being'. Workers cannot and do not 'affirm' themselves in such circumstances; indeed, they come to 'deny' their true selves. They feel unhappy (and not 'content'), as they cannot develop themselves for themselves physically or mentally, and the production process is said, in somewhat dramatic terms, to 'mortif[y the] body and ruin (...) [the] mind'. The labor provided by the worker is therefore 'not the satisfaction of a need; it is merely a *means* to satisfy needs external to it' (Marx, 1988 [1844]: 74; emphasis in the original). These and other kinds of social relations of production that Marx wrote about, and the exploitation and alienation endemic to capitalism, become hidden as the market only shows the finished product to the person acquiring them. And here we have Marx's references to fetishization as the way in which labor, as a social process integral to social relations, is concealed when commodities are exchanged for money in a market: 'they do not appear as direct social relations between persons in their work, but rather as material relations between persons and social relations between things' (Marx, 1990 [1867]: 165). As Marnie Holborow (personal communication) notes, it is important to highlight the role of money in concealing the social relations embodied in labor as most LC advocates tend to refer to generally vague notions of value rather than money.

Marx constructed his detailed analysis of various aspects of capitalism, writing with and against his predecessors in political economy, Smith and Ricardo being the most prominent. Smith, as observed above, developed the notion of commodities embedded in the market (the space in which and through which products – or commodities – are bought and sold), where they have exchange value. The observation of this simple phenomenon led to speculations about supply and demand, and eventually the idea that commodities had 'natural' value, which was the price at which they sold when supply and demand were in equilibrium. The need to pay wages (to workers), profit (to capitalists as the organizers of production) and rent (to the owners of land rented), what in modern terms might be understood as 'overheads', were all foundational to Smith's understanding of commodities and their market value.

Language Commodification

Bearing in mind the discussion thus far, however, and in particular Marx's definition of commodity, can we talk of the commodification of English, or any other language, with authority? If we accept the reasoning of Heller and others, we are framing language in general, and English in particular, as a means of communication in an ever-increasing number of political, economic, social, cultural and geographical spaces in a constant state of evolution and change, *and* as an objective skill, acquired and possessed, that affords status, recognition legitimacy, and ultimately material remuneration, to those who possess it. It can be traded in social spaces as well as employment markets, where it is required for an increasing number of jobs. However, if we stick to a narrowly Marxist interpretation of what is and what is not a commodity, serious questions arise.

For example, if we move from use value to exchange value, we see, following Marx, that 'as an exchange value, a commodity is always regarded as a result' (Marx, 1904 [1859]: 34) with a value commensurate with the cost of its production. What then is the cost of production of language as commodity? This is a difficult question to answer given the way that language is so intermeshed with other actions which are constitutive of commodified labor. A simple example makes this clear. Let us suppose that as part of her job as an academic, Silvia teaches four hours a week. These four hours of work require Silvia to use language, both alone in lecturing mode (including PowerPoint presentations) and in interactions with students. In addition, there is preparation time which goes into her teaching, which will involve a range of activities, but speaking perhaps is not one of them – reading, thinking and organizing, all mediated by language to be sure, being more likely candidates. Indeed, embedded in teaching are a lot of more subtle activities, such as physical being and bearing for the length of a seminar or even more abstract tasks such as representing the university for which she works or the ongoing management of time, space and collective behavior. These and other components of Silvia's labor are arguably not in the realm of what Josiane Boutet (2001, 2012) has called 'the language part of work (*la part langagière du travail*) labour', that is, 'the implementation of the linguistic capacities needed to do a job' (Boutet, 2012: 208).

It should be noted, however, that the favored site for researchers focusing on 'the language part of work' is not the more privileged end of the so-called 'services economy' which Silvia occupies, but contexts such as call centers. In the latter, workers are subjected to invigilated, disciplined work regimes that have more in common with regimented factories devoted to the manufacture of hard goods (automobiles, home appliances, computers) than the high-flying 'new economy', service-based jobs touted as future employment for 21st century university graduates by governments, the media and educational institutions alike (Holborow, 2015). Indeed, as has been noted by Boutet, Heller and others, call center work constitutes a new form of Taylorism based on the factory organization procedures for mass production outlined by Frederick Winslow Taylor in the early part of the 20th century (Taylor, 1998 [1911]). Taylorism, it should be noted, is an approach to labor management whereby every action forming part of a task is broken down into a series of segments (sometimes lasting just a fraction of a second), the aim being to control time and movement with a view to increasing efficiency and predictability in the workplace.

In the context of the call center, and indeed in other contexts that LC researchers focus on (e.g. the tourist industry), one question that arises is if the valuing of language and communication skills as central to work is actually a novel phenomenon. Heller acknowledges that language and communication skills have always existed as integral parts of the labor power of workers, where the latter is understood, following Marx, to be 'the aggregate of those mental and physical capabilities existing in the physical form, the living personality, of a human being, capabilities which he sets in motion whenever he produces a use-value of any kind' (Marx, 1990 [1867]: 270). However, she argues that 'in much contemporary work, language is not only an integral, if not the only, part of the work *process*; it is also frequently the work *product*' (Heller, 2010a: 350; emphasis in the original). Here, she makes reference to the rise in importance of what she calls the 'language industries', which include advertising, translation and language teaching, in which the product of labor may be considered clearly linguistic.

However, bearing in mind the example of Silvia's tasks outlined above, as well as relevant discussions by Marnie Holborow (2015) and Kevin

McGill (2013), we still may wonder about the extent to which the language part of work can indeed be separated from other parts of work which employees must carry out on a moment-to-moment basis and then be considered commodified. In this sense, Holborow (2015) argues that

> language and IT and communication skills are no different to dexterity and literacy in the past in that they are both vital parts of the work process (…) [and] language as part of human capabilities in the work potential, even if its applications have become vastly more sophisticated, has always been part of labour power within the productive process and within service industries. (Holborow, 2015: 21)

Following this line of reasoning, we see how all kinds of non-linguistic tasks are intertwined with linguistic-based ones, as call center workers, for example, proceed through their daily routines. In doing so, they are constantly pressing keyboard keys in an efficient and controlled manner to keep their computer screens updated or to connect and disconnect lines of communication with clients. Or they must constantly organize their work space, situating their keyboard, any hard documents and other objects in such a way that they do not impede the efficient and uninterrupted operation of their work. In other words, while the call center employees are hired to talk on the phone for hours on end, they must possess other qualities and skills in order to do the job. As McGill (2013) explains,

> insofar as the commodification of call center work is achieved via the commodification of the general abilities, effort and attention of the person doing the work, rather than in terms of the commodification of any specific linguistic or communicational competence, it remains worthwhile to focus on the broader nature of the alienation involved, rather than solely on its entanglement with language use. (McGill, 2013: 200)

Indeed, although they are not always spelled out in a clear and explicit manner, the chief concerns for those writing about LC in call center contexts seem to be: (1) alienation, whereby, paraphrasing Marx (1904 [1859]), workers feel unhappy, physically 'mortified' and mentally 'ruined' as a result of the rigid work regimes to which they are subjected; and (2) exploitation, or the making of surplus value or profit by the capitalist from the labor power of employees, after overheads (including rent and interest payments), taxes and depreciation of the means of production have been factored in. But alienation and exploitation are not new, nor are they qualitatively different in early 20th-century factories and 21st-century call centers. Bearing this in mind, Holborow explains a basic truth about capitalism which we ignore at our peril:

> human skills in capitalist relations of production, in the concrete, contribute towards producing surplus value, or extra value (in the system as whole) over and above what the employee has been paid in wages. This point is important because casual reference is made to post-industrial

work as if the use of different skills and networked work patterns, or 'communication power' (Castells, 2009; Hardt & Negri, 2000), have altered social relations. But extraction of surplus value still takes place even if it is through the exploitation of communication skills, multilingualism or IT skills within an overall system of production. (Holborow, 2015: 21)

If we take on board this argument, we might well wonder if LC researchers are perhaps guilty of not seeing the forest for the trees, and that it might be better to take a more general approach to the exploitation of labor power and abandon the position that the ability to communicate – which is, after all, just one of many skills required in employment today – is truly the heart of the matter.

In addition, there is the need to consider the possibility that what many are thinking about, researching and discussing is not so much LC as it is *language as skill*. Bonnie Urciuoli (2008) goes some way in this direction, even if she does invoke LC as a key construct in her discussions of the interrelationships between language and work in 21st century societies. She provides a very convincing account of the move from commodity-based in the material to commodity-based in the abstract, but mainly because she subsumes language under skills and then argues that there has been a commodification of the latter. Urciuoli charts the move in job markets in recent years from 'hard skills' to 'soft skills', the former being 'the technical requirements of the job' and the latter 'the cluster of personality traits, social graces, facility with language, personal habits, friendliness, and optimism that mark each of us to varying degrees' (Menochelli, 2006, n.p., cited in Urciuoli, 2008: 215). She discusses the way in which one item in the soft skills cluster, 'facility with language' (i.e. knowing how to communicate) has come to be valued as something that can be broken down into component parts and then taught and measured (see Cameron, 2000).

Still, framing different types of communication as skills sets, such as 'effective public speaking', allows for the itemization of component parts, which can be assembled so that there is a product, the well-delivered speech (more on this below). As the move to soft skills has become all pervasive, there is, therefore, room for adapting Marx's thinking about labor processes and products to the present, a process made easy given Marx's references to the evolution of the nature of employment in capitalist societies.[4] As Urciuoli argues, '[i]n skills discourses, social acts are cast in a transactional or entrepreneurial frame and actors' segmented selves are recast as assemblages of productive elements, as bundles of skills' (Urciuoli, 2008: 224). The bundles of skills, in turn, act as 'commodities insofar as they are aspects of productive labor with market value: as aspects of self that enhance theory possessors' worth on the labor market and as products sold by their inculcators, which command hefty fees for some hours or days of skills workshops' (Urciuoli, 2008: 224). But a bundle of skills is not the same as a vague notion of language as individual skill separable from the bundle, and Urciuoli's portrayal of what is going on in contemporary societies is not inconsistent with Marx's notion of commodified labor.

Elsewhere, Holborow elaborates another line of critique of LC, arguing that those who do focus only on the language part of work often seem to be positioning workers as having been completely dominated by their Taylorized work regimes, and therefore their labor is – irremediably – alienated from them and they are dehumanized by the exploitation of their labor power. As Burawoy (1979) notes in his classic ethnography of an engine manufacturing factory in the American Midwest, even in the most routine work environments, workers find ways to subvert norms and carve out niches of control over production not envisaged by the designers of both the premises and processes in which they toil. In this spirit, Holborow wonders if researchers are perhaps giving too much away to neoliberal thinking, noting how workers do not generally just roll over and accept their condition, but offer resistance, at different levels and with greater or lesser intensity, to the Taylorized work regimes to which they are subjected. And in doing so, they act in such a way that their language is not wrested completely from their sense of self and authenticity. Running parallel to this argument is Marx's suggestion that workers '*manage* (...) *both to alienate* (...) [their] labour-power and to avoid renouncing (...) [their] rights to ownership over it' (Marx, 1990 [1867]: 271). This does not take away from the basic fact that capitalism is about the exploitation of workers by capitalists who own and control the means of production. But it does mean that we need to be careful about creating totalizing images of the realities of Taylorized labor in contexts such as call centers.[5]

The notions of alienation and exploitation are relevant to an additional aspect of commodification, namely that it 'presumes the existence of property rights over processes, things, and social relations, that a price can be put on them, and that they can be traded subject to legal contract. The market is assumed to work as an appropriate guide – an ethic – for all human action' (Harvey, 2005: 165). And this brings us to a major question which Holborow (2015) develops in detail, namely that any work that extends the semantic space of commodification as a construct is, in effect, based on an acceptance of the market metaphor for all. For we cannot argue that language, for example, has been commodified if we do not accept the dominance of the market as an organizer of all activity. Perhaps this is, as stated above, a matter of giving too much away, a priori, to the market metaphor in any discussion of the commodification of language or culture or any number of other social and psychological phenomena. The appearance of the market or the invocation of the market in interpretation as a heuristic does not equal the ontological reality of the market, in fact.

But further to this and as a way of bringing this section of the paper to a close, it is worth focusing on the processual element in LC, as indicated by the -cation suffix. Commodification is a process which occurs in the course of production, distribution, exchange and consumption (Marx, 1973 [1858]), and is not something that one can do to an object or more abstract entity via individual or collective volition. In other words, one cannot simply declare abstractions (e.g. a thought), phenomena (e.g. communication) or events (e.g. a festival) to be commodities as the latter are constructed and constituted as such in the overall and interrelated social relations emergent in production, distribution, exchange and consumption.

Language in Language Commodification: Language as Material Product

Thus far, I have discussed LC in more social terms around production processes in particular. But what of the 'language' in LC? That is, what does the language side of LC actually refer to? In the aforementioned 'language industries', it is, in some cases, easy enough to imagine what a linguistic product might be: for example, in translation work, a written text is produced. However, in language teaching, just to cite another language industry, what is the linguistic product of a lesson taught? All of the words uttered by both teacher and students in the course of the lesson? An aspect of language learned (bearing in mind, of course, how difficult it is to establish that the learning of a specific aspect of language has taken place at a specific moment in time)? Elsewhere, in discussions of English as an international language, LC seems to mean that the command of English (in its entirety, one assumes, although it is not clear what this might mean) is seen as a sellable skill. But in such a case, can we say that the English language – everything that we understand 'the English language' to represent – has been commodified? Finally, in contexts ranging from call centers to reception desks in hotels, Boutet's (2012) notion of 'the language part of labour' deserves some consideration. Is the 'language' that is commodified a matter of instances of language use? For example, is it about participation in a spontaneous conversation in which the utterances produced are unique and not likely ever to be replicated in any other conversation occurring in the same language? Or is it about phrases repeated in a formulaic manner again and again, such as 'have a nice day'?

Another dimension or angle on language in LC is the extent to which it has 'materialness'. In a very timely and useful article, Shankar and Cavanaugh (2012) discuss language and materiality, arguing that the two converge as opposed to diverge (the divergence thesis said to be the default assumption for far too long) and they propose a new area of inquiry in linguistic anthropology – 'language materiality'. Their argument is constructed carefully on the back of a great deal of research in recent years on LC and their starting point is the very thesis that they aim to overturn, that is, how '[s]ince at least Herder and Marx, the state or quality of being material, physical, or object-like is claimed in Western thought to be different from that of the ideational realm; objects, things, and bodies are opposed to ideas' (Shankar & Cavanaugh, 2012: 356). The authors perhaps have in mind Marx and Engels's argument that rather than 'set[ting] out from what men say, imagine, conceive, (...) or from men as narrated, thought of, imagined, conceived, in order to arrive at men in the flesh (...) [, w]e set out from real, active men, and on the basis of their real life-process we demonstrate the development of the ideological reflexes and echoes of this life-process' (Marx & Engels, 1998 [1846]: 42). Here, we have, if anything, a denial of the notion that language can be material: it can be part of 'the ideological reflexes and echoes of th[e] life-process' or, as Marx and Engels go on to argue, 'phantoms formed in the human brain' (Marx & Engels, 1998 [1846]: 42), but it is not comparable with the material (and real) life processes of labor. Or, perhaps more accurately, we see Marx and Engels (and this is a strand running through Marx's work over time) highlighting the economic base, foundational and fundamental to the development of superstructural phenomena, which include social structures such as institutions and sociocultural phenomena such as language. In the case of institutions, there is ample space to argue for materiality in that institutions combine actual physical objects and locations with activities constitutive of their putative existence, as well as the multimodal discursive constructions of both. In the case of sociocultural phenomena, and in particular language, materiality is difficult to argue for if we follow Marx and Engels. This is because they make a distinction between real life as material in contrast with the realm of 'morality, religion, metaphysics, all the rest of ideology and their corresponding forms of consciousness' (Marx & Engels, 1998 [1846]: 42) – and here we can include language – as constituting another level of existence, distinguishable from the real or material. And while they accept that language has always accompanied these 'real life processes' and is ubiquitous in any account of the history of human existence, writing that that '[l]anguage is as old as consciousness, language is practical consciousness that exists also for other men, and for that reason alone it really exists for me personally as well' (Marx & Engels, 1998 [1846]: 49), they add that 'language, like consciousness, only arises from the need, the necessity, of intercourse with other men' (Marx & Engels, 1998 [1846]: 49), that is, goings on in the real (material) world.[6]

In the face of such argumentation, Shankar and Cavanaugh must look elsewhere in political economy for inspiration and support for their call for 'language materiality'. Early on, they cite David Harvey as a kindred spirit, stating:

> If, as Harvey (2005: 11) asserts, 'the neoliberal project is to disembed capital from [state regulation and ownership] constraints,' then the role of language in national and global capitalist agendas must be considered for how linguistic forms are involved in such deregulation and its effects. (Shankar & Cavanaugh, 2012: 357)

As someone long associated with research on language in society issues, I might agree with Shankar and Cavanaugh's assertion here. However, it in no way follows from Harvey's cited words nor indeed from anything written in his 2005 introduction to neoliberalism. So, yes, Harvey writes about the disembedding of capitalism from constraints, but he has precious little to say about language in neoliberalism.

But returning to Shankar and Cavanaugh's main argument, that is, that there is something of interest and indeed something real in the notion of 'language materiality', I would say that the authors do a good job of bringing together what they themselves term 'various, and as yet disparate, works' (Shankar & Cavanaugh, 2012: 356). They revisit Peirce's (1955) work on semiotics, following Agha (2011), Kockelman (2006) and others who have explored how the 'material and verbal dimensions of signification' (Shankar & Cavanaugh, 2012: 357) may be connected, all of this on the way to an understanding of how 'instances of cosignification can be considered together to reveal processes of local meaning making, value formation, and the construction and maintenance of social hierarchy' (Shankar & Cavanaugh, 2012: 359). They add to their layered argument, work on embodiment, and here we move to Bourdieu's notion that '[l]anguage is body technique, and specifically linguistic, especially phonetic, competence is a dimension of bodily hexis in which one's whole relation to the social world, and one's whole socially informed relation to the world, are expressed' (Bourdieu, 1991: 86). In this case the body is posited as material and since language, and indeed all semiotic activity, is so corporally ingrained, then language too may be seen as material.

Another way in which language may be seen as material is in the processes through which it is objectified, which is what happens when 'non objects are given object-like qualities, involving the externalization and materialization of meaning and value' (Shankar & Cavanaugh, 2012: 355). Elsewhere, Silverstein (1996: 290–291) has suggested that in some contexts 'language acquires "thinginess" such that the properties language takes on are continuous with those of other objects in the culture'. The 'thinginess' that Silverstein refers to is the way in which in political, media and education circles in the United States the 'standard' language is objectified and packaged in static form as an incontestable reality which can be talked about, learned, exchanged, and so on. But further to this is the infinity of language samples out there in the world, captured electronically by researchers and others, which can be objectified. For example, Shankar and Cavanaugh (2012) write about recordings of language samples as a materialization of language or the ways in which computer technologies convert what is, in essence, talk, into words on a screen which can be moved about as so many other objects can be moved about. And, of course, via an ever more sophisticated media which draws on ever-evolving technologies, there is much scope for chunks of language, produced orally for example, to become objectified and fixed and circulated (e.g. slogans in advertising). There are also icons interrelated with words and other semiotic forms, which can equally well be packaged for present and future consumption.

Shankar and Cavanaugh make an interesting point about a fundamental difference between objectification and commodification. Both are about the transformation of the ontological status of language, from an immaterial or abstract realm of reality to a material one, but crucially, '[w]hereas all commodified language is objectified, the reverse may not be true (...) [and] objectified language need not circulate beyond its original context, but commodified language is always ready to move beyond local communities and societies into national and global contexts' (Shankar & Cavanaugh, 2012: 362). It is therefore possible to accept that a language has been objectified or 'thingified', as is clearly the case when workers in call center are provided with scripts to follow when speaking on the phone; it is quite another to add that, *ipso facto*, this objectification means commodification. The latter process is, as I argued in the previous section, embedded in the complex workings of capitalism, and in this sense the claim that 'a language is ready to move beyond local communities and societies into national and global contexts' hardly seems sufficient support for saying that it has been commodified (and this, even if one accepts the anthropomorphism of language at work here). I would suggest therefore that the language materialization argument works and is supported convincingly by the work of scholars such as Shankar and Cavanaugh, Agha (2011) and Kockelman (2006), while the further argument in favour of LC is tenuous. Indeed, Agha (2011), despite appearances, seems to lean in this direction when he writes:

> We pay lawyers, accountants, and tax consultants for discursive services. (...) Similarly, doctors, tour guides, computer programmers, stockbrokers, NGO workers, those who canvass door to door, telemarketers, pollsters, sales personnel. (...) In all of these cases, various features of discourse (lexemes, prosody, adjacency pairs, turn-taking mechanisms, topic schedules, idioms, formulaic speech, etc.) are given a highly delimited and differentiated form (officially linked to cognitive and interpersonal task demands). And these differentiated forms are formulated as enregistered styles designed to be animated by those whose activities constitute the transaction. (Agha, 2011: 44)

Here, Agha examines discursive practices around differentiable and differentiated features of language (one prosody as opposed to another, one set of lexical features as opposed to another, etc.) and how the resultant ways of speaking come to be treated as semi-stable bundles of features which serve the reproduction of social structures and orders in the form of enregisterment. The latter is elsewhere defined as 'processes whereby distinct forms of speech come to be socially recognized (or enregistered) as indexical of speaker attributes by a population of language users' (Agha, 2005: 38). All of this is very different from saying that language is commodified, unless we mean bundles of features of language converted into some notion of skill separable from other actions constituting labor power. Agha goes on to explain how via 'ventriloquation' – the processes through which repeated semiotic performances congeal into genres which, in turn, can be drawn in the present – such bundles of features 'can be used by job-seekers to redescribe themselves in resumes and job interviews as a bundle of skills, and thus to reformulate themselves as quantifiable units of human capital' (Agha, 2011: 45).

Agha thus moves his discussion in the direction of recent critiques of neoliberal policies and practices, in particular how changes in the economy have led to changes in how individuals as workers and as citizens in general are conceptualized (Boltanski & Chiapello, 2006; Brown, 2005; Foucault, 2008 [1978–1979]). And when he refers to job-seekers 'redescribing' and 'reformulating' themselves, I am reminded of recent work on branding, in particular popularized work by style gurus such as Tom Peters (e.g. 2008), who writes about 'brand you', that is, the networked individual who in chameleonic fashion adapts constantly to his/her environment, always making sure that those who matter – employers, fellow workers and where appropriate (e.g. with celebrities) – register and value his/her achievements (Gray, 2012). In this sense, the ventriloquation that Agha discusses is not about LC; rather, it is about 'thingified' chunks of language implemented in key ways at key junctures in communicative events to create, via enregisterment processes, the effect of a particular type of person as a valued product. The language involved, therefore, is not 'commodified'; it is merely part of a more general act of self-presentation and branding.

Conclusion

In this chapter, I have attempted to engage critically with LC, first by problematizing it through a Marxist gaze – along the way discussing aspects of production, the commodity form, value, alienation and exploitation – and secondly by discussing recent work on language as a material reality. My conclusion is that LC does not hold up well as a construct in Marxist terms but that there is something of value in discussions of the objectification or 'thingification' of language which, as Shankar and Cavanaugh note, can occur without commodification taking place as well.

In the introduction to this chapter, I asked if the ways in which commodification is used by sociolinguists needed to be consistent with Marxist thought. Having read a fairly sizable sample of publications in which LC figures prominently, I have come to the conclusion that many researchers are using 'commodity' not in a Marxist sense, but in the prosaic sense of 'something that can be bought and sold', adding that that something was previously treated as not sellable and was not actually sold. In this case, 'commodification' is simply the process of something not previously sellable becoming sellable. But is this really all right? Is it enough? I think that it is neither, especially when so many LC researchers do not even attempt to define LC, treating it as something of a 'you know what I mean' issue.

In recent years, it has become common (or even fashionable) for sociolinguists to frame their work as 'interdisciplinary', where the latter term seems to mean that the sociolinguist in question has done reading in social theory, sociology, anthropology, geography, and other social science disciplines. This kind of disciplinary crossing is especially necessary in a field like sociolinguistics, which has moved from its variationist roots (and a fairly clearly defined ambit of activity) to the present in which it is many things to many people (one need only attend the biannual Sociolinguistics Symposium to come to this conclusion). Thus, publications appearing under the banner of 'sociolinguistics' are about bi/multilingualism, language policy, (critical) discourse studies, literacies, language and identity and many other relatively well-established areas of research, all of which are interdisciplinary in their own right. In the midst of all of this interdisciplinarity and overlapping fields of inquiry, political economy has come onto the scene as a possible source area to draw on (see Block, 2014, 2017, 2018 for a discussion). This has occurred perhaps because an increasing number of scholars and researchers, both alarmed and intrigued by the economic crisis of 2008, are realizing that they need a new toolkit if they are going to take on issues such as economic inequality and class conflict from a sociolinguistic perspective.

But working in an interdisciplinary way, and specifically drawing on political economy for inspiration, is not a simple affair. It requires reading beyond the seemingly obligatory source, David Harvey's (2005) *A Brief History of Neoliberalism* and a handful of sociolinguistics publications which are positioned as 'political economy' (e.g. Block *et al.*, 2012; Duchêne & Heller, 2013; Duchêne *et al.*, 2014; Flubacher & Del Percio, 2017; Park & Wee, 2012). It requires immersion in the multitude of publications coming out every day analyzing the current economic crisis. And, I would add that it requires some reading of older sources, from Smith to Ricardo to Mill to Marx, and onwards to the foundational theoretical work sustaining dominant economic developments and trends, such as neoliberalism: von Mises, Hayek, Rand, Friedman, Becker, and others. In short, it is my belief that if more sociolinguists immersed themselves more deeply in political economy, we could prevent LC from becoming little more than empty catch-all for phenomena which might be conceptualized in different ways. For example, instead of discussing LC we might more fruitfully discuss branding and/or skilling.

All of the discussion thus far has revolved around LC as a concept or construct. But what of the theme of this volume, sloganization? More specifically, has LC actually *become* a slogan? Has it actually *been* sloganized? How one answers these questions depends on how one defines the term 'slogan' and how one understands 'sloganization' as a process. In the introduction to this volume, the editors link their thinking about sloganization to David Little's call for rigor in research on learner autonomy in second/foreign language education some 25 years ago. Little (1994: 430) argued that 'any technical term that gains currency as a buzzword is in danger of losing its original, perhaps rather precisely grounded, meaning and becoming an empty slogan'. Some years later, Barbara Schmenk advanced on Little's idea, using the term 'sloganization' in her book on learner autonomy (Schmenk, 2008). Elsewhere in this volume, Aneta Pavlenko is more concerned with how buzzwords become slogans. She outlines six 'strategies' for branding a new product, which she sees as integral to the sloganization process. First, there is the *'adoption of a slogan* promoting the brand' (Pavlenko, this volume: 149). Secondly, there is *'proprietary branding* that links the brand with the names of individual scholars' (this volume: 149). Thirdly, there is the *'institutionalization* of the brand through centers, conferences, handbooks, and journals' (this volume: 149). Fourthly, there is the *'endless recycling* of the brand name in the titles of the said publications, centers, symposia, and grants' (this volume: 149). Fifthly, there is the use of *'intentionally vague language* that makes the claims exempt from critiques' (this volume: 149). Sixthly and finally, there is *'affective rhetoric*, that frames the phenomena in question in superlative terms (*radical, unprecedented, hugely complex, tremendously important*)' (this volume: 149).

As regards whether or not LC has become a slogan, my position is mixed. Reading relevant publications, attending relevant talks at conferences and engaging in conversations about LC with colleagues around the world, my general impression is that while some researchers seem to have a clear idea about what they mean by commodification (and crucially, seem able to convey this in their contacts with others), a very large number are using the term rather loosely, thus converting it into a 'buzzword (...) in danger of losing its original, perhaps rather precisely grounded, meaning' (Little, 1994: 430). Indeed, as I have noted throughout this chapter, the big problem is that in most publications LC is never defined by researchers using it.

As regards whether or not LC has been sloganized, we must move to the realm of advertising, self-promotion and other marketing-based activities. And this brings us back to Pavlenko's (this volume) branding strategies, in which there is an implied agent which, in turn, can be none other than an academic or a group of academics. A further implication is that the academics in question are working in unison around a common project which involves self-promotion and an attempt to impose a particular term (i.e. a slogan). In what I have read and been exposed to, I have seen that LC has been adopted by many researchers and I have also noted how the term is repeated in the titles of publications and conference talks and colloquia. However, I do not see these processes as part of a concerted effort on the part of a group of scholars who wish to impose their view of the world or set a research agenda which excludes other points of view. Rather, LC seems to have a certain seductive appeal because the early work in which it was used (e.g. Heller, 2002, 2003) was deemed interesting, engaging and generative of new ways of thinking by those who read it. Indeed, I have seen no evidence of any intentional use of the six branding strategies outlined by Pavlenko (this volume) in the actions of sociolinguists such as Heller and Duchêne. To conclude, then, I would say that LC has become something of a buzzword, and it is used in a relatively untheorized way by many scholars; however, crucially, there has never been anything resembling an advertising campaign in which scholars have attempted to sell or impose it. Perhaps then, it is a *casual* or *accidental* slogan, if such a thing exists.

Acknowledgments

I thank Celso Álvarez Cáccamo, Marnie Holborow, John Gray, Kori Allan, Hartmut Haberland for helpful comments on an early draft of this chapter, and Bruce Manheim, Gregory Hadley, Nasima Yamchi, Anna Kristina Hultgren, Bernhard Forchtner, Jayne Whistance and others who participated in an Academia.Edu open forum about this chapter in early 2016.

Notes

(1) This is a considerably expanded and substantially reoriented version of a discussion of language commodification in Block (2014) and Block (2017).
(2) However, my first encounter with the notion of language commodification was in Florian Coulmas's (1992) *Language and Economy*, where he wrote:

> … languages have market value That is the exchange value a certain language has as a commodity, or the index of its appreciation by a relevant group as compared to other languages. The commodity nature of languages manifests itself most clearly in the demand of foreign language learning which can be described as market (…) The factors determining the market value of a language at a given point in time are of various kinds, political, cultural, but above all economic. (Coulmas, 1992: 77–79)

> Two elements in this quote are worthy of attention in the context of this chapter. First, we see here how Coulmas makes reference to the 'exchange value' of languages and therefore anticipates by a decade the current interest in LC. Secondly, he makes reference to the world of language teaching, which Heller (2010b) classifies as an example of a 'language industry', in which language is a 'product' with a market value.

(3) Heller and Duchêne (2013: 9) define 'tertiarization' as 'the development of the economic sector that, unlike the primary sector's focus on extraction of primary resources (food, metals, wood, etc.), or the secondary sector's concentration on their industrial transformation, is instead centered on information, services and symbolic goods'.
(4) As Christian Fuchs (2014: 38) notes, in the *Grundrisse*, 'Marx argues that the development of capitalism's productive forces results in an increased role of technology

(fixed constant capital) and thereby historically increases the importance of science and knowledge work in the economy and society' and that in doing so, he 'forecast (...) what is today called information society'.
(5) To be fair, Heller and Duchene (2013) do not take such a totalizing approach. Thus, while they are no doubt interested in the move in many societies from language as identity and citizenship marker (the latter being what they call 'pride') to language as marketable skill or symbol ('profit'), they no doubt see language as taking on both roles at a given point in time. Call center employees may feel alienated from how they use a language on the job (following scripts, adopting an accent), but this does not mean that they have somehow lost this language as an identity or citizenship marker.
(6) Still, it would be unfair to position Marx (or Engels for that matter) as an unrepentant economic determinist who argued that all that is social and cultural is unidirectionally caused by the economic base of society or, as Harvey puts it, 'as some sort of fixed and immovable structuralist thinker' (Harvey, 2010: 12). More accurately, Marx saw the interrelationship between the economic base and the sociocultural, and the material and the immaterial, as dialectic in nature. As Harvey (2010: 11–12) explains, Marx aimed to 'take account of the unfolding and dynamic relations between elements within a capitalist system (...) in such a way as to capture fluidity and motion because he (...) [was] impressed with the mutability and dynamics of capitalism'. I hasten to add that Shanker and Cavanaugh do not to take the Marx-as-economic-determinist position, although, as Harvey (2010) suggests, it is one fairly widespread across the social sciences and humanities.

References

Agha, A. (2005) Voice, footing, enregisterment. *Journal of Linguistic Anthropology* 15 (1), 38–59.
Agha, A. (2011) Commodity registers. *Journal of Linguistic Anthropology* 21 (1), 22–53.
Block, D. (2010) Globalisation and language teaching. In N. Coupland (ed.) *Handbook of Language and Globalisation* (pp. 287–304). Oxford: Blackwell.
Block, D. (2014) *Social Class in Applied Linguistics*. London: Routledge.
Block, D. (2017) Political economy in applied linguistics research. *Language Teaching* 50 (1), 32–64.
Block, D. (2018) *Political Economy in Sociolinguistics: Neoliberalism, Inequality and Social Class*. London: Bloomsbury.
Block, D., Gray, J. and Holborow, M. (2012) *Neoliberalism and Applied Linguistics*. London: Routledge.
Boltanski, L. and Chiapello, E. (2006) *The New Spirit of Capitalism*. London: Verso.
Bourdieu, P. (1991) *Language and Symbolic Power*. Cambridge: Polity Press.
Boutet, J. (2001) La part langagière du travail: Bilan et évolution. *Langage et Société* 98, 17–42.
Boutet, J. (2012) Language workers: Emblematic figures of late capitalism. In A. Duchêne and M. Heller (eds) *Language in Late Capitalism: Pride and Profit* (pp. 207–229). London: Routledge.
Brown, W. (2005) *Edgework: Critical Essays on Knowledge and Politics*. Princeton, NJ: Princeton University Press.
Burawoy, M. (1979) *Manufacturing Consent: Changes in the Labor Process under Monopoly Capitalism*. Chicago, IL: Chicago University Press.
Cameron, D. (2000) *Good to Talk? Living and Working in a Communication Culture*. London: Sage.
Castells, M. (2009) *Communication Power*. Oxford: Oxford University Press.
Coulmas, F. (1992) *Language and Economy*. Oxford: Blackwell.

Duchêne, A. and Heller, M. (2012) Multilingualism and the new economy. In M. Martin-Jones, A. Blackledge and A. Creese (eds) *The Routledge Handbook of Multilingualism* (pp. 369–383). London: Routledge.

Duchêne, A. and Heller, M. (eds) (2013) *Language in Late Capitalism: Pride and Profit*. London: Routledge.

Duchêne, A., Moyer, M. and Roberts, C. (eds) (2014) *Language, Migration and Social Inequalities: A Critical Sociolinguistic Perspective on Institutions and Work*. Bristol: Multilingual Matters.

Flubacher, M.-C. and Del Percio, A. (eds) (2017) *Language, Education and Neoliberalism: Critical Studies in Sociolinguistics*. Bristol: Multilingual Matters.

Foucault, M. (2008 [1978–1979]) *The Birth of Biopolitics: Lectures at the Collège de France 1979–1979*. London: Palgrave Macmillan.

Fuchs, C. (2014) *Digital Labour and Karl Marx*. London: Routledge.

Gray, J. (2012) Neoliberalism, celebrity and 'aspirational content' in English language teaching textbooks for a global market. In D. Block, J. Gray and M. Holborow (eds) *Neoliberalism and Applied Linguistics* (pp. 86–113). London: Routledge.

Hardt, M. and Negri, A. (2000) *Empire*. Cambridge, MA: Harvard University Press.

Harvey, D. (2005) *A Brief History of Neoliberalism*. Oxford: Oxford University Press.

Harvey, D. (2010) *A Companion to Marx, Capital, Volume 1*. London: Verso.

Heller, M. (2002) Globalization and the commodification of bilingualism in Canada. In D. Block and D. Cameron (eds) *Globalization and Language Teaching* (pp. 47–63). London: Routledge.

Heller, M. (2003) Globalization, the new economy and the commodification of language. *Journal of Sociolinguistics* 7 (4), 473–492.

Heller, M. (2010a) Language as resource in the globalized new economy. In N. Coupland (ed.) *The Handbook of Language and Globalization* (pp. 349–365). Malden: Blackwell.

Heller, M. (2010b) The commodification of language. *Annual Review of Anthropology* 39, 101–114.

Heller, M. and Duchêne, A. (2013) Pride and profit: Changing discourses of language, capital and nation-state. In A. Duchêne and M. Heller (eds) *Language in Late Capitalism: Pride and Profit* (pp. 1–21). London: Routledge.

Heller, M., Pujolar, J. and Duchêne, A. (2014) Linguistic commodification in tourism. *Journal of Sociolinguistics* 18, 539–566.

Holborow, M. (2015) *Language and Neoliberalism*. London: Routledge.

Kockelman, P. (2006) A semiotic ontology of the commodity. *Journal of Linguistic Anthropology* 16 (1), 76–102.

Little, D. (1994) Learner autonomy. A theoretical construct and its practical application. *Die Neueren Sprachen* 93, 430–442.

Marx, K. (1904 [1859]) *A Contribution to the Critique of Political Economy*. Chicago, IL: Kerr.

Marx, K. (1973 [1858]) *Grundrisse*. Harmondsworth: Penguin.

Marx, K. (1988 [1844]) *Economic and Philosophic Manuscripts of 1844*. Amherst, NY: Prometheus Books.

Marx, K. (1990 [1867]) *Capital: A Critique of Political Economy, Vol. 1*. Harmondsworth: Penguin.

Marx, K. and Engels, F. (1998 [1846]) *The German Ideology*. London: Lawrence & Wishart.

McGill, K. (2013) Political economy and language: A review of some recent literature. *Journal of Linguistic Anthropology* 23 (2), 196–213.

Menochelli, J. (2006) *Collateral Learning and the Soft Skills*. Electronic Document. See http://www3.telus.net/linguisticsissues/collateral (accessed 27 May 2007).

Park, J.S.-Y. and Wee, L. (2012) *Linguistic Capital and Language Policy in a Globalizing World*. London: Routledge.

Peirce, C. (1955) *Philosophical Writings of Peirce* (ed. J. Buchler). New York: Dover.
Peters, T. (2008) *The Brand You 50: Fifty Ways to Transform Yourself from an 'Employee' into a Brand that Shouts Distinction, Commitment, and Passion!* New York: Knopf.
Pietikainen, S. and Kelly-Holmes, H. (eds) (2013) *Multilingualism and the Periphery*. Oxford: Oxford University Press.
Rubdy, R. and Tan, P.K.W. (eds) (2008) *Language as Commodity: Global Structures, Local Marketplaces*. London: Continuum.
Schmenk, B. (2008) *Lernerautonomie. Karriere und Sloganisierung des Autonomiebegriffs*. Tübingen: Narr.
Shankar, S. and Cavanaugh, J.R. (2012) Language and materiality in global capitalism. *Annual Review of Anthropology* 41, 355–369.
Silverstein, M. (1996) Monoglot 'standard' in America. In D. Brenneis and R. Macauley (eds) *The Matrix of Language* (pp. 284–306). Long Grove, IL: Waveland.
Smith, A. (2012 [1776]) *The Wealth of Nations, Books 1–3*. Ware: Wordsworth Editions.
Taylor, F.W. (1998 [1911]) *The Principles of Scientific Management*. Mineola, NY: Dover.
Urciuoli, B. (2008) Skills and selves in the new workplace. *American Ethnologist* 35, 211–228.
Urciuoli, B. and LaDousa, C. (2013) Language management/labor. *Annual Review of Anthropology* 42, 175–190.

8 Superdiversity and Why It Isn't: Reflections on Terminological Innovation and Academic Branding

Aneta Pavlenko

In 2013, the UN announced that the number of international migrants worldwide had reached 232 million, up from 154 million in 1990. To capture the effects of this increase on the UK, Vertovec (2007) proposed a term superdiversity, *which was then taken up by the sociolinguistic community (e.g. Blommaert, 2013; Blommaert & Rampton, 2011). The purpose of this paper is to examine the process of sloganization by following the emergence of this term and its uptake in the field. I will show that, in contrast to terms such as 'autonomy' which have become empty slogans over time, 'superdiversity' has been conceived as a slogan from the start, in response to increasing pressure on scholars to distinguish their work via scholarly* branding. *The rapid and uncritical uptake of the term will be linked to the traditional roles of slogans – to rally, unite and sell.*

Most of the words examined in this volume have a common trajectory – they began their lives as academic terms and then morphed into slogans. *Superdiversity* makes an interesting case study in this context as a word whose sloganization potential was apparent from the start. Coined by a scholar of migration, Vertovec (2007), to refer to the 'diversification of diversity' of migrants in the UK, the term soon expanded meaning and crossed disciplinary boundaries. In the span of five years, between 2011 and 2016, sociolinguists witnessed the appearance of two (!) books, one special issue, one conference and several research projects all bearing the same title: *Language(s) and Superdiversity(ies)*. Other titles are not far behind, sporting permutations of *superdiversity* and *linguistic* and *sociolinguistics* (Table 8.1). On the face of it, all that's conveyed by these near-identical titles is that *superdiversity* – whatever it is – is real and important for sociolinguistics. On a closer look, however, the uniformity and

Table 8.1 Language and superdiversity: Selected publications, conferences and grants, 2010–2016

Year	Selected publications	Selected conferences	Selected funded projects and research institutes
2010	Blommaert, J. (2010) *The Sociolinguistics of Globalization*. Cambridge: Cambridge University Press. Creese, A. and Blackledge, A. (2010) Towards a sociolinguistics of superdiversity. *Zeitschrift für Erziehungswissenschaft* 13, 549–572 (Special Issue).		International Consortium for Language and Superdiversity (InCoLaS) formed with core members of Tilburg University, King's College London, Birmingham University, Copenhagen University, University of the Western Cape and University of Jyväskylä.
2011	Blommaert, J., Rampton, B. and Spotti, M. (eds) (2011) Language and superdiversities. *Diversities* 13 (2) and 14 (2) (Special Issue). Revised versions republished in a volume edited by Arnaut, K., Blommaert, J., Rampton, B. and Spotti, M. (2016b)		Project 'Superdiversity and Digital Language Practices' funded at the University of Hamburg (2011–2012).
2012	Mutsaers, P. and Swanenberg, J. (2012) Super-diversity at the margins? Youth language in North Brabant, The Netherlands. *Sociolinguistic Studies* 6 (1), 65–89.	Several colloquia and papers at the *Sociolinguistics Symposium* 19, Berlin, August 2012.	Academy of Finland funds 'Language and Superdiversity (Dis) identification in Social Media', a project at the University of Jyväskylä, Finland (2012–2016).
2013	Blommaert, J. (2013) *Ethnography, Superdiversity and Linguistic Landscapes: Chronicles of Complexity*. Multilingual Matters. Duarte, J. and Gogolin, I. (eds) (2013) *Linguistic Superdiversity in Urban Areas*. John Benjamins. Møller, J. and Jørgensen, J. (2013) Organizations of language among adolescents in superdiverse Copenhagen. *International Electronic Journal of Elementary Education* 6 (1), 23–42.	*Language and Superdiversity: Explorations and Interrogations*. Conference at the University of Jyväskylä, Finland, June 2013.	Institute for Research on Superdiversity (IRiS) established at the University of Birmingham, UK, with funded project 'Translation and Translanguaging: Investigating Linguistic and Cultural Transformations in Superdiverse Wards in Four UK Cities'.

(Continued)

Table 8.1 (Continued)

Year	Selected publications	Selected conferences	Selected funded projects and research institutes
2014	Androutsopoulos, J. and Juffermans, K. (2014) Digital language practices in superdiversity. *Discourse, Context & Media* 4–5 (Special Issue).	*Superdiversity: Theory, Method, and Practice in an Era of Change.* IRiS Conference at the University of Birmingham, UK, June 2014.	
	Cadier, L. and Mar-Molinero, C. (2014) Negotiating networks of communication in a superdiverse environment: Urban multilingualism in the city of Southampton. *Multilingua* 33 (5–6), 505–524.		
2015	Goebel, Z. (2015) *Language and Superdiversity: Indonesians Knowledging at Home and Abroad.* Oxford University Press.	*Diversity and Superdiversity.* Georgetown University Round Table, March 2015.	
	Faudree, P. and Schulthies, B. (2015a) The social life of diversity talk. *Language & Communication* 44 (Special Issue). (Some of the papers.)		
2016	Arnaut, K., Blommaert, J., Rampton, B. and Spotti, M. (eds) (2016b) *Language and Superdiversity.* Routledge.		
	Toivanen, R. and Saarikivi, J. (eds) (2016) *Linguistic Genocide or Superdiversity?* Multilingual Matters.		
	Jaspers, J. and Madsen, L. (2016a) Sociolinguistics in a languagised world. *Applied Linguistics Review* 7 (3) (Special Issue). (Some of the papers.)		

pervasiveness of the titles suggest that the launch of *superdiversity* as the 'it' word in the field is a strategic effort known as *academic branding*.

I do not question the usefulness of the word for migration studies – it is not my area of expertise and not my place to do so. Nor do I deny the reality of the so-called 'new migration'. I am a 'new migrant' as a matter of fact. Having fled the Soviet Union on the verge of its collapse, I celebrated my son's first birthday in a refugee settlement in Torvaianica, Italy. And I should have been thrilled to see that Western sociolinguists are interested in studying, 'legitimizing' and, dare I say, celebrating the experience of 'new migrants'. But instead of running out to get a badge *Je suis superdiversity*, I feel uneasy about the process that transformed a newly coined word into 'a fact on the ground' and the accompanying affective rhetoric, better suited for advertising than academia (*radical* changes, *unprecedented* increases, *hugely complex* linguistic practices). The purpose of this chapter is to articulate the reasons for this unease. I will begin with an overview of processing features that differentiate slogans from academic terms and strategies that turn slogans into academic brands. Then I will examine the meanings and functions of *superdiversity*, highlighting the referential indeterminacy of the term which renders it impervious to critique, and its use as a 'hot' brand name which adds market value and distinction to preexisting lines of research and promotes a new academic hierarchy and elite.

What's in a Name: How to Craft a Successful Slogan

In the increasingly corporatized and competitive environment of today's academia, scholars scramble to publish ever more articles in an ever-increasing number of journals to make an ever-greater 'impact on the field'. 'Modern academics', argues Billig (2013: 26), 'must be able to keep writing and publishing even when they have nothing to say'. But if all of us are busy writing, how do we achieve the desired impact? One way for senior academics to promote their approaches is to create new academic terms (or to borrow them from other fields), while junior scholars distinguish their research by adopting trendy keywords (Ahearn, 2013; Billig, 2013; Williams, 1983). But what makes some words sexier than others? The introduction to the volume *Language and Superdiversity* provides the following rationale for favoring *superdiversity* over potential competitors, such as *translocality*, *liquid modernity* and *global complexity*:

> When compared with the range of other terms on offer (...) Vertovec's 'superdiversity' comes across as a primarily descriptive concept, limited in 'grand narrative' ambitions or explicit theoretical claims. (...) It spotlights the 'diversification of diversity' as a process to be investigated but it doesn't pin any particular explanation onto this. Indeed, the term 'superdiversity' is itself relatively unspectacular – 'super' implies complications and some need for rethinking, but 'diversity' aligns with a set of rather long-standing discourses. (Arnaut *et al.*, 2016a: 3–4)

The authors are being modest – the term is not *unspectacular* and there may be more thinking that went into its selection than this paragraph reveals. To probe this thinking, let us compare *superdiversity* and its competitors on features that differentiate slogans from academic terms. Studies of marketing define *slogans* as attention-grabbing and catchy words or phrases, used to distinguish a brand, a product, a cause or an individual and create demand for the things they refer to. The key processing features of successful slogans are simplicity, memorability and emotionality (Alter, 2013; Ghanem & Selber, 2009; Strutton & Roswinanto, 2014).

Simplicity refers to the ease with which we recognize, pronounce and understand a word. Research shows that the ease of word processing (*processing fluency*) influences our attitudes towards people, objects and phenomena they name: drugs with easy-to-read names are deemed less risky; financial stocks with simple names outperform the rest; and people with easy-to-pronounce names are judged more positively and promoted faster than those whose names are long or irregularly spelled (Alter, 2013; Alter & Oppenheimer, 2009; Laham *et al.*, 2012). The words in our professional toolkit are not known for simplicity – they are often hard to articulate and even harder to understand, at least for the uninitiated (witness the cumbersome *performativity* or forbidding *entextualization*). In contrast, successful slogans are short, easy to pronounce and have transparent meanings, easily derived from their components (hence, the success of *Universal Grammar* over *generative* and *new media* over *digital*). The competitors of *superdiversity* do not rank highly on these criteria: *global complexity* is the opposite of *simplicity*, *liquid modernity* is anything but transparent, and *translocality* is neither transparent nor easy to utter due to pesky consonant clusters. *Superdiversity*, on the other hand, fits the criteria very nicely: its components are short and frequent English words with CV and CVC syllables, whose combined meaning is easily computed as 'diversity, only bigger and better than ever before'.

Memorability describes words and phrases that can be retained after a single exposure. This criterion rarely affects the making of linguistic terms (as witnessed by anyone who ever tried to teach *epenthesis* or *subcategorization*) and it does not distinguish either *translocality* or *global complexity*. Successful slogans have to be catchy. Simplicity, transparency and ease of processing go a long way towards memorability, but to make slogans truly memorable experts often appeal to mnemonic devices, such as rhythm, alliteration, parallel constructions, word play, rhymes and jokes (e.g. *The news you can use* or Wendy's *Where's the beef?*) (Ghanem & Selber, 2009; Strutton & Roswinanto, 2014). A common strategy in the humanities these days is to add modifiers *new*, *super* and *big* to already familiar terms (e.g. *big data*, *new speakers*) (Reyes, 2014). The modifier *super* is particularly useful, for it is increasingly popular in the 'real world', where young people are *super hungry*, *super busy* and *super sad* (Ferris, 2014). Contrary to the claim we saw earlier, *super* does not imply complications and the need for rethinking – rather, it suggests that the said *diversity* exceeds the implied norm in excellence *and* size. What makes *superdiversity* memorable is the witty polysemy of *super* – reminiscent of Orwell's (1949) *doubleplus* – combined with its contemporary feel and sheer novelty in sociolinguistics.

Yet we could also make new words that would be simple and memorable, so why not *glonk* or *frump*? The third criterion that distinguishes slogans is *emotionality*, i.e. the ability to trigger positive associations and a cheerful emotional response. Academic terms can become affectively loaded yet at the outset they are neither evaluative nor emotion-laden (frankly, it is hard to get excited about *loan translation* or *scalarity*). In contrast, slogans have to compel people to buy the product, support the campaign or join the movement they represent. The best way to trigger such response in the English-speaking world is by crafting a 'positive message', encoded in short 'power words' loaded with positive affect, such as *pro*, *yes* or *great* (Storey, 1997). This strategy explains the success of the labels *Pro-life* and *Pro-choice*, De Beers' ever-lasting *A diamond is forever*, Nike's irresistible trademark *Just Do It*, and slogans that won US presidential elections, such as Obama's *Yes We Can* and Trump's *Make America Great Again*.

The emphasis on bright-sidedness also made inroads in Western academia, as seen in the increased use of *new*, *super* and *big* (Reyes, 2014), the popularity of *the bilingual advantage* and *conviviality*, and the rise of the science of happiness, *positive psychology* (for an illuminating discussion of this rise, see Ehrenreich, 2009). Of course, slogans can also harness negative affect, as seen in *language endangerment*, yet it is not accidental that linguists are rallied to *save* endangered languages (for insightful analysis of the rhetoric of language endangerment, see Duchêne & Heller, 2007). *Global complexity*, *liquid modernity* and *translocality* do not convey positive messages and neither do *glonk* and *frump*, nor the prefix *hyper-*, rejected by Vertovec:

> The (...) reason why hyperdiversity is an unfortunate term is that 'hyper-' can inherently suggest that something is overexcited, out of control and therefore generally negative or undesirable (like hyperactivity or hyperinflation). Again, 'super-' is our preferred modifier in order to emphasize the sense of superseding, or addressing what is 'above and beyond' what was previously there. (Meissner & Vertovec, 2015: 545)

In the end, *superdiversity* is superior because it is likeable (*glonk* and *frump* not so much). *Diversity* connotes a desirable (at least in academic circles) state of affairs and the superlative prefix *super-* takes the positive charge through the roof, linking *superdiversity* to other perennial favorites, from Superman to the Super Bowl. The change in affective footing – away from depressing treatments of linguistic diversity as an endangered phenomenon (e.g. Evans, 2010; Harrison, 2007; Skutnabb-Kangas, 2000) towards happy celebrations of increasing linguistic diversity – makes the slogan even more appealing and memorable. 'Superdiversity', argues Makoni (2012: 193), appeals to us because it 'contains a powerful sense of social romanticism, creating an illusion of equality in a highly asymmetrical world, particularly in contexts characterized by a search for homogenization'. Simple, catchy, youthful and relentlessly optimistic and bright, *superdiversity* resonates with those who look for positive messages and causes for celebration in ways *translocality, commodification* or *linguistic landscapes* do not.

Now I am not saying that terminological innovation is a problem – in academia, it is par for the course. Rather than an egregious culprit, simple words are a welcome development in the sea of murky jargon, replete with *enregisterment, semiotization* and endless *problematizing* (for a brilliant critique of academic rhetoric and long nouns that dress up banalities as profundities, see Billig, 2013). The problem arises when keywords are turned into slogans whose function is to promote academic brands. To follow this transformation, let us now turn to the strategies that made *superdiversity* a hot item in the sociolinguistic marketplace.

The Art of the Sell: How to Make an Academic Brand

Slogans have several aims: (a) to distinguish the product from competing products (e.g. *Nike's Just Do It*, <u>new</u> *media*); (b) to create a positive impression of the product or the individual (e.g. Trump's *Make America Great Again*, <u>positive</u> *psychology*); (c) to deliver a message that shapes public opinion (e.g. De Beers' *A diamond is forever*, the bilingual <u>advantage</u>); and (d) to create the need and desire for the brand, product, cause or individual they serve (all of the above). Summed up in one word, slogans have to *sell* (after all, Trump did win the election, De Beers' slogan of the century made diamond engagement rings a must, Nike's *Just Do It* campaign resulted in a larger share of the exercise gear market and *positive psychology* cornered a lucrative niche in the corporate world). Clearly, even the best-crafted slogans cannot accomplish this task on their own – they need to be integrated into promotional campaigns. *Superdiversity* allows us to examine one such campaign and to identify ten strategies behind the academic art of the sell.

As seen in Table 8.1, the trajectory of *superdiversity* follows a regular academic path: publications, conferences and grants. What is remarkable about it is its speed: left to their own devices, scholarly ideas take years or even decades to gestate before they inspire conference themes, Wiki entries and handbooks (the one on languages and *superdiversity* is on the way). *Governmentality*, for instance, took two decades to become a popular keyword (Billig, 2013). Yet there is also a way to speed up the process. Writing like academic advertisers, 'self-declared experts can commercially market big new words as big new ideas', since we 'cannot have a new approach, theory or insight, unless we have a new noun to promote' (Billig, 2013: 11). But how do we know whether the enthusiastic uptake of *superdiversity* is spontaneous or a result of an academic branding campaign? To answer this question, let us compare the rise of *superdiversity* to that of other keywords, such as *Universal Grammar* and *linguistic landscapes*.

The first step in a branding campaign is *adoption of a slogan* promoting the brand. In academia, the best brand names function as their own slogans (e.g. *positive psychology*), as is the case sometimes in the 'real world' (e.g. *Pro-life, Pro-choice*). *Universal Grammar* and s*uperdiversity* make excellent slogan-brands promoting everyone's grammar and good, no, great diversity. In contrast, *commodification* triggers negative associations, *new speakers* remind us of Newspeak, and *linguistic landscapes* fail to deliver a message or elicit an emotional response.

The second step involves *proprietary branding* which links the brand with the names of individual scholars. Such links are effortless when the individuals in question did come up with the actual idea, theory, finding or, at least, term: the *Universal Grammar* is undisputedly Noam Chomsky's baby, the *bilingual advantage* is a signature finding of Ellen Bialystok and *positive psychology* is the brainchild of Martin Seligman. *Linguistic landscapes*, on the other hand, are not linked to a single name. *Superdiversity* was coined by Vertovec, yet an imported name can be rebranded once it is attractively repackaged. The repackaging for sociolinguistics took place in the special issue of an online journal *Diversities* (2011). Then, the ownership was claimed by Blommaert (2015) who distanced himself from both Vertovec and his own co-author by stating: 'my approach to superdiversity (e.g. Blommaert & Rampton, 2011) differs quite substantially from the original formulations proposed by Steven Vertovec' (Blommaert, 2015: 86).

The third and fourth strategies involve *institutionalization* of the brand through centers, conferences, handbooks and journals, combined with *endless recycling* of the brand name in the titles of the said publications, centers, symposia and grants. The endless recycling strategy raises the visibility of the brand and enhances its acceptance, based on the cognitive effect documented in studies of marketing and truth-value judgments: frequently repeated and easy-to-recall statements are perceived as more truthful (Alter & Oppenheimer, 2009). The conflation of repetition with truthfulness is particularly useful in contexts where the audience is asked to accept claims as articles of faith, as is the case with *superdiversity* which – unlike *commodification* or *linguistic landscapes* – became a keyword *before* it became subject to research.

To secure such acceptance, academic branding relies on the fifth strategy, *intentionally vague language* which makes the claims exempt from critiques, and the sixth strategy, *affective rhetoric*, which frames the phenomena in question in superlative terms (*radical, unprecedented, hugely complex, tremendously important*). I will return to these strategies later on but first let us consider a peculiarity of the trajectory in Table 8.1 that reveals a strategy unique to academia and one that distinguishes *superdiversity* from *commodification* and *linguistic landscapes*.

Strikingly, the majority of sociolinguistic publications with *superdiversity* in the title have appeared as monographs, edited volumes or articles in special issues, working papers and journals not known for rigorous peer-review (and, in some cases, not known at all), or simply as 'research materials' available on academic networking sites, such as Academia, and the sites of the various research centers. Missing from the record are articles in top sociolinguistic journals, such as *Language in Society* or *Journal of Sociolinguistics*. The rationale for the heavy reliance on web publishing is found on the site of Babylon, the Center for the Study of Superdiversity:

> In order **to lower the threshold of publishing** for junior researchers, to stimulate the dialogue and debate on research materials across disciplines, and **to improve and expedite the circulation of research materials**, we started the electronic working papers series Tilburg Papers in Culture Studies (TPCS) in the Fall of 2011. (https://www.tilburguniversity.edu/research/institutes-and-research-groups/babylon/about-babylon/, emphasis added)

The same strategy of, um, *lowering the threshold of publishing* is adopted by senior researchers and rationalized by Blommaert (2014) as a breakaway from commercial publishers. What remains unacknowledged is the fact that the free-for-all also skips peer-review, making research articles an equivalent of academic blog posts. The haste is particularly apparent in the special issue of *Diversities* (2011), which – in an unusual move – was revised and republished five years later as an edited volume (Arnaut *et al.*, 2016b). Revisions made in the papers respond to some of the criticisms of *superdiversity* made since 2011 but now they are addressing a paradigm in existence, a fait accompli.

The strategy of uniting and rallying supporters by *lowering the threshold of publishing* for both junior *and* senior scholars is far from novel – in the 1960s and 1970s, Chomsky and his followers also circulated unpublished work to make Generative Grammar the dominant paradigm in linguistics (Huck & Goldsmith, 1995). Today, as then, the launch of a new paradigm requires social networking and it is often the charisma of the leaders, the sense of belonging to the in-group and the excitement of privileged access to new ideas (so new they have not been published yet!) that account for success of new academic brands. The game-changing role of the 'new' media is in 'expediting the circulation of research materials' and simplifying the access for potential consumers and prosumers. The eighth and ninth branding strategies, therefore, are *social networking* and *creation of the digital footprint* that facilitate distribution of published, semi-published and unpublished work and generate excitement and support. The tenth strategy, successfully used by Chomsky and his supporters to squash the opposition, involves ruthless ad hominem attacks on those who oppose the new paradigm. But perhaps those who launch revolutionary new paradigms have no choice but to publish rapidly, skipping reviews by their more orthodox and conservative peers?

To answer this question, we need to go beyond analyses of why *superdiversity* makes a good slogan and how it was transformed into a brand and determine what *superdiversity* is. Is it a novel finding, like *the bilingual cognitive advantage*? Or perhaps a research focus and a method, like *linguistic landscapes*? Or is it a theoretical paradigm, like *Universal Grammar*? And what are the differences between the ways in which it is treated by Vertovec and Blommaert?

What is *Superdiversity*?

Manufacturing of consent: *Superdiversity*, the diversity we can believe in

Pinning down the meaning of *superdiversity* is not an easy task. In his much-cited paper, Vertovec (2007) introduced the keyword (with a dash) as a way to describe new patterns of migration in the UK that surpassed anything the country had experienced in the past. His goal was to capture the complexity of recent sociodemographic phenomena and it still appears to be one intended meaning of the term, reconfirmed by Meissner and Vertovec (2015):

> Super-diversity is a term coined to portray changing population configurations particularly arising from global migration flows over the past thirty-odd years. The changing configurations not only entail the movement of people from more varied national, ethnic, linguistic and religious backgrounds, but also the ways that shifts concerning these categories or attributes coincide with a worldwide diversification of movement flows through specific migration channels ... (Meissner & Vertovec, 2015: 542)

The same meaning was then adopted in sociolinguistics (Blommaert, 2013; Blommaert & Rampton, 2011; Duarte & Gogolin, 2013), with pre-1990 migration described as follows:

> Migration prior to the early 1990s was a **well-regulated phenomenon**, organized on a cross-national basis in such a way that the profiles of 'migrants' into Western European societies were rather **clearly defined and predictable**. (Blommaert, 2013: 4, emphasis added)

An expanded version of this claim can be found on the site of the eponymous conference:

> During the past few decades, the face of social, cultural and linguistic diversity in **societies all over the world** has changed **radically,** producing **complexity of a different kind** than what has traditionally been captured in the notion of multiculturalism. Superdiversity manifests itself in such demographic and social changes as the **tremendous** increase in the categories of migrants, in terms of nationality, ethnicity, language and religion, and also in terms of motives, patterns and careers as migrants, processes of insertion into, settling in and interactions with the host societies. (https://www.jyu.fi/en/congress/superdiversity/theme, emphasis added)

Brand name consultants often say that a great name takes reality and alters it just a little bit (Colapinto, 2011). This formula also applies to *superdiversity* in its guise as a descriptive term. The reality is incontrovertible: international migration reports reveal that between the years 1990 and 2013 the number of international migrants has increased by 50%, from 154 million to 232 million (UN DESA, 2013; WMR, 2015). What is altered is the significance of these raw numbers on the global stage. The analysis of global migration patterns by Czajka and de Haas (2014) shows that, while an absolute number of international migrants *has* increased, the world population grew even faster; as a consequence, the proportion of global migrants has *decreased* from 3.1% of the world population in 1960 to 2.7% in 2000. They also found that in the Americas and the Pacific the numbers have increased but the diversity of the categories has not.

These findings are echoed in recent migration reports that highlight marked differences between the developed North, where migrants constitute 10.8% of the population, and developing regions where they constitute only 1.6% and where some countries are neither an important source nor destination for migration flows. They also show that in 2013, 51% of the world's migrants were living in ten countries: USA, Russian Federation, Germany, Saudi Arabia, United Arab Emirates, UK, France, Canada, Australia and Spain (UN DESA, 2013; WMR, 2015). The concentration of migrants in a 'shrinking pool of prime destination countries' (Czajka & de Haas, 2014: 315), many of them small countries in Western Europe, led Czajka and de Haas (2014: 314) to conclude that 'the idea that immigration has become more diverse may partly reveal a Eurocentric worldview'.

The bias becomes even more apparent when we face the fact that *Europe* in discussions of *superdiversity* is a stand-in for Western Europe, while Eastern Europe is ignored as its bland and irrelevant periphery. Yet a closer look at Eastern European – or, for that matter, Central Asian – trends offers a salutary insight for Western European sociolinguistics: migration does not necessarily increase ethnolinguistic diversity. The efforts to create ethno-nationalist states from the ruins of Yugoslavia and the USSR triggered the process Brubaker (1998) termed *ethnic unmixing*, a bilateral exchange involving out-migration of ethnolinguistic minorities and in-migration of the titulars. As a result, the proportion of titulars has increased in successor states of the former Yugoslavia and USSR, with the exception of the Russian Federation. In Kazakhstan, for instance, in 1959 Kazakhs constituted 30% of the population; by 2009 the proportion of Kazakhs rose to 63.1%. Even stronger homogenization can be observed in Azerbaijan, where the proportion of Azeris rose from 67.5% in 1959 to 91.6% in 2009 (CIS Statistics, 2013). A similar trend can be observed in Croatia, where between 1991 and 2011 the proportion of Croats increased from 78.1% to 90.4% and the proportion of Serbs decreased from 12.2%

to 4.4% (Croatian Bureau of Statistics, 2012). This census data may undoubtedly conceal some diversification on the ground yet it is as legitimate as the data used to 'reveal' *superdiversity*.

But if migration cannot be assumed to increase ethnolinguistic diversity, how do we know which societies are *superdiverse*? One answer to this question can be found on the website *Ethnologue*, dedicated to the study of linguistic diversity. The makers of *Ethnologue* are very open about the ambiguity of the construct of *language*, problems inherent in counting languages by their areas of origin and the difficulties of counting them at all (Lewis *et al.*, 2016). Nevertheless, they do offer a general assessment, based on Greenberg's (1956) *linguistic diversity index*, which computes the probability that any two people of the country, selected at random, would have different mother tongues. The highest score on this scale is 1 (no two people have the same mother tongue) and the lowest 0 (everyone has the same mother tongue). The calculation of the score – far from perfect but fully transparent – is based on population statistics.

The countries with the highest linguistic diversity score – over 0.8 – are Benin, Bhutan, Cameroon, Central African Republic, Chad, Congo, Côte d'Ivoire, East Timor, Ethiopia, Gabon, Ghana, India, Indonesia, Kenya, Liberia, Mali, Mozambique, Namibia, Nigeria, Pakistan, Papua New Guinea (off the charts at 0.988%), Sierra Leone, Solomon Islands, South Africa, South Sudan, Togo, Vanuatu and Zambia. The UK with a score of 0.15 is on the lower end of the chart. The list is consistent with the spread of the world's languages, whereby Asia, Africa and the Pacific house the majority (32.4%, 30.1% and 18.5%, respectively), while Europe is home to a measly 4% (Lewis *et al.*, 2016). These statistics are undoubtedly familiar to scholars of *superdiversity*, given the number of Africanists in their midst, yet they do not affect their research since European funders are more interested in Belgium than in Papua New Guinea.

In sum, even a very brief look at worldwide migration trends reveals a few inconvenient truths: (a) the intensity and diversity of migration have *not* increased worldwide but they have increased in Western Europe; (b) migration does *not* necessarily increase ethnolinguistic diversity, as seen in Eastern European and Central Asian census data, but it did increase it in Western Europe; (c) the rise in the number of languages spoken is particularly tangible because of the *low* linguistic diversity in Europe – the centers of *linguistic diversity* are located in Africa, Asia and the Pacific. These facts raise an uncomfortable question: Why should we look at the world through a Western European lens? An equally uncomfortable answer is that many influential sociolinguists reside in the countries affected by the new migration (for an overview of Westernizing mechanisms in sociolinguistics, see Smakman, 2015). This privileging of the local in the guise of the global reminds me of the response the namesake of American TV series *Ally McBeal* gave to the question: 'Ally, what makes your problems bigger than everyone else's?' 'They are MINE!'

But there is an even bigger problem in using *superdiversity* as a descriptor: 'diversity defies definition' (Meissner, 2015: 559). While some authors use census data to prove that their contexts are *superdiverse* and others differentiate between more and less *superdiverse* contexts, there is no heuristic that determines at what point *diversity* morphs into *superdiversity*. 'The use of "superdiverse" as a descriptive adjective', argues Deumert (2014: 116), 'is a theoretical cul-de-sac, because the complexities brought about by diversity in the social world ultimately defy numerical measurement.' Tagging on *super-* does not solve the problem but amplifies it, requiring us to accept that which cannot be defined as an article of faith.

The adepts of *superdiversity* recognize the dangers of reliance on the intangible *je ne sais quoi*. The purpose of the affective rhetoric (*radical, tremendous, unprecedented*) is to facilitate the process an American journalist Walter Lippman aptly called *the manufacture of consent*. They also have an alternative definition: a 'superdiverse society is a society in which ethnicity, culture, language and religion have no guarantees' (Juffermans *et al.*, 2014: 49). The difference between linguistically diverse and *superdiverse* societies, therefore, is one of quality, not of quantity:

> *Superdiversity* differs from diversity or mere societal multilingualism, a characteristic of just about all African societies, in the way it reflects the unmooring of correlations between populations and languages that is then magnified through digital mediation. (McLaughlin, 2014: 36–37)

Exposing the naiveté of those who saw *superdiversity* as 'the increasing presence of "more ethnic groups"' (Meissner & Vertovec, 2015: 543), the new definitions free us from the need to define categories and calculate numbers and make *superdiversity* a feature of our age.

Truthiness: The times they are a-changin'

Echoing Bob Dylan's timeless lyrics, the work on *superdiversity* reminds us that times are a-changin' or have already changed, as seen in Blommaert's (2010) confident claim:

> Now that **times have changed** and we are looking at **a world that can no longer be neatly divided into clear and transparent categories**, the theoretical paradigms need to be revised as well. (Blommaert, 2010: xiv, emphasis added)

This *age of superdiversity* can apparently be summed up in three words: 'mobility, complexity and unpredictability' (Blommaert, 2013: 6; see also http://superdiversity.net/). Historians – not surprisingly – take exception to such claims of contemporary exceptionalism and 'dismiss the entire superdiversity debate as yet more hype' (De Bock, 2015: 583). Studies of globalization history show compellingly that each historic development – be it the emergence of the first cities, the invention of writing, the Roman road-building craze or the Victorian telegraph – created unprecedented surges of mobility and connectivity, with new flows of ideas, people and goods creating ever more expanded and far-flung transcultural networks (e.g. Bellwood, 2013; Frankopan, 2015; Jennings, 2011). The sense of time-space compression experienced by users of today's Facebook has parallels among the recipients of Mesopotamian clay letters, the beneficiaries of the Ptolemaic postal system, and Londoners for whom the telegraph was as revolutionary as the internet is for us (Standage, 1998, 2013).

The 'diversification of existing diversity' is also far from novel, for it characterizes any sequence of migrations. Take, for instance, the USA. Prior to the 1880s, immigrants to the New World hailed primarily from Western and Northern Europe and, with the exception of the Catholic Irish, were seen as reasonably assimilable. In the period between 1880 and 1924, this diversity was diversified by almost 24 million of the 'new migrants', largely from Southern and Eastern Europe and from the lower economic strata. These new arrivals were seen as racially, morally and culturally inferior to the mainstream population and migrants of the old. They also came in much greater numbers: by 1910, 14.8% of the total US population was foreign born and so were 58% of school-age children in the nation's largest cities and 72% of the kids in New York (Weiss, 1982). This unprecedented influx raised numerous concerns about national unity and the capacity of the American society to assimilate such a large body of newcomers, not unlike the anxieties raised by the refugee flows of today. The same diversification is documented in the recent Western European past: De Bock's (2015) study of migration in Ghent in 1960–1980 shows that 'the image of post-war immigrant populations as largely undifferentiated groups of people is related to an ahistorical and static approach towards these populations' (De Bock, 2015: 585).

Historians also know that it is human nature to experience one's own era as unique, to yearn for the Golden Age when the world was, in Blommaert's (2010: xiv) unforgettable words, 'neatly divided into clear and transparent categories', and to experience the invasion of 'others' as unprecedented. Roman historian Pompeius Trogus lamented that Gaul had been turned into Greece and English chronicler William of Malmesbury complained bitterly that 'England has become a dwelling place of foreigners and a playground for lords of alien blood' (Morris, 2016: n.p.). These lines could easily invoke the refugee camps of Calais (Will Brexit rid us of the troublesome throng?) and real estate prices in London, inflated by the oil money of Arab potentates and ubiquitous new Russians, if not for the fact that they were written circa 1125. The vacuous terms *mobility*, *complexity* and *unpredictability* apply to human lives in any era of human history, an insight not lost on Silverstein (2015: 9), who gently reminds us that what we call the English language has existed under conditions of *superdiversity* since the end of the 8th century CE. A historian of globalization Jennings (2011: 17) warns that 'we need to be wary of this sense of radical difference. Although every age is indeed unique, people in each age have tended to accentuate the differences with the past and downplay the similarities'. The times, they are always a-changin' and the use of slogans to trigger the sense of contemporary exceptionalism is a prime example of a rhetorical strategy the American comedian Stephen Colbert calls *truthiness*, an appeal to gut feeling without any regard for evidence, logic or facts.

Historians' concerns have been heard by the makers of *superdiversity*, prompting them to hedge their bets and argue that the spread, speed and scale of many social processes 'are at least perceived to be more elaborate today' (Meissner & Vertovec, 2015: 547) and that the difference is in ways diversity is perceived and talked about (Juffermans *et al.*, 2014: 49). In fact, treating these phenomena as 'real' may be distracting:

> referring to superdiversity as a social phenomenon obscures the notion's analytic potential – that is, its potential to unveil and make accessible for study social complexity as it relates to migration but with the possibility to address issues beyond the impacts of migration alone. (Meissner & Vertovec, 2015: 547)

And here it is: just when we thought we caught its slippery tail, *superdiversity* makes a feint, sheds its old skin and reappears as an analytical lens or a symbiosis of the lens and the social context it is applied to. This approach enables scholars to have their cake and eat it too: they can 'uncover' *superdiversity* by bringing in the right tools or decide a priori that the context and participants they are interested in are *superdiverse*. It also appears that some groups are more *superdiverse* than others: in her perceptive analysis of the *superdiversity* craze, Piller (2016) points out that the locus of diversity is invariably migrants and descendants of *certain* migrants, like Jews who – after residing in England for more than a millennium – are treated as *old diversity*, while the descendants of Romans, Angles, Saxons, Vikings and Normans have managed to blend in. But perhaps this is all for the greater good because calling things *superdiverse* allows us to notice and theorize new forms of multilingual behavior, right?

Where's the beef? Newspeak as the emperor's new clothes

In his book *Ethnography, Superdiversity and Linguistic Landscapes*, Blommaert (2013) makes an intriguing claim: *superdiverse* environments are distinguished by new multilingual behaviors, which forced sociolinguists to develop new vocabulary:

> the many **new forms of multilingual communicative behavior** that seem to characterize the present world, and for which scholars have developed terms such as 'languaging,' 'polylanguaging,' 'crossing,' 'metrolingualism,' 'transidiomatic practices' and so forth. (…) In **superdiverse**

environments (both online and offline), people appear to take any linguistic and communicative resource available to them – a broad range typically, in **superdiverse contexts** – and blend them into **hugely complex** linguistic and semiotic forms. (Blommaert, 2013: 8, emphasis added)

These new behaviors, evidenced both offline and online, appear to follow the *new polylingual norm*, according to which

Language users employ whatever linguistic features are at their disposal to achieve their communicative aims as best they can, regardless of how well they know the involved languages; this entails that the language users may know – and use – the fact that some of the features are perceived by some speakers as not belonging together. (Jørgensen *et al.*, 2011: 34)

In fact, *superdiverse* environments appear to have produced whole new languages, *supervernaculars*, the term coined and defined by Blommaert (2011) as

a descriptor for new forms of semiotic codes emerging in the context of technology-driven globalization processes. Supervernaculars are widespread codes used in communities that do not correspond to 'traditional' sociolinguistic speech communities, but as deterritorialized and transidiomatic communities that, nonetheless, appear to create a solid and normative sociolinguistic system. (Blommaert, 2011: 2)

Leaving aside facile uses of *semiotic* as an adjective that continue to puzzle scholars of semiotics (e.g. Gottdiener, 2012: 107), let's see what *the many new forms of multilingual communicative behavior* actually are. Taking a closer look at the studies listed in Table 8.1, I made a striking discovery: the new migrations made *no impact* on the languages of the host populations. Unlike the Norman conquest of the British Isles, the Muslim invasion of Spain, Sicily and Malta or colonial expansions of the modern era, the languages of new migrants do not seem to affect the repertoires of their hosts, beyond a cameo appearance in youth vernaculars – the only people who engage in the 'new' multilingual practices are immigrants themselves. Even *superdiversity* scholars who write about them do so in standard academic English: 'sociolinguists' deconstruction of languages as bounded codes', note Jaspers and Madsen (2016b: 237), 'does not seem to preclude their continuing professional commitment to this idea.'

Even more disappointingly, migrants' practices fail to deliver the promised *hugely complex linguistic forms*: the dominant trends are towards homogenization and normativity (Belling & De Bres, 2014; Sharma, 2014) and creation of new enclaves of homogeneity (Juffermans *et al.*, 2014; Mutsaers & Swanenberg, 2012). Most importantly, the *new polylingual norm* and the *unprecedented unmooring* of relations between language, ethnicity and religion turn out to have numerous historic precedents, for they describe business as usual in multilingual contexts and are extensively documented in the ancient and medieval worlds (e.g. Adams, 2003; Beale-Rivaya, 2012; Bresc, 2001; Constable, 1997; Forster, 1970;

Hsy, 2013; Léglu, 2010; Metcalfe, 2003; Mullen & James, 2012). The only reason why the claims of novelty went as far as they did is the ahistoricity of the field of sociolinguistics, firmly rooted in the present moment and resolutely divorced from its historical counterpart and sociolinguistic explorations by classicists and medievalists (for critiques of ahistoricity of the *superdiversity* approach, see also Flores & Lewis, 2016; Piller, 2016).

But if you are beginning to suspect that *crossing* and *translanguaging* are not really *new*, the makers of *superdiversity* are one step ahead of you. Effortlessly contradicting their own earlier statements, they explain that the practices are not new but the vocabulary is:

> Translanguaging and crossing are different from codeswitching **not phenomenologically but theoretically** in that codeswitching *grosso modo* takes a structural perspective on bilingual text or talk whereas translanguaging focuses primarily on what speakers actually do and achieve by drawing on elements from their repertoires in situated contexts. A translanguaging perspective looks at people not as *having* or *using* a language or identity but as *performing* repertoires of identities by means of a range of linguistic–semiotic resources acquired over the course of one's life trajectory through membership of or participation in various communities of practice. (Juffermans *et al.*, 2014: 49, emphasis added)

The 'new ways of doing sociolinguistics' (Juffermans *et al.*, 2014: 48) enable us to 'grapple head-on with complexity' (Deumert, 2014: 118), but to do so we need to acquire Newspeak and relegate Oldspeak to the memory hole:

> So although notions like 'native speaker,' 'mother tongue' and 'ethnolinguistic group' have considerable ideological force (and as such should certainly feature as *objects* of analysis), they should have no place in the sociolinguistic toolkit itself. (Blommaert & Rampton, 2011: 5)

These clarifications forced me to reread the publications listed in Table 8.1 with an eye on their contributions to sociolinguistic theory. In doing so, I made another startling discovery: some studies with *superdiversity* in the title never mention it in the text and few, if any, actually use the recommended apparatus in more than a perfunctory way. It is, in fact, shocking to see how much the new sociolinguistics depends on the Oldspeak, including the – presumably undesirable and theoretically inadequate – notion of *language*.

The list begins with Blommaert's (2013) own study of linguistic landscapes which relies – as pointed out by Hinrichs (2015) – on the very approach disparaged by the author: reifying languages as emic units, Blommaert counts the total number of languages on signs in Oud Berchem, yielding Dutch and French, plus 22 others. Other studies of *superdiversity* are equally permeated by references to *languages* and *language varieties* (e.g. Cadier & Mar-Molinero, 2014; Charalambous *et al.*, 2016; Creese & Blackledge, 2010; Goebel, 2015; Maly, 2016; McLaughlin, 2014; Spotti, 2013; Varis & Wang, 2011), *lingua francas* (e.g. Belling & de Bres, 2014;

Jacquemet, 2015), *code-switching* and *code-mixing* (e.g. Belling & de Bres, 2014; Manosuthikit & De Costa, 2016; Swanwick *et al.*, 2016), *loan words* (e.g. Jørgensen *et al.*, 2011), and *heritage* and *second language speakers* (e.g. Manosuthikit & De Costa, 2016; Rampton, 2016). This lack of engagement parallels migration studies, where Meissner's (2015) meta-analysis identified four strands: (1) studies that use *superdiversity* to recognize multidimensionality (39%); (2) studies that use it to refer to increased ethnic diversity (38%); (3) studies that use it as a catch phrase, without explaining why they use it (17%); and (4) studies that employ it in their empirical analysis (6%).

One likely reason for this reluctance is the difficulty in deciding what *superdiversity* is. What started out as a modest reference to 'diversification of diversity' in the UK has expanded to global demographics (*superdiverse societies*), time (*the era of superdiversity*), people (*superdiverse participants*), language (*superdiverse practices*), media (*digital superdiversity*), and a theoretical paradigm all in one. Unlike *linguistic landscapes* and *language commodification* – both of which have a limited scope of reference – the referential indeterminacy of *superdiversity* allows its users, in a manner reminiscent of Lewis Carroll's Humpty Dumpty, to make it mean whatever they want it to mean.

Note, though, that while semantic excess may be a disadvantage for academic terms, it is an asset for slogans: vagueness allows them to reach the widest range of consumers (Strutton & Roswinanto, 2014). In academia, referential indeterminacy and the ever-changing definitions also have an additional plus: they make slogans impervious to critique. *Universal Grammar* is a great example of this moving target strategy: shifting the goal posts with each new reincarnation of his theory, Chomsky has managed to protect his brand for more than half a century, making linguists utterly dependent on his latest – often unpublished – manuscripts. The only things that have remained constant since the 1960s are the impenetrable writing style and reification of a metaphor as a real entity (albeit elusively out of reach).

Billig (2013) argues that impenetrable writing is an extremely useful strategy for social scientists, for it confers an aura of intellectual superiority: 'the persistently obscure writer' is, for him, 'like a bully, who tries to humiliate others into submission' (Billig, 2013: 4). Reification is equally useful but in a different way: 'by depicting the concepts as agents in the world', writers distance themselves from their own creations and succeed in making discursively constructed notions appear real ('something that has established itself') and in 'accentuating their importance, or, to use current slang, bigging them up' (Billig, 2013: 139, 141).

Now the same strategies are used by the makers of *superdiversity* who reify an abstract noun as an agent and an astroturfing voice that 'questions the foundations of our knowledge' (Blommaert, 2013: 6). Blommaert's (2015) latest reincarnation of *superdiversity* rescinds all and any claims about new phenomena and fixed concepts and reintroduces *superdiversity*

> as a paradigmatic project, a *tactic* in other words, not a subdiscipline – it is defined primarily by a theoretical and methodological explorative perspective rather than by a set of specifically 'superdiverse' phenomena or a fixed set of concepts. (...) This perspective revolves around the acceptance of *uncertainty* in sociolinguistic analysis. (Blommaert, 2015: 83)

Uncertainty is indeed the keyword here, for it captures the very purpose of the moving target strategy – to place us in a situation where meanings are uncertain and have to be defined for us by those who know best and can confidently instruct us to 'use this, not that'. The only difference between the two slogan-brands is that *Universal Grammar* is a bona fide theory, whose reiterations are diligently applied by its adepts, while *superdiversity* is a theory look-alike.

The troubling discrepancy between the enthusiastic uptake of the keyword and the obvious reluctance (or even inability) to use it as an analytical lens suggests that *superdiversity* fails as a theoretical framework because it 'reproduces the same normative assumptions that it purports to be critiquing' (Flores & Lewis, 2016: 108). 'The vocabulary may have changed', quips Orman (2012: 350), but 'the ultimately flawed conceptualization of what goes on during linguistic communication has not'. The very terms *translanguaging, polylanguaging, crossing* and *truncated repertoires* are anchored in the idea of languages as codes, whose idealized norms and wholes we *truncate* and whose boundaries we may or may not *cross* (Flores & Lewis, 2016; Jaspers & Madsen, 2016b; Makoni, 2012; Orman, 2012, 2013). 'Couched in the terms of an iconoclastic formula ("the end of synchrony")', argues Hinrichs (2015: 263), 'this argument dresses itself as a new departure', while, in reality, it is a sociolinguistic version of the emperor's new clothes. Billig (2013: 51) makes similar arguments with regard to other terms whose purpose is 'not to identify a discovery, but to cover over a lack of discovery'.

Together, these critiques provide a compelling explanation for why the devotees of *superdiversity* retain traditional theoretical commitments and methodologies, yet they fail to explain why so many studies whose research aims, methods and findings can stand perfectly well on their own add *superdiversity* to the title and the list of keywords. Perhaps the question we should have been asking all along is not what *superdiversity* **is** but what it **does**.

Making Sociolinguistics Great Again: *Cui Bono*?

In his critique of contemporary academia, Billig (2013: 133) hits the nail on the head when he states that 'the problem is not the words themselves' but what we do with words:

> Academics also have products to promote and they will praise their own theories and approaches, recommending them to readers. They will want

to say that the product operates well – has insights, produces findings, exposes what is hidden. Anyone using the product will have these benefits and understandings. (Billig, 2013: 142)

What he doesn't say is that benefits can be of two kinds. 'Exposing what is hidden' is an explicit benefit and one freely acknowledged in *superdiversity* work. Yet the adoption of certain keywords or, if you wish, paradigms, also confers other benefits, some of them less openly acknowledged. Here, a comparison with *Universal Grammar* becomes particularly instructive, as there was more to it than Chomsky's personal charisma and the appeal of a radical new theory:

> Prior to Chomsky, to be an American linguist almost obligatorily entailed one or two years of living among a minority language community and writing a grammar of their language. This was nearly a rite of passage in North American linguistics. But since Chomsky himself did no field research and apparently had learned more interesting things about language than any fieldworker, many students and incoming professors working under the influence of Chomsky's assumptions understandably believed that the best way to do research might be to work deductively rather than inductively – from the institution rather than the village, starting with an elegant theory and predetermining where the facts best fit. (Everett, 2008: 253)

The *Universal Grammar* not only enhanced the status of linguists, making them key players in the new field of cognitive science, but it also facilitated their lives – abandoning linguistic fieldwork, they could now accrue significant benefits in the comfort of their offices through 'theoretical modeling of fragments of well-known languages' (Evans, 2010: 222).

Superdiversity facilitates our lives in more ways than one. Activists concerned about *language endangerment* would have sent us to far-away places, while the *new sociolinguistics* legitimizes research in our own backyard and makes 'uncovering' of its own traces through the office window more rewarding – in terms of academic benefits – than the decidedly unsexy documentation of indigenous languages of Australia and North America or the labor-intensive ethnography of multilingual communication in Papua New Guinea and Vanuatu. As a framing device, rather than a theory, *superdiversity* also makes lives easier by allowing scholars of multilingualism to retain their traditional questions, concepts and methods (this maintenance is immediately apparent when one compares studies of *superdiversity* with the earlier studies by the same authors). Most importantly, it soothes disciplinary anxiety by aligning us with the wider world. The key advantage of the slogan – proudly flagged by Arnaut, Blommaert, Rampton and Spotti (2016a: 4) – is its 'strategic purchase in the field of social policy'. A convenient euphemism, *superdiversity* hits the spot with European governing bodies concerned about the refugee crisis, the new migration and the management of ethnolinguistic diversity. The best-hidden secret of *superdiversity* is that it does not change the way linguistic diversity operates and is researched – what it does is to improve the lives of those who signal allegiance to Newspeak.

The reward for the allegiance is the 'rising scholarly currency of the superdiversity framework' (Faudree & Schulties, 2015b: 3) and generous funding for research on languages and *superdiversity* (Table 8.1), which is exactly what Billig (2013) sees as branding success:

> An approach with thousands of recruits across the world will be a successful approach. And success will bring further success. The adherents of a successful approach are likely to run regular conferences, publish their own journals, attract funding, convene postgraduate workshops, present awards to the founders and so on. (Billig, 2013: 59)

As with any popular brand, its makers may benefit more than others, as seen in Blommaert's (2013) confident statement:

> Mobility, complexity, and unpredictability (...) enable me to imagine a sociolinguistics of superdiversity as organized on an entirely different footing from that which characterized the Fishmanian and Labovian sociolinguistic world. (Blommaert, 2013: 13)

This is arguably the most telling phrase in the book: all that remains is to replace the names of the 'old' founding fathers with the names savvy readers can put in the empty slots.

The benefits for migrants and refugees are less obvious. As a former refugee and interpreter in a Refugee Assistance program, I sincerely doubt that migrants derive benefits from Newspeak that relabels their linguistic practices in obscure journals (or, for that matter, in prominent ones). The only beneficiaries are Western scholars, for it is 'the powerful who celebrate the notion of diversity' as Makoni (2012: 192) reminds us: 'those of us from other parts of the world feel the idea of diversity is a careful concealment of power differences', including the power to imagine and define us (for a critique of *superdiversity* as a colonial project, see also Ndhlovu, 2016).

Tellingly, the first questions 'raised by *superdiversity*' are: 'who is the Other? And who are We?' (Blommaert, 2013: 5). The answers link the Otherness to *migrants* and, even more troublingly, 'second and third generation immigrants' who still display 'immigrant accent' (Blommaert, 2013: 72, 75) and 'daughters and sons, grand-daughters and grand-sons, great-grand-daughters and great-grandsons of immigrants' (Creese & Blackledge, 2010: 550). Following this impeccable logic, my son, my grandchildren and even my great-grandchildren will still be Russian immigrants in the USA because the Other has to remain the Other to ensure the existence of the powerful We (for an insightful analysis of *diversity* rhetoric, see Piller, 2016). It is the 'listening subjects' – 'the perceiver, the overhearer-now-reporter, the knowledge producer' (Reyes, 2014: 367) – who observe the change in the face and the soundscapes of

Western cities, who interpret signs without consulting their authors, who analyze interactions in languages they do not know and who derive benefits from the construction of difference. The Newspeak may not be many things but one thing it certainly is: the movement to make sociolinguistics great again under the banner of *superdiversity* is an exercise in rhetorical power that calls for the dismantling of boundaries, while surreptitiously erecting the Great Wall.

'Choice of keywords', notes Ahearn (2013: 7), 'has implications in terms of intellectual interactions that the author might have with other scholars' and 'repercussions in terms of the scholar's social status and job security'. In the context of such risk-benefit analysis, the uptake of the slippery slogan-brand is not surprising and the accompanying language of profit (*rising currency, strategic purchase*) not accidental. Cashing in on our anxieties, *superdiversity* enables us to repackage our research as cutting edge, to receive funding from governments anxious about immigrant influx, to move up the academic ladder, and to create a new academic hierarchy, with new hegemonic orders of normativity and indexicality, and a new elite.

Yet, readers who think that this unenlightened migrant is urging the field to abandon *superdiversity* could not be more wrong. I am not a fan of banning words. Given the natural trajectory of buzzwords in academia, I have no doubt that eventually *superdiversity* will join its peers in the repository of terms that make publications look decidedly *passé*. What concerns me is the idea of *scholarly currency* and – to stay with the fiscal metaphor – the price we pay as a research community for accepting new words as substitutes for new ideas, terminological innovation as a viable stand-in for theory, slogans as means of adding value to research, and branding, marketing, selling and self-promotion as unavoidable facets of academic life.

Acknowledgments

The purpose of this chapter was not to criticize or embarrass individual authors – some of the scholars working on *superdiversity* are colleagues and friends, who are genuinely concerned about migrants and whose work contributes to the study of multilingualism, with or without the trendy keyword. I also think very highly of Blommaert's early contributions to sociolinguistics. My purpose was to illustrate the difference between keywords, slogans and brands and to raise concerns about academic branding. To maintain this focus, this chapter was subjected to three forms of peer-review: editorial review, informal review by colleagues and a crowd-sourced review by readers on Academia and Research Gate, which allowed me to get feedback not only from like-minded peers but from opponents and critics of my arguments. I am deeply grateful to: Raphael Berthele, Alexandre Duchêne, Robert Gibb, François Grin,

François Grosjean, Monica Heller, Lars Hinrichs, Julien Danero Iglesias, Jürgen Jaspers, Sinfree Makoni, Sebastian Muth, Jon Orman, Robert Phillipson, Ingrid Piller, Angela Reyes, Francesco Screti and Martina Zimmermann for their insightful comments on the first draft of this chapter (and to Martina for drawing my attention to Billig's [2013] book); to Marian Sloboda and his colleagues and students for a superb critique; to Ofelia García, William Labov and Li Wei for kindly answering questions related to the chapter; to Alex Mullen whose Oxford workshop on multilingualism in antiquity gave me an opportunity to present my concerns to Jan Blommaert in person; and to Barbara Schmenk, Stephan Breidbach and Lutz Küster for the visionary idea to address sloganization in the field, for the invitation to the conference in Berlin and for being patient and open-minded editors. All remaining errors and inconsistencies are exclusively mine.

References

Adams, J. (2003) *Bilingualism and the Latin Language*. Cambridge: Cambridge University Press.
Ahearn, L. (2013) Commentary: Keywords as a literacy practice in the history of anthropological theory. *American Ethnologist* 40 (1), 6–12.
Alter, A. (2013) *Drunk Tank Pink and Other Unexpected Forces that Shape how we Think, Feel, and Behave*. New York: Penguin.
Alter, A. and Oppenheimer, D. (2009) Uniting the tribes of fluency to form a metacognitive nation. *Personality and Social Psychology Review* 13 (3), 219–235.
Androutsopoulos, J. and Juffermans, K. (2014) Digital language practices in superdiversity. *Discourse, Context & Media* 4–5 (Special Issue).
Arnaut, K., Blommaert, J., Rampton, B. and Spotti, M. (2016a) Introduction: Superdiversity and sociolinguistics. In K. Arnaut, J. Blommaert, B. Rampton and M. Spotti (eds) *Language and Superdiversity* (pp. 1–17). London: Routledge.
Arnaut, K., Blommaert, J., Rampton, B. and Spotti, M. (eds) (2016b) *Language and Superdiversity*. London: Routledge.
Beale-Rivaya, Y. (2012) The written record as witness: Language shift from Arabic to Romance in the documents of the Mozarabs of Toledo in the twelfth and thirteenth centuries. *La Corónica* 40 (2), 27–50.
Belling, L. and de Bres, J. (2014) Digital superdiversity in Luxembourg: The role of Luxembourgish in a multilingual Facebook group. *Discourse, Context & Media* 4–5, 74–86.
Bellwood, P. (2013) *First Migrations: Ancient Migration in Global Perspective*. Chichester and Oxford: Wiley Blackwell.
Billig, M. (2013) *Learn to Write Badly: How to Succeed in the Social Sciences*. Cambridge: Cambridge University Press.
Blommaert, J. (2010) *The Sociolinguistics of Globalization*. Cambridge: Cambridge University Press.
Blommaert, J. (2011) Supervernaculars and their dialects. *Working Papers in Urban Language & Literacies*, King's College London.
Blommaert, J. (2013) *Ethnography, Superdiversity, and Linguistic Landscapes: Chronicles of Complexity*. Bristol: Multilingual Matters.
Blommaert, J. (2014) The power of free: In search of democratic academic publishing strategies. *Tilburg Papers in Culture Studies* 114, Tilburg University.

Blommaert, J. (2015) Commentary: Superdiversity old and new. *Language & Communication* 44, 82–88.
Blommaert, J. and Rampton, B. (2011) Language and superdiversity. *Diversities* 13 (2), 1–21.
Blommaert, J., Rampton, B. and Spotti, M. (eds) (2011) Language and superdiversities. *Diversities* 13 (2) (Special Issue).
Bresc, H. (2001) *Arabes de Langue, Juifs de Religion: L'Évolution du Judaïsme Sicilien dans l'Environnement Latin, XIIe – XVe Siècles*. Paris: Editions Bouchène.
Brubaker, R. (1998) Migrations of 'ethnic unmixing' in the 'New Europe'. *International Migration Review* 32 (4), 1047–1065.
Cadier, L. and Mar-Molinero, C. (2014) Negotiating networks of communication in a superdiverse environment: Urban multilingualism in the city of Southampton. *Multilingua* 33 (5–6), 505–524.
Charalambous, P., Charalambous, C. and Zembylas, M. (2016) Troubling translanguaging: Language ideologies, superdiversity and interethnic conflict. *Applied Linguistics Review* 7 (3), 327–352.
CIS Statistics (2013) Статистика СНГ [CIS Statistics]. *Статистический бюллетень* [*Statistical Bulletin*] 5, 31–38.
Colapinto, J. (2011) Famous names: Does it matter what a product is called? *New Yorker*, 3 October. See http://www.newyorker.com/magazine/2011/10/03/famous-names (accessed 31 October 2017).
Constable, O. (1997) Cross-cultural contracts: Sales of land between Christians and Muslims in 12th century Palermo. *Studia Islamica* 85, 67–84.
Creese, A. and Blackledge, A. (2010) Towards a sociolinguistics of superdiversity. *Zeitschrift für Erziehungswissenschaft* 13, 549–572 (Special Issue).
Croatian Bureau of Statistics (2012) *Census of Population, Households and Dwellings 2011*. Zagreb: Croatian Bureau of Statistics.
Czajka, M. and de Haas, H. (2014) The globalization of migration: Has the world become more migratory? *International Migration Review* 48 (2), 283–323.
De Bock, J. (2015) Not all the same after all? Superdiversity as a lens for the study of past migrations. *Ethnic and Racial Studies* 38 (4), 583–595.
Deumert, A. (2014) Digital superdiversity: A commentary. *Discourse, Context & Media* 4–5, 116–120.
Duarte, J. and Gogolin, I. (eds) (2013) *Linguistic Superdiversity in Urban Areas*. Amsterdam and Philadelphia, PA: Benjamins.
Duchêne, A. and Heller, M. (2007) *Discourses of Endangerment: Ideology and Interest in the Defence of Languages*. London: Continuum.
Ehrenreich, B. (2009) *Bright-sided: How the Relentless Promotion of Positive Thinking has Undermined America*. New York: Metropolitan Books/Henry Holt.
Evans, N. (2010) *Dying Words: Endangered Languages and What They Have to Tell Us*. Malden, MA: Wiley-Blackwell.
Everett, D. (2008) *Don't Sleep, There are Snakes: Life and Language in the Amazonian Jungle*. New York: Pantheon Books.
Faudree, P. and Schulthies, B. (2015a) The social life of diversity talk. *Language & Communication* 44 (Special Issue).
Faudree, P. and Schulthies, B. (2015b) Introduction: 'Diversity talk' and its others. *Language & Communication* 44, 1–6.
Ferris, L. (2014) Super! *Chronicle of Higher Education*, 1 December. See http://chronicle.com/blogs/linguafranca/2014/12/01/super/?cid=at&utm_source=at&utm_medium=en (accessed 31 October 2017).
Flores, N. and Lewis, M. (2016) From truncated to sociopolitical emergence: A critique of super-diversity in sociolinguistics. *International Journal of the Sociology of Language* 241, 97–124.
Forster, L. (1970) *The Poet's Tongues: Multilingualism in Literature*. Cambridge: Cambridge University Press.

Frankopan, P. (2015) *The Silk Roads: A New History of the World.* London: Bloomsbury.
Ghanem, S. and Selber, K. (2009) An analysis of slogans used to 'sell the news'. *Newspaper Research Journal* 30 (2), 16–29.
Goebel, Z. (2015) *Language and Superdiversity: Indonesians Knowledging at Home and Abroad.* Oxford: Oxford University Press.
Gottdiener, M. (2012) Review of Adam Jaworski and Crispin Thurlow (eds) *Semiotic Landscapes: Language, Image, Space,* Continuum Publishing. *Applied Linguistics* 33 (1), 107–111.
Greenberg, J. (1956) The measurement of linguistic diversity. *Language* 32, 109–115.
Harrison, D.K. (2007) *When Languages Die: The Extinction of the World's Languages and the Erosion of Human Knowledge.* Oxford: Oxford University Press.
Hinrichs, L. (2015) Review of Jan Blommaert *Ethnography, Superdiversity and Linguistic Landscapes: Chronicles of Complexity,* Multilingual Matters. *Journal of Sociolinguistics* 19 (2), 260–265.
Hsy, J. (2013) *Trading Tongues: Merchants, Multilingualism, and Medieval Literature.* Columbus, OH: Ohio University Press.
Huck, G. and Goldsmith, J. (1995) *Ideology and Linguistic Theory: Noam Chomsky and the Deep Structure Debates.* London and New York: Routledge.
Jacquemet, M. (2015) Asylum and superdiversity: The search for denotational accuracy during asylum hearings. *Language & Communication* 44, 72–81.
Jaspers, J. and Madsen, L. (2016a) Sociolinguistics in a languagised world. *Applied Linguistics Review* 7 (3) (Special Issue).
Jaspers, J. and Madsen, L. (2016b) Sociolinguistics in a languagised world: Introduction. *Applied Linguistics Review* 7 (3), 235–258 (Special Issue).
Jennings, J. (2011) *Globalizations and the Ancient World.* Cambridge: Cambridge University Press.
Jørgensen, J., Karrebaek, M., Madsen, L. and Møller, J. (2011) Polylanguaging in superdiversity. *Diversities* 13 (2), 23–37.
Juffermans, K., Blommaert, J., Kroon, S. and Li, J. (2014) Dutch-Chinese repertoires and language ausbau in superdiversity: A view from digital media. *Discourse, Context & Media* 4–5, 48–61.
Laham, S., Koval, P. and Alter, A. (2012) The name-pronunciation effect: Why people like Mr. Smith more than Mr. Colquhoun. *Journal of Experimental Social Psychology* 48, 752–756.
Léglu, C. (2010) *Multilingualism and Mother Tongue in Medieval French, Occitan, and Catalan Narratives.* University Park, PA: Pennsylvania State University Press.
Lewis, P., Simons, G. and Fennig, C. (eds) (2016) *Ethnologue: Languages of the World* (18th edn). Dallas, TX: SIL International. See http://www.ethnologue.com (accessed 24 November 2017).
Makoni, S. (2012) A critique of language, languaging, and supervernacular. *Muitas Vozes* 1 (2), 189–199.
Maly, I. (2016) Detecting social changes in times of superdiversity: An ethnographic linguistic landscape analysis of Ostend in Belgium. *Journal of Ethnic and Migration Studies* 42 (5), 703–723.
Manosuthikit, A. and De Costa, P. (2016) Ideologizing age in an era of superdiversity: A heritage language learner practice perspective. *Applied Linguistics Review* 7 (1), 1–25.
McLaughlin, F. (2014) Senegalese digital repertoires in superdiversity: A case study from Seneweb. *Discourse, Context & Media* 4–5, 29–37.
Meissner, F. (2015) Migration in migration-related diversity? The nexus between superdiversity and migration studies. *Ethnic and Racial Studies* 38 (4), 556–567.
Meissner, F. and Vertovec, S. (2015) Comparing super-diversity. *Ethnic and Racial Studies* 38 (4), 541–555.

Metcalfe, A. (2003) *Muslims and Christians in Norman Sicily: Arabic Speakers and the End of Islam.* London and New York: Routledge.
Møller, J. and Jørgensen, J. (2013) Organizations of language among adolescents in superdiverse Copenhagen. *International Electronic Journal of Elementary Education* 6 (1), 23–42.
Morris, M. (2016) What the Normans did for us. *BBC History Magazine*, 6 October. See https://www.pressreader.com/uk/bbc-history-magazine/20161006/281590945048571 (accessed 31 October 2017).
Mullen, A. and James, P. (eds) (2012) *Multilingualism in the Graeco-Roman Worlds.* Cambridge: Cambridge University Press.
Mutsaers, P. and Swanenberg, J. (2012) Super-diversity at the margins? Youth language in North Brabant, The Netherlands. *Sociolinguistic Studies* 6 (1), 65–89.
Ndhlovu, F. (2016) A decolonial critique of diaspora identity theories and the notion of superdiversity. *Diaspora Studies* 9 (1), 28–40.
Orman, J. (2012) Not so super: The ontology of 'supervernaculars'. *Language & Communication* 32, 349–357.
Orman, J. (2013) New lingualisms, same old codes. *Language Sciences* 37, 90–98.
Orwell, G. (1949) *1984.* New York: Harcourt Brace Jovanovich.
Piller, I. (2016) *Linguistic Diversity and Social Justice: An Introduction to Applied Sociolinguistics.* Oxford: Oxford University Press.
Rampton, B. (2016) Drilling down to the grain in superdiversity. In K. Arnaut, J. Blommaert, B. Rampton and M. Spotti (eds) *Language and Superdiversity* (pp. 91–109). London: Routledge.
Reyes, A. (2014) Linguistic anthropology in 2013: Super-new-big. *American Anthropologist* 116 (2), 366–378.
Sharma, B. (2014) On high horses: Transnational Nepalis and language ideologies on Youtube. *Discourse, Context & Media* 4–5, 19–28.
Silverstein, M. (2015) How language communities intersect: Is 'superdiversity' an incremental or transformative condition? *Language & Communication* 44, 7–18.
Skutnabb-Kangas, T. (2000) *Linguistic Genocide in Education – or Worldwide Diversity and Human Rights?* Mahwah, NJ: Lawrence Erlbaum.
Smakman, D. (2015) The Westernising mechanisms in sociolinguistics. In D. Smakman and P. Heinrich (eds) *Globalising Sociolinguistics: Challenging and Expanding Theory* (pp. 16–35). London and New York: Routledge.
Spotti, M. (2013) The primary classroom as a superdiverse hetero-normative space. In J. Duarte and I. Gogolin (eds) *Linguistic Superdiversity in Urban Areas* (pp. 161–177). Amsterdam and Philadelphia, PA: Benjamins.
Standage, T. (1998) *The Victorian Internet: The Remarkable Story of the Telegraph and the Nineteenth Century's On-line Pioneers.* New York: Walker.
Standage, T. (2013) *Writing on the Wall: Social Media – the First 2,000 Years.* New York and London: Bloomsbury.
Storey, R. (1997) *The Art of Persuasive Communication.* Aldershot: Gower.
Strutton, D. and Roswinanto, W. (2014) Can vague brand slogans promote desirable consumer responses? *Journal of Product & Brand Management* 23 (4–5), 282–294.
Swanwick, R., Wright, S. and Salter, J. (2016) Investigating deaf children's plural and diverse use of sign and spoken languages in a super diverse context. *Applied Linguistics Review* 7 (2), 117–147.
Toivanen, R. and Saarikivi, J. (eds) (2016) *Linguistic Genocide or Superdiversity?* Bristol: Multilingual Matters.
UN DESA (2013) *International Migration Report 2013.* New York: United Nations, Department of Economic and Social Affairs, Population Division.
Varis, P. and Wang, X. (2011) Superdiversity on the internet: A case from China. *Diversities* 13 (2), 71–83.

Vertovec, S. (2007) Super-diversity and its implications. *Ethnic and Racial Studies* 30 (6), 1024–1054.
Weiss, B. (ed.) (1982) *American Education and the European Immigrant: 1840–1940*. Urbana and Chicago, IL: University of Illinois Press.
Williams, R. (1983) *Keywords: A Vocabulary of Culture and Society*. New York: Oxford University Press.
WMR (World Migration Report) (2015) *Migrants and Cities: New Partnerships to Manage Mobility*. Geneva: International Organization for Migration. See www.iom.int (accessed 26 November 2017).

9 Sloganization: Yet Another Slogan?

Barbara Schmenk, Stephan Breidbach and Lutz Küster

The term around which all the contributions in this volume are centered is *sloganization*, a noun that expresses a process of both slogan making and slogan using. Since the volume introduces this term, we would like to clarify and discuss its meanings in this concluding chapter, referring to the ways in which the authors of the individual chapters have interpreted and used it. A critical discussion of the term itself also seems necessary in light of Billig's (2013: 7) explicit warning about using 'big words' in academic writing: 'Beware of long words ending in "ization" or "ification"' (Billig, 2013: 173). This can be taken as a reminder that a term like sloganization is itself prone to be sloganized. Given the general critical outlook shared by all contributors to this volume, the notion of *sloganization* and its inherent slogan-potential ought to be discussed critically, too. Finally, another question arising from the study of sloganization will be addressed, namely, why it should be studied further and what the goals of such research could be.

Coming to Terms: Conceptualizing Sloganization

The current volume is dedicated to the exploration and investigation of *sloganization*. It arose from the concern with an increasingly sloganized use of specific terms in language education discourse, such as learner autonomy or communicative language teaching. Arguing that these terms often appear sloganized does not mean that they are slogans per se, as outlined in the introductory chapter. The intention was to capture and scrutinize the phenomenon of sloganization in language education discourse, which can be observed on many occasions, in academia and in other domains of knowledge production and dissemination (curricula, policy papers, universities, schools, etc.) and which are problematic for language education theory and practice.

Calling this phenomenon *sloganization* rests on the assumption that there are a number of terms in language education discourse that appear undertheorized, fuzzy, often trivialized and simplified, yet also appealing and catchy. In contrast to notions such as trivialization or simplification, which are implied by *sloganization*, it also entails the notions of branding and marketing. *Sloganization* thus pays tribute to the fact that 'academics work in an increasingly commercial culture, as universities, disciplines and individuals compete economically. In this competitive culture, it has become second nature to promote oneself and one's work' (Billig, 2013: 5). The analyses of the sloganization of innovation (Gramling), paradigm shift (Rösler), language commodification (Block), input (Plews) and superdiversity (Pavlenko) demonstrate that these terms have often been used for academic branding in scholarly discourse, showcasing 'the grand promotional metafunction, which is very much a part of contemporary academic communication' (Billig, 2013: 53). Deliberately or not, labeling one's research as innovative or declaring one's own or others' approaches paradigm shifts bears witness to the fact that what language education presumably needs most is 'newness' and change – at the expense of acknowledging, reflecting on and ultimately remembering the 'old'. The constant need to innovate and to produce something new (better, improved) can thus be directly linked to what Pavlenko calls 'the ahistoricity of the field' (this volume: 158). In other words, the use of slogans serves the sloganizer, to the extent that it makes historical considerations superfluous, *and* it is more easily sellable and palatable.

While these considerations suggest that sloganization has become almost a necessity in today's academic world, it is equally obvious that neither scholarly work nor educational practice can or ought to be based on slogans. Yet it makes it all the more challenging to investigate sloganization critically.

The contributions to this volume indicate that there are at least two kinds of sloganization that can, to some extent, be distinguished. On one hand, there are concepts that have, in the course of their frequent usage, turned into slogans due to a lack of critical reflection of their historical, cultural and conceptual background(s). Phrases such as *intercultural learning, communicative language teaching, autonomy, multiple intelligences* or *paradigm shift* fall into this category. They are often used as slogans in scholarly works as well as in other texts, e.g. in policy papers, teaching manuals, curricula and standards; yet at the same time there are also many instances in which authors take great care to conceptualize and contextualize these terms. As a result, we encounter sloganized as well as non-sloganized versions of widely used phrases in language education discourse. Tracing the process of their sloganization requires identifying the original meaning(s) attached to these terms and taking into account the specific contexts within which they were developed. On this basis it is possible to distinguish between more or less sloganized versions of the respective terms, and thus to keep up an ongoing dialogue about meanings and meaning-making of core notions in our field.

The second kind of sloganization identified in this volume refers to deliberate coinage and use of terms that are primarily aimed to brand a particular approach or theory. Examples of this are *language commodification* and *superdiversity*. Both notions are relatively new to scholarly discourse in applied linguistics and come across as slogans rather than as clearly defined and to varying degrees well-reflected terms. Especially in the case of *superdiversity*, Pavlenko (this volume) shows very clearly how this notion has been used to sell a 'new' field of study, and how its use renders it a slogan rather than a clear-cut term. Another example of this kind of sloganization is the rapid success of the notion of *input* over the course of the 1980s, a term that gained international currency through its most famous disseminator (although not 'coiner'), Stephen Krashen. John Plews (this volume) traces the process of establishing the slogan *input*, which was accompanied by successively eliminating the notion of exposure, most likely because the former strikes many as more scientific than the latter. This second kind of sloganization entails the coining and distribution of new (appealing, trendy) words, a process that bears witness to today's increasing need of self-branding in the world of academia, to marketize ideas and research in ways with which previous generations of scholars were unfamiliar. Sloganization thus fulfills the need to increase one's 'academic capital', while it is also instrumental in the accumulation of economic capital. Both kinds of capital can in turn help to promote the respective slogans even further, which increases the likelihood that they will be put on political and educational agendas and circulated yet more widely. Slogans thus turn out to be valuable assets; that is, they can be regarded as academic, political and economic currency.

Generally, questioning language education discourse and attempting to identify instances of sloganization requires focusing our attention on our own field and the discourse it produces. As such, it owes much to critical discourse analysis (Fairclough, 2001; Wodak & Meyer, 2009) and to Pennycook's (2001) notion of critical applied linguistics. Pennycook highlights the complex interrelationships of theory and practice at the micro- and macro-levels and underlines the necessity of critical inquiry, self-reflexivity and problematizing givens (Pennycook, 2001: 2–10), all of which are crucial concerns for the study of sloganizations in language education discourse. Not only is the field itself inherently interdisciplinary, situated at the crossroads of language study, multilingualism, education and pedagogy, as well as social, cultural and psychological fields of inquiry, but language education discourse is also produced and constantly reinterpreted and reconstructed at the micro-level of classrooms and schooling, in teacher education and professional development, and on the macro-levels of academic inquiry and research, political interventions and programming, which are often aligned with economic and commercial concerns. Amid this complexly interwoven network of interests and interdisciplinary perspectives, terms such as *autonomy* or *intercultural and transcultural competence* are often prone to be interpreted differently and invested with meanings that are primarily owed to their users' intentions and objectives. Britta Viebrock's chapter illustrates this, arguing that the widespread sloganization of *intercultural and transcultural competence* can in part be attributed to the fact that these terms are used by different stakeholders and adjusted to fit their respective agendas. At the same time, there is a considerable volume of publications dedicated to these notions, whose authors carefully reflect on the meanings of *inter- and transcultural competence* and acknowledge their complexity. This non-sloganized use of the terms is, however, often ignored in publications on language education, possibly because the meaning of the terms is taken for granted, and they are thus treated as unquestionable givens. In such instances, we encounter a simultaneous occurrence of both kinds of sloganization we have identified; apparently, the terms *inter-* and *transcultural competence* are used as slogans either because authors are not aware of their background and histories in diverse academic fields and treat them as new and appealing phrases (the second kind of sloganization outlined above), or because authors are aware that these terms have been around for a while but assume that their meaning is stable and thus does not need to be questioned or problematized (the first kind of sloganization). The simultaneous occurrence of both kinds of sloganization can also be observed with regard to other terms, e.g. communicative language teaching or paradigm shift.

The dilemma scholars are faced with today is obvious: on one hand it is often necessary to use slogans to brand oneself and one's work, and to sell ideas or approaches to administrators and funding institutions, which often amounts to a question of survival in academia. It is also true that many funding organizations and administrators request slogans rather than carefully reflected thoughts and discussions. On the other hand, the use of slogans has encroached on language education discourse as well, and as a result it has become more and more important to distinguish between marketizing strategies and research: 'Generally, we should aim to keep separate the activities of advertising and analyzing' (Billig, 2013: 215).

The study of sloganizations seems to us a necessary task in order to make this distinction and to continue to discuss, to question and to revise core notions in our field so as to 'keep them alive' and open to critical reflection.

Another Slogan?

In light of the discussion of sloganizations and the increasing use of slogans in scholarly discourse, the thorny question arises to what extent the term *sloganization* can itself be viewed as a slogan. Arguably, it falls into the category labeled 'big words' in Michael Billig's critical analysis of academic rhetoric and, moreover, is itself a somewhat catchy noun. Both points need to be addressed here.

It is true that nouns ending in -ification and -ization have seen a considerable increase in recent humanities discourses. Billig's critique of such nouns applies to *sloganization* as well, and it is worth thinking about *sloganization* in light of his warning:

> Here, then, is the centre of my argument: the big concepts which many social scientists are using – the ifications and izations – are poorly equipped for describing what people do. By rolling out the big nouns, social scientists can avoid describing people and their actions. They can then write in highly unpopulated ways, creating fictional worlds in which their theoretical things, rather than actual people, appear as the major actors. (Billig, 2013: 7)

The focus of Billig's critique is the passive voice of -ization and -ification nouns, which conceals the agent, a critique that led Dwight Bolinger (2014: 86) to call the passive voice 'one of the worst plagues of irresponsible journalism'. Indeed, *sloganization* foregrounds the making and use of slogans, rather than the agents, the sloganizers. This observation is important because it allows us to clarify two things. First, while it is necessary to point out instances of sloganization in scholarly discourse, the focus is less on individual authors and colleagues who may be 'guilty' of sloganizing, and more on the discourse produced in our field. The study of sloganization, as the contributions in this volume suggest, does not aim to point the finger at someone, charging them with sloganization. This is related to the second point, namely, that sloganization often happens unintentionally and goes unnoticed, simply because many take it for granted that the terms they use are known to their audience and will be understood. Instead of accusing them, it seems more important to raise awareness among scholars and students of applied linguistics so as to sensitize them to the phenomenon of sloganization. Keeping the passive construction of -ization therefore foregrounds the need to look critically at the discourse we produce and participate in. This entails a call for self-critical scrutinizing of one's own writing and speaking, and a warning to watch out for the use of slogans and sloganization in our field.

The second point mentioned above concerns the slogan-potential of *sloganization*. The intention of this volume is not to merely throw out a catchy new term. However, the conceptualization of sloganization has yet to be elaborated further. The contributions to this volume approach sloganization in different ways. What they have in common is a general concern about the use of slogans in scholarly discourse; however, each author approaches this task somewhat differently. Depending on the terms chosen, they all trace back some of the histories of the respective terms they investigate. It is also important to note that the terms and phrases addressed in this volume are but a few examples of what is arguably a more extensive list of potential and actual slogans which are still awaiting further discussion and critical investigation with regard to their sloganization and academic branding.

Another important point in the context of sloganization is the global spread of concepts and approaches, a development which more often than not involves the unidirectional distribution of Western theories and educational thoughts to the 'Global South', i.e. Africa, Latin America and the Caribbean, the Middle East and Asia. As one reviewer of this volume pointed out, these regions 'have been and continue to be the "dumping ground" of so-called new theories of language education that are largely generated from the Global North'. The contributors to this volume all work at European and North American universities and thus indeed represent only the 'Global North', yet the use and spread of the slogans scrutinized in the respective chapters are of course not restricted to Western discourses of language education. Viewed in this light, the global spread of slogans is a form of conceptual or educational imperialism, adding another dimension to the points discussed in the previous chapters that warrant further discussion and scrutiny: What do sloganizations look like in places where Western slogans are 'dumped' on non-Western practices and traditions of language education and research? To what extent do slogans impact on local practices? To what extent can responses to sloganizations within non-Western contexts be described as strategies to counter sloganizations? Are there such responses in the first place?

These considerations suggest that the study of sloganization is a work in progress, with regard both to investigating more sloganizations in language education discourse in different contexts, and to conceptualizing the notion of sloganization further. Finally, going back to the original Gaelic meaning of *slogan*, which denoted a Scottish Highland war cry, sloganization can indeed be regarded as a kind of slogan: although not a war cry, it does call for a heightened awareness of meanings, contexts and conceptualizations of the notions on which we build our theories, our research and our practices.

Why Study Sloganizations?

The contributions to this volume demonstrate that casting a critical eye on sloganizations in language education discourse yields insights into the production and dissemination of this discourse. As participants in this discourse, we are inadvertently involved in or confronted with sloganizations. This underlines the importance of critical reflection of our own use of terms, as well as an awareness of their cultural and historical embeddedness. The study of sloganizations is thus geared towards more transparency in the use of terms and meaning-making processes, and it requires us to take the time and effort to theorize them adequately and not take their meanings for granted. Of course there are limitations to that, and we cannot always explain everything from scratch. In this regard sloganization is always lurking behind every sentence we utter. And yet that is no reason to declare the entire project obsolete. Rather, knowledge about sloganization as a phenomenon serves as a constant reminder that we should be as clear as we can be in order to situate our own research and our own thoughts, analyses and interpretations within the wider field of scholarly discourse in language education, and acknowledge their cultural and historical contingency.

Studying sloganizations foregrounds the importance of attending to cultural and historical difference: people do not use the same terms, all in the same vein and consistently across times, cultures and contexts. Rather than homogenizing terminology use, the study of sloganizations identifies the use of slogans and the concomitant loss of conceptual clarity and precision in scholarly discourse and highlights the importance of the fact that many terms are used differently by different authors and in different contexts. Given the many different contexts and histories of scholars in the field of applied linguistics and language education, some heterogeneity in the use of terms is unavoidable and can even be seen in a positive light. Such unavoidable heterogeneity means that there is all the more reason for scholars to notice differences in the use of terms, and to reflect on these differences in light of the diverse contexts within which they take on different meanings. The study of sloganization is concerned with the limits of clarity and consistency and seeks to understand them rather than glossing over inconsistencies and fuzziness. It teaches us to clarify and reflect on how we and others use a particular term and to notice and address terminological inconsistencies and difficulties. The study of sloganization is thus fundamental to critical, scholarly inquiry in our field.

References

Billig, M. (2013) *Learn to Write Badly. How to Succeed in the Social Sciences.* Cambridge: Cambridge University Press.
Bolinger, D. (2014) *Language – The Loaded Weapon: The Use and Abuse of Language Today.* New York: Routledge.
Fairclough, N. (2001) *Language and Power* (2nd edn). London and New York: Routledge.
Pennycook, A. (2001) *Critical Applied Linguistics. A (Critical) Introduction.* Mahwah, NJ: Lawrence Erlbaum.
Wodak, R. and Meyer, M. (2009) *Methods of Critical Discourse Analysis* (2nd edn). Los Angeles, CA: Sage.

Index

academic capital 171
accountability 2
Adorno, Theodor W. 10–11
agency 100, 117
Agha, Asif 133–135
alienation 125, 128, 130, 135
assessment 5, 24–26, 67, 70, 153
audit culture 21
authenticity 3, 45–46, 49

behavioral economics 60
behaviorism 3, 69
Benson, Phil 3, 6, 8, 10
Block, David 14, 123, 136, 139, 170
border literacies 82–83
Bourdieu, Pierre 133
Boutet, Josiane 127, 131
brand you 135
branding
    academic branding 144, 148–149, 163, 170, 174
    proprietary branding 137, 149
bundle of skills 129, 135
Burawoy, Michael 130
buzzword 4–7, 121–122, 137–138
Byram, Michael 3, 73–77, 81, 83–84

call center 127–128, 130–131, 134
Cavanaugh, Jillian 131–135
classroom
    classroom practices 62
    language classroom 44, 74–75, 83–84, 89, 100
code 102–103, 107, 160
cognitive domain 57
cognitive psychology 3, 5, 119
collaboration 28
collateral damage 50
commodification 14, 121–137, 149, 159, 170–171

communicative approach 42, 45–49, 51
communicative competence 45, 47, 53–54, 63–64, 74–76, 84, 105
    intercultural c.c. 74–76, 78, 81, 83–84
    transcultural c.c. 82
communicative language teaching 3, 13, 25, 45, 169–170, 172, 180–181, 183
community of practice 50, 51
complexity 13, 20, 43, 154–155, 162
compliance 9
confidence
    over-confidence axiom 61–62
contact 98–117
convention 2
conversation (see also: interaction) 100–101, 106–107
creativity 21
critical transcultural awareness 83
culture 13, 73–74, 76–89
curricula 85

decontextualization 9, 11, 85
de-sloganizing 50, 81
digital footprint 150
dogma 44
Duchêne, Alexandre 122–124, 136, 138, 147, 163

economic capital 171
education discourse 2–14, 169, 171
educational landscapes 2
educational philosophy 9, 11
emic perspective 94, 97, 115, 118
emotion 75
emotionality 146–147
Engels, Friedrich 132
ethnic unmixing 152
evaluation 27
exploitation 125, 128–130, 135
exposure 14, 94–118

Fairclough, Norman 2, 81, 171
fashion 2–3
focus on form 48–50, 53–54
Foucault, Michel 81, 135
Fuchs, Christian 138

global knowledge 81–82
Global North 174
Global South 174
grammar translation method 44–46

Harvey, David 130, 132–133, 136, 139
Heller, Monica 122–123
Holborow, Marnie 126–130, 138
Holec, Henri 5–6, 9
homogenizing 175
Hu, Adelheid 26, 73, 75, 77–78, 80, 83
hype cycle 90

immersion 95, 100–102, 112, 117, 136
implementation 23–25, 38, 65
industrial age 59
in-group 23, 25–27, 29, 150
out-group 23, 25–26
innovation 12, 19–39, 57–58, 170
terminological innovation 148, 163
input
   comprehensible input 103–106,
      108, 112
   input hypothesis 14, 103–104, 108
   input processing 108–109
institutionalization 137, 149
instruction
   formal instruction 101, 104, 113
   grammar explanation 100
instructional scenarios 69
intake 104, 108–109
intelligence
   multiple intelligences (MI) 13, 57,
      62–65, 67–71
   MI theory 63–65, 68, 70
   MI taxonomies 64
interaction
   interaction hypothesis 109
intercultural learning 3, 72–75, 77–81, 87
intercultural speaker 3
invention 31

Kant, Immanuel 9, 11
knowledge construction 50

Kockelman, Paul 133–134
Kulturkunde 73–74

label(ing) 10, 13, 70
labor power 127–130, 135
labor, commodified 126, 130
Landeskunde 73–74
language
   language as skill 129
   language awareness 3, 63
   language commodification 14,
      121–121, 126, 159, 171
   language labs 69
   language materiality 131–133
   language part of work 127–128, 130
   language portfolio 62
   language program 27, 35
learner autonomy 3–11, 44, 137, 169
learner centeredness 3
learning
   core operations 63–64
   dispositions 69
   learning styles 13, 45, 62–63, 65, 69
   learning skills 58
   learning strategies 13, 58, 62–63, 69
life-long learning 8
linguistic diversity 147, 151, 153, 162
linguistic landscapes 143, 148–149, 151,
   156, 158–159

mainstream(ing) 6, 36, 45, 70, 73, 155
maintenance 38, 133, 161
market 12, 14, 19, 25–28, 30–31,
   35, 37, 123–126, 129–130, 138,
   145, 148
   market saturation 25–26
marketability 2
marketing 1, 12, 21, 32, 43, 50, 137,
   145, 149, 163, 170
marketize 1, 171
Marx, Karl 14, 121–132, 136, 138–139
McGill, Kevin 128
memorability 15, 146
method 3, 5, 12, 25, 30–33, 38, 44–46,
   49, 51, 85, 96, 150–151, 160–161
methodology 4, 35, 57, 74, 95
Meyer-Drawe, Käthe 10–11
mother tongue 44–45, 48–49, 103,
   153, 158
multiple literacies 81–82

neoliberalism; neoliberal discourses 1, 14, 121–122, 130, 133, 136
new economy 127
new speakers 146, 149

objectification 134–135
optimism 19, 129
output 2, 28, 29, 104, 110, 112–114, 117
  comprehensible output 105
ownership 27–28, 132, 149

paradigm; paradigm shifts 3, 12, 13, 25–26, 42–53, 56, 58, 61, 65, 68, 73–74, 78, 91, 150–151, 154, 159, 161, 170, 172
Pavlenko, Aneta 14, 20, 80, 137–138, 142, 170–171
Pennycook, Alastair 6–7, 79, 171
PISA 67, 71
political economy 14, 124, 126, 132, 136
polylanguaging 156, 160
positive psychology 147–149
power relations 11, 81
processing fluency 146
processing instruction (PI) 108
proclivities 65, 69
profitability 2

Realienkunde 73–74
resistance 23–24, 28, 34, 36, 130

savoir apprendre 75–76
savoir être 75
savoir faire 76
savoir s'engager 76
savoirs 76
Schmenk, Barbara 1, 4, 9, 44, 46–47, 73, 137, 164, 169
Schumpeter, Joseph 20, 30–31, 37

second language acquisition (SLA) 5, 13, 31, 73, 94–95, 97, 99, 106, 108
second language education (SLE) 14, 43–44, 94–95, 97, 99
self-branding 2, 171
setting; naturalistic setting 21, 25, 27–29, 65, 68, 98, 100–102, 104, 106–107, 109–112, 116
Shankar, Shalini 131–135
shared commitments 50
Silverstein, Michael 133, 155
simplification 6, 72, 77, 85–86, 89, 170
social networking 70, 150
stereotyping 77, 86
study abroad 13, 94–95, 97, 111–113, 115–118
superdiversity 14–15, 80, 142–163, 171
supervernaculars 157

task-based language learning 48
Taylorism 127
teacher identity 7, 23–25
thingification 135
thinking 2, 10, 59, 84, 116, 122, 127
  thinking skills 66
tradition 19, 37, 174
transcultural learning 13, 72–73, 75, 79–81, 84, 86–90
translanguaging 143, 158, 160
trivialization 72, 89, 170
turn 3, 12, 42, 43, 45, 50–53, 57

universalist 67, 69
universal grammar 146, 148–149, 151, 159–161
Urciuoli, Bonnie 2, 26, 31–32, 122, 129

ventriloquation 135

war on terror 19, 27–28
Welsch, Wolfgang 78–81, 84, 87, 89
WYSIATI 61–62

For Product Safety Concerns and Information please contact our EU Authorised Representative:

Easy Access System Europe

Mustamäe tee 50

10621 Tallinn

Estonia

gpsr.requests@easproject.com